PRAISE FOR TERRY THOMPSON AND CAJUN-CREOLE COOKING

"Thompson learned her trade by chopping, chatting, cleaning, and cooking with some of the best Creole and Cajun cooks."
Greensboro News & Record

" ... Presents a look at the roots of this interesting cuisine and explains the ethnic nuances that gave birth to it. The necessary ingredients are described, as are the people who developed them.... Thompson is as steeped in the ways of the Cajuns and Creoles as file gumbo is in tradition."
The Philadelphia Inquirer

"Blending the best of French theory, technique, and discipline with Cajun and Creole cooking to produce a new style ... From the French, she acquired their love of delicately balanced sauces. From the Cajuns and Creoles, she borrowed their use of spices, their repertoire of fresh ingredients, and their unique combinations of herbs."
Bon Appetit

CAJUN-CREOLE COOKING

Terry Thompson

BALLANTINE BOOKS • NEW YORK

Library of Congress Catalog Card Number: 86-68999

ISBN 0-345-34260-7

This edition published by arrangement with HPBooks, Inc., A Subsidiary of Knight-Ridder Newspapers, Inc.

Manufactured in the United States of America

First Ballantine Books Edition: May 1987

Contents

Introduction

Ensconced among the moss-draped oaks and cool, still bayous of South Louisiana, the Cajuns and Creoles live —noted for their traditions of fine dining and slow, easy living. Here it is believed that in the savoring of exquisite food among good friends and close families, life seems a little fuller.

With the same fervor or *joie de vivre* for which they are famous, the Cajuns and Creoles resist change. Perhaps that is why South Louisiana retains its old-world flavor and why its cuisine has been largely sheltered from the ravages of changing food trends.

The area's history, both political and otherwise, has been nothing shy of tempestuous—often marked by bloodshed, revolt, chicanery and general foolishness.

The city of New Orleans began as what may have been the world's first "worthless swamp-land swindle." Early attempts to populate and develop the entire Louisiana territory were hindered by charter holders whose only concern for the struggling colony was how many francs they could extract from its lagging economy.

History cannot explain exactly how or why these determined people stayed and dredged up one of the world's most interesting cities from an Indian clearing on an island between the Mississippi River and Lake Ponchartrain. Nor can we say what took the Cajuns into the primeval, mosquito- and alligator-infested marshlands and bayous to establish a way of life unlike that found anywhere else upon the earth.

If you have an *envie*, as the Cajuns would say, or yearning or covetous desire to cook and eat Cajun-Creole foods, come with me and explore these unique people and their foods.

1

The first European to reach what is now New Orleans was the French explorer LaSalle in 1682. He erected a cross and claimed the land for France. Various plans were tried to develop the land into a thriving colony; most failed.

Thousands of unsuspecting German farmers, mainly from poverty-stricken Alsace-Lorraine, were lured to the colony with the promise of free land, transportation, and tools to farm the soil. Within 10 years, 8,000 German settlers were brought to Louisiana, voluntarily or otherwise. It is estimated that half of them perished as the swampy settlement hovered at the brink of extinction. Their settlement became known as the Cote des Allemands or "the German Coast." They gave a German influence to the culture and the cuisine.

New Orleans managed to survive the weather, financial ruin and the devastating epidemics of yellow fever, cholera, typhus and smallpox, each one claiming sizeable chunks of the population.

In 1763, Louis XV gave the Louisiana territory to Spain. The colony had been deemed more trouble than profit. Lawlessness abounded despite attempts at bringing order, and the population was simply not increasing.

Through the years, the Spanish tried desperately to populate the colony. In 1785 they imported 1600 Acadians from France. These Acadians were originally citizens of French Nova Scotia forced from their homeland by the conquering British. Devoutly Catholic, they had refused to worship in the Anglican church. The English scattered them in small groups over the British colonies. Having heard about the French territory of Louisiana, many were drawn to that area by the hope that they would be welcome in a French colony. But even though the colony was comprised mostly of Frenchmen, it was now ruled by Spain. When these Acadians got together with the large group that the Spaniards had imported from France, they decided to leave New Orleans and establish their own settlement. They journeyed to the bayou country and established early settlements in the areas of Lafayette, Breaux Bridge and St. Martinville. These Acadians came to be known as "Cajuns" by the Indians, who could not pronounce the word properly.

At the same time, a title had been bestowed on the

residents of New Orleans. The Spanish word "Criollo" was given to all residents of European descent and their direct heirs. The name soon became "Creole."

Adversity struck the city of New Orleans once again on Good Friday of 1788. A candle ignited an altar cloth in a house on Chartres Street. The usual practice for fires was to ring the huge bells of the St. Louis Cathedral to summon volunteers to man the bucket brigades. This being a holy day, however, the priests would not allow the bells to be rung. The ensuing holocaust burned down four-fifths of the town. Six years later, a second fire destroyed many of the shops and warehouses spared in the first great fire!

After the fact, the fires were seen as a blessing for the Vieux Carre, which was subsequently rebuilt under Spanish rule. It was rebuilt using the European-style architecture still standing in the French Quarter today. Two-story, brick-walled houses with wide galleries edged with wrought-iron railings overlooking the streets replaced the one-story wooden structures. These intricate works of art came to be known as iron lace. The interior courtyard was also incorporated into houses during this rebuilding.

The Spanish now adopted a general policy of open immigration and welcomed virtually anyone who would come: British fleeing the American Revolution, Canary Islanders who settled downriver from New Orleans in what is now St. Bernard Parish, 500 Malagans who settled along the Bayou Teche in what is now New Iberia—and many other ethnic groups.

In the 1790s, the city's culture was further broadened by the arrival of thousands of French refugees who fled the slave uprisings of Santo Domingo (now Haiti). The Santo Domingans brought blacks and mulattoes, who introduced voodoo to Louisiana.

Meanwhile in France, Napoleon now in power, decided that Spain must return Louisiana to France. Napoleon deduced that he was bound to lose the colony to either England or America. He moved quickly to turn this possession into cash before fate could intervene.

Once again, Louisiana and her residents were traded off. In 1803 the Louisiana Purchase was completed. The United States bought the entire territory from France for

11.25 million dollars and the cancellation of a 3.75 million-dollar debt.

The Americanization of Louisiana began under its first governor, William Charles Cole Claiborne. Businessmen from the East came in droves and settled in the new Faubourg St. Mary District, across Canal Street from the Vieux Carre. This area, and eventually St. Charles Avenue, became known as the American Sector. The Creoles stayed rigidly within the old quarter, guarding their dignified European society against the vulgarity of the Americans. Louisiana began to grow by leaps and bounds, spurred perhaps by the promise of commerce or the success of the cotton and sugar plantations. Maybe it was the lure of the West Indian atmosphere, the European elegance or its strong reputation for vice.

In 1812 Louisiana became the 18th State, and in 1815 it was forced to defend itself against the British. In the years after the War of 1812, Louisiana prospered. With the invention of the steamboat, a new way of life on the Mississippi emerged. New Orleans became a major world port and a leading world supplier of cotton, sugar and indigo. Gambling flourished in the city, with casinos open 24 hours a day. Bourré, a win-or-lose-it-all card game, ruled lives in the Cajun country.

During the great potato famine in Ireland, some 25,000 Irish settled in New Orleans. They were clannish people and kept to themselves, forming their own sector of the city. The "Irish Channel" still exists today, a neighborhood inhabited by the descendants of these hardworking, fun-loving people.

Dark days began in 1861 when Louisiana seceded from the union. In February of 1862, Union troops laid siege for over a month, crippling New Orleans and its commerce. New Orleans, the Confederacy's largest city, fell. Many historians believe the South was doomed by the loss of this vital port and center of commerce.

Occupation of the city, under Major General Benjamin Butler, brought hard times for the city and the entire state. Occupation continued for 15 years, extending into the Reconstruction Era after the war.

The last two decades of the 19th century saw a rapidly booming economy for the State. Carpetbaggers from the North came in droves to set up businesses, lured by the plight of the broken land owners. Industry flourished, and traffic on the Mississippi almost choked the port of New Orleans. The era came to be known as the "Gilded Age."

In the late 1800s, large numbers of immigrants from Sicily began to settle mainly in New Orleans and in the town of Independence, about 50 miles upriver. The Sicilians quickly became involved in the food enterprises of the city. They added an entirely new and exciting dimension to the city's culture and to its cuisine.

The early part of the 20th century saw political turmoil in Louisiana and poverty in many of its rural areas. However after World War II, Louisiana became a leader in the petrochemical industry, and many poor Cajun farmers became millionaires overnight with the discovery of oil and gas on their lands. Many, sadly, were duped into selling for peanuts.

New Orleans has meant many different things to many people. Exotic, captivating and exciting are but a few of the words often used to describe her. New Orleans has always been an entity unto herself—in, but not entirely of, the South, or for that matter, the state of the nation! She is a little bit of each ethnic group which formed her.

But she always maintains her dignity, even during the Carnival Season. Called "the greatest free show on earth," Mardi Gras begins each year on Twelfth Night, January 6th. The season is marked by a succession of elaborate private balls and by the lavish street parades which begin about two weeks before *Fat Tuesday*. With the dawning of *Ash Wednesday*, a period of religious fasting begins, and the city reflects the somber mood of the Lenten Season.

New Orleans has always been a unique city of neighborhoods, beginning with the original division between the Creoles of the Old City and the Americans of the Faubourg St. Mary District. As other ethnic groups arrived, they too formed their own neighborhoods.

The neighborhood gave birth to two of New Orleans' best assets, the neighborhood grocery and meat market and the neighborhood restaurant and bar. Many remain today, selling and serving true Creole food in its own element.

When one goes to the food store to shop in New Orleans, it is referred to as "making groceries" and is a truly unique experience. At the small markets, such as Langenstein's, Puglia's and Meme's, there are real, old-fashioned meat counters with meats cut to order and sausages made by hand. These markets have honest-to-goodness butchers who have spent their lives selling fine meats to generations of New Orleanians. These are markets where smiling Creoles lean over the counter to ask: "Wotcha' need today, dawlin?" And if you don't know, they can make suggestions, tell you how much you need to buy for the number of people you want to feed, how to cook and season it and what to serve with it. A dying art!

For the most mind-boggling shopping trip, quite comparable to a hallucinogenic experience, Schwegmann Brothers Giant Supermarket is your destination. There are several of the markets, all independently owned by the Schwegmanns. The largest Schwegmann's is in the Gentilly area of eastern New Orleans. Under its roof you will find literally everything from appliances to cleanser —with dry cleaning, watch repair, tax preparation and veterinary services thrown in. It takes an hour just to walk, gape-mouthed, through the place, much less think about "making groceries." The mere massiveness of the place is intimidating; choosing groceries from the myriad selections and facing the 30-basket-deep checkout lanes looms as an insurmountable task. But not to worry, brother John Schwegmann has taken your fears into consideration. Just past the place where you fight for a shopping cart stands one of the biggest bars in New Orleans. You can sip Bloody Marys as you wind your merry way through the maze!

Grocery shopping in Cajun country is also unique, but in a very different respect. Small grocery stores and meat markets are plentiful. The common thread in these markets is that everybody—butchers, checkers and customers alike—speaks Cajun-French Patois. If you don't happen to speak it yourself, just wave your hands and look forlorn. They'll understand right away that you probably don't speak their language. The bad news is that you probably won't be able to understand their English either!

With such a rich and mixed historical background in

mind, it is possible to unravel the mysteries that together make up Cajun-Creole cuisine. It was formed with French roots, livened with Spanish spices, inspired by African vegetables and general magic, "Caribbeanized" by West Indian hands, laced with black pepper and pork by the Germans, infiltrated with potatoes by the Irish, blasted with garlic and tomatoes by the Italians, and even touched in some small ways by the Swiss, Dutch, Malagans and Malaysians. Small wonder that what emerged was a complex taste!

The question most often asked of South Louisiana residents is *What is the difference between Cajun and Creole food?* The answer, quite simply, is that Cajun food is the "rough-around-the-edges," robust food of country people. It is most often characterized by a very dark roux and very spicy flavor with a lot of animal fat thrown in. Creole food is a more refined "city" food with greater emphasis on the use of cream and butter. Some say that the Creoles use more tomatoes than the Cajuns, but that point is debatable from Cajun to Cajun.

As a matter of fact, many of the differences between the cuisines are often hotly debated. Cajuns and Creoles love to argue about food.

Any cookbook attempting to teach Cajun-Creole cookery, food that will bring people begging back to your table, must first explain *la bouche Creole*, or "the Creole mouth." It is a complex matter, but basically it is a sense of taste that is developed by a deep-seated love for the cuisine, a definitive palate, an inherent affinity for seasoning foods and lots and lots of tasting. Thankfully, the Creole mouth may be attained by diligent dedication to eating and cooking things Cajun and Creole.

If you have visited South Louisiana and have fallen in love with the food, then concentrate with all your might on one particular dish you enjoyed. Can you bring the taste back to your "mind's tongue" so sharply that your mouth begins to water? If so, get out your pots and pans and start cooking!

A few important pointers are in order before you start "cookin' Cajun," or "preparing Creole." Cajuns and Creoles take their food and its preparation very seriously. It is said that they don't just like to eat; they really like to cook as well!

Many of the Cajun-Creole dishes require tedious, time-consuming steps in their preparation. Shortcuts will result in a loss of flavor. Complex tastes are being developed and coaxed out of the foods by the long-cooking methods. Before attempting to prepare ANY recipe, read it through to be certain that you understand the various procedures. Then prepare all of your ingredients before you begin cooking. Chop the meats and vegetables as instructed. Gather spices, herbs and seasonings. Sift flours, grease pans, set ovens, heat fat and assemble all pots, pans and utensils that you will need. It becomes critically important to "get it together first" when dealing with complex recipes containing many ingredients.

South Louisianians do a lot of frying. There is a definite art to successful frying, and the subject demands a few pointers in this book. Although it may seem that slipping a piece of food into hot fat and cooking it would be one of the simpler culinary operations, I find that cooks in many parts of the country know absolutely nothing about proper frying procedures. Their efforts, more often than not, produce limp, soggy and grease-laden products—hardly a tribute to the crispy, golden-brown fried foods of South Louisiana. However, if foods are fried properly, there will be a minimum amount of fat absorption. For more information on frying, see box page 00.

Building Blocks of the Cuisine

Every regional or ethnic food has certain rules that make it unique and set it apart from other styles of cooking in ways that are sometimes vast, sometimes very subtle. Each major cuisine seems to have its own pastries and breads, its own particular seasonings, flavors, and, certainly, its own character.

Cajun-Creole food is no exception. The building blocks of Cajun-Creole cuisine are simple to master and yet are very important to the success of "cookin' Cajun."

Indeed, we have a standard reply in South Louisiana when asked "What is your recipe?" for this or that dish. We say, "Well, cher, first you make a roux...." Classically, the roux is the basis for the oldest and most authentic of the Cajun-Creole dishes, gumbos, etouffées, stews, courtbouillons and sauce piquants. If you start with a weak and underdeveloped roux, you will produce a very ho-hum dish. If you start, on the other hand, with a burned or scorched roux, you will create a dish with an overpowering bitter taste.

I am adamantly classic about roux! An actual revolution of thought has occurred within the Cajun-Creole cuisine in favor of the fast, high-heat method of roux-making. Well, I say, that method is okay, but it's not the best. And it doesn't taste the same! It is my no-longer-secret theory that the love and dedication given to that slowly cooked pot of roux are somehow magically transferred into the taste. Often we seem to be so intent upon finding shortcuts that we sacrifice a most essential thing —perfection of taste.

Once you have mastered the roux—and you'll probably burn two or three batches before you get the hang of it, then turn your attention to the stocks. In all likelihood, the stocks used in most Cajun-Creole foods are very different from those you have worked with. They are quite dark and have an assertive taste.

The Seafood Stock bears no resemblance to the delicate French fish fumet which is cooked 20 minutes and is almost clear with a faint essence of seafood and white wine. The Cajun-Creole variety of Seafood Stock contains many bold-flavored creatures and is cooked three hours! The stock is almost black in color, and the aroma and taste are indescribable.

Ingredients

Food experts who sample South Louisiana cuisine may try with all their culinary might to identify the various elements of the taste, but they invariably encounter a great deal of difficulty. Many Cajun-Creole dishes have lengthy ingredient lists. The unique cooking methods result in tastes not found outside of the Cajun-Creole kitchen. To really understand some of the ingredients used in this cuisine, it is necessary to understand the people.

Both Cajuns and Creoles are thrifty people who feel

that it is an abomination to waste food. Even seemingly useless scraps are put to delicious use in the South Louisiana household. Leftover rice and French bread are treasures. From the rice will come tomorrow morning's Rice Calas; from the bread scraps, crisp and tasty bread crumbs or, eventually, a bread pudding. Meat and vegetable scraps will find their way into the next day's soup, gumbo or jambalaya. Bones and carcasses are saved for stocks, as are shrimp and crawfish heads and shells. Onion, green onion, celery and carrots scraps are saved for the stock pot.

The most controversial ingredient in the cuisine is animal fat, and we use a lot of it in the form of lard, butter or beef suet. It is possible to substitute cholesterol-free, polyunsaturated vegetable oils and margarine in the recipes, but you will do them irreparable damage. It has often been said that when you remove the animal fat and the time-consuming stocks from the Cajun-Creole cuisine, you have removed much of its magic. I heartily agree. Since you will probably not be preparing Cajun-Creole dishes on a regular basis, save up your cholesterol allotment to splurge on a South Louisiana feast.

Cajun-Creole foods are steadfastly un-trendy. The adherents of the cuisine could care less what color peppercorns are "in" this year, or what obscure fruit has been discovered on a remote South Pacific island to command five dollars apiece in New York markets. And now for the big jolt to the world of haughty—or haute—cuisine. It doesn't even matter if you use canned artichoke bottoms or garlic powder or premixed Cajun-Creole seasonings. *The taste of the completed dish is the final judge*. If it tastes wonderful, isn't that what it's all about?

When shopping for ingredients, let freshness, rather than rigid compliance to recipes, be your guide. If the recipe calls for "ripe, fresh tomatoes," but the only ones available at the market are the cardboard-skinned, pale pink hothouse variety, then by all means, use canned tomatoes! Fresh does not always mean unfrozen either. If you live in a part of the country where the supplies of fresh fish and shellfish are questionable at best, use frozen fish and shellfish from a reputable source.

On the subject of freshness—you will note throughout this book that the recipes call for unsalted butter, and I am fairly adamant on the subject. Unsalted butter is the freshest butter available. It contains no additives and therefore has fewer liquids, a fact to consider when preparing delicate pastries. When you purchase unsalted butter, keep all but the portion currently in use in the freezer to prevent spoilage. It will remain fresh indefinitely. Cajuns and Creoles, Cajuns especially, rarely, if ever, clarify butter before using. Actually, the taste of the browned bits of milk solids forms an important aspect of the taste in many classic dishes. Cajuns rarely seed their tomatoes, either.

The five most important vegetables in Cajun-Creole cookery are onions, celery, bell peppers (known as the holy trinity), green onions and parsley, preferably the flat-leaf variety.

After a lengthy cooking process, many Cajun-Creole dishes are finished off with chopped green onions and parsley. The green onions lend a subtle onion taste and a bit of crunch to the dish. Here's a bit of trivia. Many of the junior league, church and service organization-published cookbooks in South Louisiana call for *shallots* in their recipes. That's not what they really mean, however. Cajuns and Creoles rarely, if ever, use real shallots. What these recipes really mean is green onions. To confuse matters even more, if you talk to a Cajun housewife, she might refer to green onions simply as *onion tops*, but what she really means is green onions—tops, bottoms and all!

Parsley is another serious subject in South Louisiana. Parsley is in, or on top of, literally every dish except breakfast cereal and desserts. This common herb is an important flavor enhancer.

If possible, use the flat-leaf variety, often called "Italian parsley." It has more flavor than the curly variety, which is generally used for garnishing. Do not use "Chinese parsley" or cilantro. Use only fresh parsley, never dried parsley flakes.

What cuisine that was strongly influenced by both the Spanish and the Italians would not be a garlic-laden one? When using garlic, mince the cloves almost to a pulp. Never brown or scorch it, lest you develop a bitter taste that will overpower the entire dish. It is for this reason that garlic powder, never garlic salt or garlic flakes, is often used in Cajun-Creole food. Often there are instances when you wish a batter to contain a hint of garlic. If you were to use fresh minced garlic, it would burn during the process of frying and impart a bitter taste.

Fish & Shellfish

Blue Crab—Crab is available in many forms. You can buy whole live crabs to boil and pick yourself. You can buy boiled crabs, or you can buy the picked meat by the pound. When preparing dishes using a lot of crabmeat, the time saved can significantly offset the purchase price. It takes from 12 to 16 crabs to produce 1 pound of crabmeat!

Crabmeat is usually available in four categories—claw meat, plain white crabmeat, lump crabmeat and backfin lump crabmeat. The backfin lump meat is the most expensive because there are only two backfin lumps per crab. They are attached to the small "flippers" on the back part of the crab.

When you purchase live crabs, place the crabs in a cooler; cover with ice. Let sit for an hour or so. They will be stunned from the cold and will be very inactive!

Many people think that softshells are a separate species of crab doomed to live their entire lives with paper-thin shells and no protection from predators. This is not the case. As crabs mature, they simply outgrow their shells, so they shed the whole thing and grow a new one! The entire process of shedding the old shell and hardening the new one takes only a few hours and is one of nature's true miracles. It is during this brief period that the softshell crab is harvested.

To prepare softshell crabs for cooking, use kitchen shears, remove the small "feelers" in the front and the eyes and eye stalks. Lift the top shell from each side using the points as handles. Remove the gills or "dead man's fingers" which will be right under the shell. Pat the shell back into place and your crab is ready to cook. And yes, you do eat the whole thing!

Crawfish—Crayfish or "mudbug" as it is affectionately known in South Louisiana. Crawfish are freshwater crustaceans which thrive in almost every area of the world. Louisiana, however, is the only place in the world where crawfish are revered.

The crawfish season runs from about the end of November to the first part of June. With sophisticated processing and freezing techniques, peeled crawfish tails are generally available the entire year.

Crawfish may be purchased in three forms: Live, boiled in the shell or peeled tails. The peeled tails are sold in 1-pound packages and have the vitally important fat from the head of the crawfish spread over the meat. The fat is the golden-colored substance; don't waste a drop. Squeeze every bit of it out of the bag. Peeled tails may seem expensive when compared to live crawfish. But consider that you must peel about 8 pounds of whole crawfish to get 1 pound of tails. The price for peeled tails suddenly becomes rather insignificant. When purchasing live crawfish, discard any that are dead before you boil them. When serving boiled crawfish as a meal, allow 3 to 5 pounds per person, depending upon appetite.

To eat boiled crawfish, first put on your jeans and T-shirts, because it is a messy affair! Hold the head with one hand; separate it from the rest of the crawfish. Gently squeeze the thorax or middle section between your thumb and forefinger to crack the shell. Then turn over and pull the shell in half. Remove the meat; pull out the dark vein on the outside curve. To sample the tasty fat, place your little finger inside the body. Gently pull out the golden fat to enjoy a Cajun treasure.

Oysters—Oysters purchased in the shell should be alive, indicated by a tightly closed shell. Discard any opened shells. If purchased by the jar, the oysters should be plump and creamy in color with viscous, clear—not cloudy—liquid. They should have a pleasant odor with no hint of sourness. If you buy oysters by the jar, pick them over carefully with your fingertips to remove any small bits of shell.

Store oysters in the shell at about 39F (5C), not directly on ice. They must be kept dry. Store shucked oys-

ters at the same temperature, covered by their own
"liquor" as it is called in Louisiana. If bought *FRESH*,
shucked oysters may be kept up to 5 days.

When shucking oysters save all of the oyster liquor
from the shells. It is worth its weight in gold to flavor
sauces, soups, gumbos or gravies. It freezes very well.

Oysters are available year around, but during the
warm months, they become very fat. This makes them
difficult to fry, but dry them thoroughly on paper towels
before breading and you will increase the odds for success.

Shrimp—When purchasing shrimp, purchase "heads-on"
shrimp whenever possible. The tomalley of the shrimp is
contained in the head and is an important taste ingredient
both in boiled shrimp and in seafood stock. Fresh shrimp
should have a translucent appearance. The flesh should
never appear dry and opaque. Fresh shrimp should not
have a strong odor. Shrimp are sold by graded categories
known as count. Shrimp labeled *15 to 20 count* will yield
15 to 20 shrimp per pound. Medium shrimp, the size
most often available, are usually 26 to 35 count.

When serving boiled, heads-on shrimp for a meal,
allow 2 to 2½ pounds per person. Two pounds of heads-
on shrimp makes 1 pound of peeled shrimp.

Catfish—Fried catfish with hush puppies is a staple meal
in southern Louisiana and Mississippi. And the demand
is spreading. Fast-food fried-catfish restaurants are pop-
ping up all over the country. Catfish are so popular that
to meet the demand, they are commercially raised on
large catfish farms.

The two varieties of catfish normally cooked are the
blue catfish and the channel catfish. They are both
white-fleshed, medium-oily fish and are excellent cooked
in any manner, either whole or filleted. The head and
skin must be removed. If served whole, they are usually
fried. Large catfish can be cut through the backbone into
steaks.

Flounder—The Gulf Coast flounder is actually a member
of the fluke family, a strange-looking group of flatfish.
Most whole flounder found in markets weigh from 12

ounces to 3 pounds. Flounder, either fresh or frozen, is available in most areas of the country.

Flounder is one of the most delicate tasting of all Gulf fish. Its flesh is pure white with a very fine texture. It lends itself to any method of preparation, either whole or filleted. It is often served whole, stuffed with a crabmeat dressing and baked, a worthy dish by anyone's standards!

Pompano—Pompano is one of the most regal, and certainly one of the most expensive, fish used in Creole cookery. Gourmets the world over acclaim the taste of the pompano.

While it lives in both the Atlantic and the Caribbean, more pompano is consumed in New Orleans than in any other place in the world. In the market, pompano is usually from 1 to 3 pounds. It is an oily fish and does not fry well. But it lends itself to any other type of preparation, including charcoal grilling, a cooking method which really makes its flavor shine.

Pompano has a one-of-a-kind taste. However, if it's not available, substitute your favorite fish in the elegant *en papillote* dish. I often use flounder fillets. While the flavor, of course, is not the same, the dish is still impressive.

Redfish—A cousin to speckled trout and a member of the drum family, found on the Atlantic and the Gulf coasts. On the Eastern seaboard, it is called the red drum. Redfish is easily identifiable by the large black spot or spots on its tail.

Like its relative, speckled trout, redfish is a white-fleshed fish with a delicate taste and low-fat content. An individual redfish can weigh as much as 25 to 30 pounds, but smaller fish are more desirable for home cooking. Speckled trout works well in redfish recipes, or you may substitute grouper, tilefish, drum or croaker.

Red Snapper—One of the most distinctive-appearing fish in the Gulf of Mexico. Its bright red body is familiar throughout the country. It is the most widely available Gulf fish. Red snapper is a tasty fish with a low fat content. It is often baked whole, but lends itself equally well to cooking as fillets. As a substitute for red snapper, use grouper, tilefish or redfish.

Shark—Shark meat is delicious and is becoming more widely available. Shark meat is available either as steaks or fillets. The meat is white and has a very mild flavor similar to that of redfish. The flesh is firm textured, much like swordfish or dolphin, and is delicious charcoal grilled.

The most commonly processed shark is the relatively small, about 40 pound, bull shark. Several varieties of shark are very poor in quality and high in uric acid, which gives the meat a strong and unacceptable taste. Use your nose to select, or reject, shark meat. If the meat has a strong and unpleasant ammonia odor, it is not likely to improve with cooking.

Speckled Trout—Or "spec" as it is called by Gulf fishermen, is the most sought-after fish in South Louisiana. It is a member of the weakfish family, which also includes croakers, drum and redfish. Its flesh is firm, white, delicate in taste and non-oily. The speckled trout is available year around. Its average size of about 1½ pounds makes its fillets just the right size for single servings.

Speckled trout can be prepared using any cooking method. Because it has a very delicate flavor, it has a natural affinity for a wide variety of herbs and all types of shellfish. As a substitute for speckled trout, use any white, firm-fleshed, non-oily fish, either salt or freshwater. Rainbow trout is an excellent substitute.

Cajun Roux

Roux freezes well, and no respectable Cajun household would be without a good supply. When you prepare roux, make a little extra; freeze it in one-cup containers.

1 cup lard   **1 cup all-purpose flour**

Melt lard in a heavy Dutch oven or a 12-inch skillet over medium heat. When lard is hot, add flour all at once; stir or whisk quickly to combine flour and lard. If necessary, use back of a wooden spoon to smooth out any lumps of flour. Reduce heat to low. Cook, STIRRING OR WHISKING CONSTANTLY, until roux is desired color and has a nut-like smell. Cook about 45 minutes for peanut-butter-colored roux or 55 minutes for the dark mahogany-colored roux. The process should not be rushed. If small black or dark-brown flecks appear in roux, it has been burned and must be discarded. A burned roux will impart a bitter and scorched taste to any dish in which it is used. To stop the cooking process, either add the vegetables called for in the recipe or immediately pour finished roux into a metal bowl. Stir or whisk 10 minutes in bowl. To make ahead, cover and refrigerate 2 days. Or freeze up to 6 months. Makes 1 cup.

Variations

Substitute vegetable oil for lard, if desired. However, the taste of the finished dish will not be as good as one prepared with a lard-based roux. Substitute another fat, such as rendered duck fat or a combination of duck fat and lard, for lard.

Making Roux

- When stirring and handling the roux, be extremely careful not to splash any of it onto your skin. Roux sticks to the skin and can cause a very serious burn.
- If you are preparing a larger quantity of roux, use a pan large enough to hold all of the fat and flour and allow enough room for stirring or whisking without splash-overs.
- The choice of a stirring implement is a personal one. I find that a long-handled metal whisk covers more of the pan surface. If you are more comfortable with spoons, then use a wooden spoon. Metal spoons be-

come extremely hot during the long cooking process.
- Even after the roux has been removed from the pan to a metal bowl, you must still be very careful with it. Do not set the bowl on a polyethylene or plastic cutting board or on your plastic laminate counter top. These materials will melt and burn. Remember that you are dealing with a substance that is in excess of 500F (260C)!

Preparing Stocks

- It is important to give as much time and thought to the preparation of your stocks as you do to each finished dish in which you will use them. If you start with a mediocre or bad stock, things generally go downhill from that point!
- Never use internal organs such as livers, hearts, gizzards or kidneys in making stock. They contain blood which gives stock a very strong and unpleasant taste.
- Chicken fat will smoke during browning. The kitchen will smell like fried chicken about a day. Do not make stock on a day when you plan to have guests.
- Stock is never salted until it is used in its final product, such as a sauce or soup. Otherwise, the saltiness would increase as the stock is reduced during cooking.
- Bring stock to a full boil and skim the surface before adding your seasonings or herbs so that you don't skim them all away!
- Cooling stock quickly is very important. Improperly cooled stock will spoil rapidly. To cool a large amount of stock, strain first. Place in smaller containers. Place containers in a sink of cold water, changing water as it becomes warm. Do not put hot stock directly in the refrigerator.
- Remove all traces of fat after stock is chilled and fat has solidified on surface of stock. Stock stored with fat remaining in it will have a fatty, oily taste. Fat be-

comes rancid rapidly, affecting the taste of the stock.

- To avoid the risk of bacterial growth, do not leave prepared stock in the refrigerator longer than two days. Freeze for longer storage. Do not freeze stocks longer than six months. After that length of time the poultry and veal stocks begin to lose their flavor, and fish stocks get very *fishy*.
- When preparing fish stock, it is important to remove the heads of any fish carcasses and to rinse the entire bony carcass under running water to remove every last trace of blood from the bones, lest your stock be a bit too "aromatic."
- When straining stocks for use or storage, be sure to press firmly on the bones and vegetables to release the flavor.
- If you use fresh herbs, save all of your herb stems— even parsley—in a bag in the freezer. Use the stems for making stocks. They contain even more flavor than the leaves, and you get a smug feeling of being economical.

Louisiana Brown-Poultry Stock

The secret to the greatness of this stock is the use of as many types of poultry bones as possible. And be sure that you have duck bones in there—they add a wonderful flavor.

10 to 12 lbs. uncooked mixed poultry bones and carcasses, such as chicken, duck, game hen, quail, dove and turkey
2 carrots, coarsely chopped
2 large onions, unpeeled, coarsely chopped

1 large leek, coarsely chopped
1 celery stalk with leafy top, coarsely chopped
6 parsley sprigs
6 thyme sprigs or 2 teaspoons dried leaf thyme
1 bay leaf

Preheat oven to 425F (220C). Place all bones and carcasses in large roasting pans. Brown bones and carcasses in preheated oven until very dark, but not burned, turning often. This takes about 2 hours. Do not burn the bones, or the stock will have a very bitter taste. Place browned bones in a 20-quart stockpot. Leaving a *thin* film of fat in 1 pan, pour off and discard fat from pans. Place carrots, onions and leek in pan with thin film of fat, spreading evenly. Cook in preheated oven, stirring frequently, until well browned. Add browned vegetables to stockpot. Pour off all remaining fat from pan; place pan over high heat. Add 1 cup water to pan to deglaze, scraping up all browned bits from pan bottom. Repeat with remaining pan. Add browned mixture to stockpot. Add enough water to stockpot to completely cover bones and vegetables by about 2 inches. Bring to a boil; skim grey foam from surface often. Boil until no more foam forms. Reduce heat; add seasonings. Simmer 8 hours. Skim fat from surface occasionally. Cool slightly. Strain stock 3 times through a fine strainer or cheesecloth; discard bones and vegetables. Pour into shallow pans; cool in sink of cold water to room temperature. Refrigerate until chilled. Remove all fat from surface. Pour into quart containers; seal tightly. Refrigerate up to 2 days or freeze up to 6 months. Makes 8 to 10 quarts.

Seafood Stock

There is no truly acceptable substitute for real seafood stock, but if you simply must use an alternative, bottled clam juice is your best bet. Any type of non-oily, white-fleshed fish bones may be used, but avoid deep-sea fish or any fish with dark meat. Whenever possible, include whole crab carcasses and shrimp heads and shells. If you have crawfish shells and heads, they are an extra treat. The more varieties you use, the more complex the taste will be. A couple of big lobster carcasses would be sublime!

10 lbs. mixed shellfish
   shells or fish carcasses
   and bones
5 onions, unpeeled,
   quartered
1 tablespoon whole cloves
2 celery stalks, coarsely
   chopped

5 garlic cloves, unpeeled,
   smashed
1 large lemon, sliced
1 (3-oz.) box shrimp and
   crab boil
1 tablespoon peppercorns

Place all ingredients in a 15- to 20-quart stockpot. Add enough water to cover by 4 to 5 inches. Bring to full boil over high heat. Skim grey foam from surface; reduce heat. Simmer 3 hours. Cool slightly. Strain 3 times through a fine strainer or cheesecloth; discard bones and vegetables. Pour into shallow pans; cool in sink of cold water to room temperature. Refrigerate until chilled. Remove all fat from surface. Pour into quart containers; seal. Refrigerate up to 2 days or freeze up to 6 months. Makes 8 to 10 quarts.

Brown Veal & Pork Stock

The use of pork bones in a veal stock may seem a very radical thing to non-Southerners, but the flavor derived from them is marvelous and is right at home in the hearty dishes of South Louisiana. If you cannot find pigs' feet, substitute 4 pounds pork neck bones.

8 lbs. veal bones and
   knuckles, cut in half
4 lbs. veal shoulder and
   shanks
5 pigs' feet, cut in half
6 onions, coarsely
   chopped
3 carrots, coarsely
   chopped

3 celerys stalks, coarsely
   chopped
6 thyme sprigs or 2
   teaspoons dried leaf
   thyme
2 bay leaves
Parsley stems
1 tablespoon peppercorns
1 (6-oz.) can tomato paste

Preheat oven to 425F (220C). Place all bones, meat and pigs' feet in large roasting pans. Brown in preheated oven until very dark, but not burned, turning often. This takes about 2 hours. Melting fat will create a lot of smoke in the oven. If too much melted fat collects in the pan during cooking, skim it off using a non-plastic bulb-baster. Do not let it overflow into the oven, because it could cause a fire. Place browned bones in a 15- to 20-quart stockpot. Leaving a *thin* film of fat in 1 pan, pour off and discard fat from pans. Place onions, carrots and celery in pan with thin film of fat, spreading evenly. Cook in preheated oven, stirring frequently, until well browned. Add browned vegetables and tomato paste to stockpot. Pour off all remaining fat from pan; place pan over high heat. Add 1 cup water to pan to deglaze, scraping up all browned bits from pan bottom. Repeat with remaining pan. Add browned mixture to stockpot. Add enough water to stockpot to completely cover bones and vegetables by about 2 inches. Bring to a full boil, skimming grey foam from surface often. Continue boiling until no more foam forms. Reduce heat. Add seasonings; simmer 10 hours. Cool slightly. Strain 3 times through a fine strainer or cheesecloth. Pour into shallow pans; cool in sink of cold water to room temperature. Refrigerate until chilled. Remove all fat from surface. Pour into quart containers; seal. Refrigerate up to 2 days or freeze up to 6 months. Makes 8 to 10 quarts.

Frying

The two methods of cooking foods in fat in the Cajun-Creole cuisine are sautéeing, which is also known as pan-frying or panéeing, and deep-frying. Sautéeing involves cooking food in a small amount of hot fat in a heavy skillet. The fat should be hot and the food dry.

But if the vegetables to be sautéed are soggy, they will lie in a pool of fat diluted with, and cooled by, their own liquid. They will be steaming or boiling rather than sautéeing. The taste is not the same and the texture will lack the crunch of a sautéed food. Vegetables which are chopped in the food processor become very watery; they simply will not sauté properly. The sauté is of extreme importance in Cajun-Creole cooking, and if not done properly, the final taste is altered. In those many instances in which the vegetables will be sautéed in a roux, it becomes downright dangerous to toss soggy vegies into a pan of hot fat which registers in excess of 500F (260C). So get out your chef's knife, please, and hand chop vegetables for a sauté.

To fry means to immerse completely in deep fat heated to a high temperature. The object of deep frying is to quickly sear the outside of the food in order to seal it with a crisp crust. Then the oil cannot seep in to make the food soggy and greasy. The juices of the food cannot seep out to make the food tasteless.

Any type of food to be sautéed or deep-fried must be free of surface moisture. If the meat or vegetables to be sautéed or fried are not coated, then they must be patted very dry with paper towels. If the vegetable or fruit to be fried or sautéed has a high liquid content, such as strawberries, eggplant or zucchini, you must batter it or coat with an egg wash and flour or bread crumbs before frying or sautéeing.

UNUSUAL INGREDIENTS
1. Creole cream cheese—A special cream cheese with a texture that is similar to sour cream but more tart. Used as a topping or for Frozen Creole Cream Cheese.

2. Crab and shrimp boil—A special blend of spices used for boiling seafood.

3. Coffee with chicory—A blend of coffee and the ground, dried root of the chicory plant. Chicory adds a slight bitterness.

4. Satsumas—Mandarin oranges that are grown in South Louisiana and other areas.

5. Lard—Rendered pork fat used to make Cajun Roux and for frying.

6. Herbsaint—An anise-flavored liqueur developed in New Orleans.

7. Picante sauce—A spicy tomato-and-chili sauce. Use the Tabasco brand if it's available. If not, substitute a thick local brand.

8. Red (cayenne) pepper—Ground, dried cayenne peppers.

9. Pickled okra—Pickled okra pods. Available in regular or hot flavors.

10. Yellow corn meal—Ground yellow corn. Used in hush puppies, corn bread and spoon bread.

11. Red beans—An essential ingredient in Red Beans & Rice.

12. Corn flour or unseasoned fish fry—A fine corn flour used for coating ingredients for frying.

13. Filé powder—A woody seasoning ground from the dried leaves of the sassafras tree. It was originally used by the Indian tribes living in the bayou country. It is readily available in specialty markets.

14. Creole mustard—A stone-ground mustard. Use Zatarain's, if it's available.

15. Hot-pepper sauces—Both red and green hot-pepper sauces are used extensively in Cajun-Creole cooking and at the table.

16. Peychaud Bitters—Alcoholic liquor containing a blend of herbs developed by A. A. Peychaud, a New Orleans' pharmacist. Used in making Sazeracs.

17. Tasso—A smoked pork or beef seasoning meat made from poor quality cuts which are coated with a very spicy seasoning mixture and smoked until hard and flavorful. You may substitute smoked ham.

18. Andouille sausage—A spicy smoked pork sausage. Available in some meat markets and by mail order.

Appetizers

Mardi Gras Pre-Parade Party

Blue-Crab Stuffed Mushrooms
Shrimp in Mustard Sauce
Patty Shells with
Mushroom & Oyster Fillings
Jezebel Sauce over Cream Cheese
Cajun Glazed Mushrooms
Paula's Dill Dip with
Vegetable Crudités
Cayenne Toasts
Cajun Mimosas, page 279

Having been raised in a part of the country where you didn't "go visiting" without a proper invitation, I was totally unprepared for life in Cajun country.

When I first moved to Louisiana many years ago, I lived in Lafayette—right in the heart of Acadia. I remember the day the moving van arrived with our belongings. Within 30 minutes, every neighbor on the block had been through the house to meet us and say "Welcome." They came with thermos jugs of rich black coffee and boxes of croissants and goodies from Poupart's Bakery.

Late that afternoon, when the movers had gone and we were tired and dirty and hungry, they came back. This time each lady had a little plate or bowl containing a shared portion of her family's supper. There was even a small portion of the best carrot cake in the world. My, did we feast that night—and for two days!

26

As soon as my house was in reasonable order, I planned a Friday evening party to pay back all the gracious hospitality. I cooked and cooked, preparing my best party foods. I garnished the platters and used mountains of greens and parsley. At the appointed hour, the guests began to arrive—each one carrying a platter of his or her very best party food! We had enough food that night for an army.

Well, it never changed, thank goodness. In South Louisiana you never need an excuse to get together with friends and neighbors. And through the years I have learned the element common to all Cajun and Creole get-togethers. The occasion or location may vary, the conversation and activities may change with the times, but there is always lots of food. An entire reputation can be based on one's collection of party-food recipes! When I moved to New Orleans, it took a week to return all the platters, plates and bowls from various events and to collect all of mine.

Party food need not be fancy, expensive or require hours of preparation time. It should be food that can be eaten with one hand, and ideally, should not require the use of silverware. It should be one or two bites in size and not oily, sticky or drippy. Foods that are not totally edible, such as strawberries with tops, require plates for leftover bits or wooden picks.

There are two standard party foods in Cajun country —pepper jelly and Jezebel Sauce. As long as you have a jar of pepper jelly on hand and a block of cream cheese to pour it over, you can have a party. My personal standby is Jezebel Sauce over cream cheese. Your favorite cracker goes well with both.

This chapter provides a wide range of party foods, from plain to fancy, easy to complex, delicate to spicy; but there's something for every occasion and every budget.

Cleaning Oyster Shells

Most raw-oyster bars or seafood markets will be happy to save oyster shells for you. Get more than you actually need because you will want to sort through them, discarding the flat top shells or the grossly large ones. Place shells in the sink under running water. Scrub vigorously, inside and out, using a stiff brush. Next fill the sink with water; add enough bleach to make a strong solution. Soak the shells in the bleach solution overnight. Drain and place them in the top rack of the dishwasher. Run them through a full cycle. Each time you use the shells, merely scrape out the bits of food, and put them in the dishwasher!

Blue-Crab-Stuffed Mushrooms

Visitors to South Louisiana fall in love with the delicate, sweet flavor of the Louisiana blue crab. Just boiled with spices is one of our favorite ways to eat it. However, blue-crab meat is used to prepare some of the most elegant dishes New Orleans has to offer.

40 medium or large mushrooms	1 teaspoon salt
1 lb. backfin lump blue-crab meat or other crabmeat	1 teaspoon red (cayenne) pepper
¾ cup dry bread crumbs	1½ cups shredded Monterey Jack cheese (6 oz.)
6 green onions, thinly sliced	1 cup unsalted butter or margarine
¼ cup minced parsley, preferably flat-leaf	About 10 toast points, if desired

Preheat oven to 350F (175C). Remove stems from mushrooms; reserve for another use. Place mushroom caps in a colander; quickly rinse under running water. Drain rinsed mushroom caps upside down on paper towels. Gently pat dry with paper towels; set aside. Using your fingertips, pick over crabmeat; remove and discard any small pieces of shell or cartilage. Place crabmeat in a large bowl; add bread crumbs, green onions, parsley, salt, cayenne and cheese. In a saucepan, melt ¾ cup butter or margarine; pour melted butter or margarine

over crabmeat mixture. Toss gently to combine. Do not
break up lumps of crabmeat. Melt remaining ¼ cup butter or margarine in a shallow baking pan large enough to
hold mushrooms in a single layer. Tilt pan to coat with
melted butter or margarine. Fill each mushroom cap with
stuffing; round off stuffing about ½ inch above cap.
Place stuffed mushrooms in pan. Bake in preheated oven
until mushrooms are dark and juicy and stuffing is
slightly browned, about 10 minutes. To serve as appetizers, arrange on platters. To serve as a first course,
arrange 4 to 6 mushrooms and toast points on each small
plate, drizzling drippings from the baking pan over top of
each serving. Makes 40 stuffed mushrooms.

Shrimp in Mustard Sauce

This is a great make-ahead recipe. At the last minute,
you need only garnish, serve and reap the compliments.

¼ cup tarragon-flavored vinegar	¼ cup minced parsley, preferably flat-leaf
¼ cup red-wine vinegar	6 green onions, chopped
1 teaspoon freshly ground black pepper	2½ lbs. uncooked medium shrimp, peeled, deveined
¼ cup dry mustard	1 (3-oz.) pkg. crab and shrimp boil
2 teaspoons hot red-pepper flakes	Cucumber slices
2 teaspoons salt	Crackers
½ cup vegetable oil	

In a 3-quart bowl, whisk together vinegars, black pepper,
mustard, pepper flakes and salt. While whisking, slowly
pour in oil until slightly thickened. Stir in parsley and
green onions. Set sauce aside. To cook shrimp, fill a 6-
quart pot half full of water; add crab and shrimp boil.
Bring mixture to a boil; boil 3 to 4 minutes. Add shrimp
to boiling water; cook just until pink, 2 to 3 minutes.
Quickly pour shrimp into a colander; shake to remove
excess water. Immediately stir drained shrimp into re-

served sauce. Cover and refrigerate overnight or up to 2 days. To serve, spoon into a glass serving bowl. Place bowl in center of a platter. Serve with cucumber slices and crackers. Serve with wooden picks or cocktail forks. Makes 8 to 10 appetizer servings.

Fried Fish Tails

A unique party finger food, this appetizer has the sauce built into the batter. The tails, about 2 inches long, are left over when fish are filleted. They are a bonus for fishermen, or ask your fish market to save them.

1¾ cups all-purpose flour	1½ tablespoons ketchup
2 eggs	2 tablespoons prepared
1½ teaspoons salt	horseradish
1½ teaspoons baking	1½ teaspoons fresh lemon
powder	juice
2 tablespoons vegetable	2 teaspoons
oil	Worcestershire sauce
¾ cup beer	3 tablespoons minced
1 teaspoon red (cayenne)	green onions
pepper	Peanut oil
	36 fish tails with meaty
	portion above fin

In a medium bowl, combine all ingredients except oil and fish tails to form a batter. In a heavy 12-inch skillet over medium heat, heat 3 inches peanut oil to 350F (175C) or until a 1-inch bread cube turns golden brown in 65 seconds. Holding fin portion of tails, dip meaty sections into batter, swirling to coat entire surface. Leave fin free of batter to use as a handle. Carefully slide battered tails into hot oil. Do not crowd tails in skillet. Fry to a rich golden brown on both sides, about 4 minutes, turning once. Remove fried fish tails from oil with a slotted spoon. Drain on paper towels. Keep warm while frying remaining fish tails. Makes 36 appetizers.

Cajun Party Spareriblets

Your party guests will never forget you for these incredible, falling-off-the-bone treats. They evoke a response similar to potato chips—nobody can eat just one.

2 lbs. pork spareribs
1 tablespoon peppercorns
1 large onion, coarsely
**   chopped**

Marinade, see below
2½ cups peanut oil

Marinade:
½ cup honey
½ cup soy sauce
½ cup dry sherry
½ cup red-wine vinegar
2 large garlic cloves,
**   minced**

2½ teaspoons grated
**   gingerroot**
4 green onions, minced
1½ teaspoons Tabasco
**   sauce**
Pinch of salt

Have butcher split sparerib rack in half horizontally for easier eating. Cut spareribs into individual ribs. Place ribs, peppercorns and onion into a 6-quart pot. Cover with cold water; bring to a boil over medium heat. Reduce heat to simmer; cook 45 minutes. Drain ribs well. Place drained ribs in a 13″ × 9″ baking pan; set aside. Prepare Marinade. Pour marinade over ribs in baking pan; cover and refrigerate at least 4 hours or up to 8 hours. Drain ribs, reserving marinade. Place reserved marinade in a 2-quart saucepan; cook over high heat until reduced by ½, about 8 minutes. Heat a wok or deep 12-inch skillet until hot. Add oil; heat until oil is almost smoking. Add drained ribs to hot oil in batches; stir about 3 minutes or until slightly crisp and mahogany colored. Remove with a slotted spoon; drain on paper towels. Arrange on a serving platter; drizzle reduced marinade over top. Serve hot. Makes 8 to 10 servings.

To prepare Marinade, combine all marinade ingredients in a heavy 2-quart saucepan over medium heat; bring to a boil. Reduce heat to low; simmer 15 minutes.

Cayenne Toasts

Watchout! These party crackers are addictive. They are an excellent use for leftover French bread. I have students all over the country who couldn't live without these spicy little toasts. For best results, do not prepare toasts more than a day or two before serving.

3 French-bread loaves	Topping, see below

Topping:

1 cup olive oil	½ teaspoon finely ground black pepper
2 teaspoons red (cayenne) pepper	1 teaspoon paprika
1½ teaspoons salt	1½ teaspoons garlic powder
1½ teaspoons sugar	1½ teaspoons onion powder

Preheat oven to 200F (95C). Prepare topping; set aside. Using a serrated bread knife or electric knife, cut French bread into slices about ¼ inch thick. Lay slices in single layers on ungreased baking sheets. Using a pastry brush, lightly coat 1 side of each bread slide with topping. Whisk mixture often while using so that seasonings do not settle to bottom of the bowl. Dry in preheated oven until very crisp, about 1 hour. The texture should be similar to Melba toast. Remove from baking sheets; cool on wire racks. When completely cool, store in airtight containers until served or up to 2 days. Cooled toasts can be packed in freezer containers and frozen up to 2 months. Recrisp frozen toasts in preheated 350F (175C) oven 5 to 7 minutes. Serve with a salad or soup. Makes 12 to 18 servings.

To prepare Topping, in a 2-quart bowl, whisk all topping ingredients until blended.

Baked Cajun Meat Pies

Meat pies are a staple item in Louisiana. One of the state's nicest little towns has its reputation built entirely around meat pies! So if you're ever passing through Natchitoches (pronounced NAK-o-tish), you owe it to yourself to stop and sample the best. Meat pies, like many Cajun dishes, can be made from whatever you have on hand, or whatever suits your fancy. They can be baked or fried.

Pastry, see below
Pork Filling, see below

1 egg, slightly beaten
2 tablespoons milk

Pastry:
2½ cups all-purpose flour
1 teaspoon sugar
1 teaspoon salt

½ cup unsalted butter or margarine, frozen
½ cup milk

Pork Filling:
¼ cup bacon drippings or lard
½ lb. lean ground pork
¼ cup all-purpose flour
½ medium onion, finely chopped
4 green onions, finely chopped
1½ teaspoons rubbed sage or 1½ tablespoons chopped fresh sage
2 tablespoons minced parsley, preferably flat-leaf

12 shucked oysters with their liquor (1 pint), finely chopped, liquor reserved
¾ cup Brown Veal & Pork Stock, page 00, or canned beef broth
½ teaspoon red (cayenne) pepper
Salt to taste
Freshly ground black pepper

To prepare Pastry, in a food processor fitted with the steel blade, process flour, sugar and salt until blended. Cut butter or margarine into 1-inch chunks; add to flour mixture. Process just until butter or margarine has been broken into pea-sized bits. Then, with motor running, pour milk through feed tube, processing just until dough begins to come together. Place dough on a lightly floured surface; shape into 2 flat pieces. Wrap in plastic wrap; refrigerate until chilled or up to 24 hours.

To prepare Filling, heat bacon drippings or lard in a heavy 10-inch skillet. When fat is hot, add pork. Cook, stirring, until all traces of pink are gone, 6 to 7 minutes. With a slotted spoon, place cooked pork into a medium bowl; set aside. Return skillet containing fat to medium heat. Add flour all at once; stir to blend. Cook, stirring constantly, until roux is a light peanut-butter color, about 15 minutes. Add onion, green onions, sage and parsley to browned roux; cook until vegetables are slightly wilted, about 15 minutes. Stir in reserved oyster liquid and stock. Cook over medium heat until mixture has thickened, about 5 minutes. Add oysters; cook 2 minutes. Stir in reserved pork and seasonings. Spoon mixture into bowl. Refrigerate until chilled.

To complete pies, preheat oven to 375F (190C). Lightly grease 2 baking sheets. On a floured surface, roll out 1 pastry piece to a 1/16-inch-thick circle. Using a 4-inch-round cutter, cut 12 circles from dough. Place a tablespoon of chilled mixture in center of each circle. In a small bowl, beat egg and milk until blended. Using a pastry brush, paint a 1/2-inch border of egg mixture around edge of each circle; fold dough in half, encasing filling. Seal edge with tines of a fork. Turn pie over; seal edge on opposite side. Place pies on greased baking sheets. Repeat with remaining pastry piece, reserving dough scraps. Gather up dough scraps; gently press together. Roll out pastry; cut and fill as before. Bake in preheated oven 15 minutes. Turn and bake until golden brown on both sides, about 10 minutes. Serve hot. To freeze, cool completely on wire racks; place in plastic freezer bags. To serve, place frozen pies on lightly greased baking sheets; bake in preheated 350F (175C) oven until heated through, about 15 minutes. Makes 24 meat pies.

Sun-Dried Tomato Spread

This is a sinfully delicious party food. The spread will keep up to 3 days.

1½ oz. dried tomatoes	½ teaspoon salt
1 cup olive oil	Pinch of sugar
2 large garlic cloves	1 green onion, coarsely
2 parsley sprigs	chopped
5 basil leaves or 1	2 (4-oz.) goat-cheese
teaspoon dried leaf	rounds
basil	Cayenne Toasts, page 00,
¼ teaspoon red (cayenne)	or crackers
pepper	

To rehydrate dried tomatoes, place tomatoes on a steamer rack over simmering water until tomatoes are completely soft and have no hard spots, about 45 minutes. Check water level often to keep bottom of steamer from drying out. Place steamed tomatoes in a 2-cup container with a tight-fitting lid. Add all remaining ingredients except goat cheese and toast or crackers. Cover container; shake to blend ingredients. Refrigerate 2 days to blend flavors. To serve, in a food processor fitted with the steel blade, process contents of container until almost smooth, leaving some texture. Place goat cheese on 1 or 2 serving dishes; pour tomato spread over cheese. Use small knives to spread on Cayenne Toasts or crackers. Makes 8 to 10 servings.

Cajun Glazed Mushrooms

These mushrooms are one of my favorite foods. They may be served with wooden picks as appetizers during the cocktail hour. Or serve two or three with each entree or first course. They can be habit-forming with steaks. Beware—these mushrooms are on the spicy side!

1½ lbs. small button
  mushrooms
1 cup unsalted butter or
  margarine
1 (5-oz.) bottle
  Worcestershire sauce

¼ cup finely ground
  pepper
½ teaspoon salt
5 to 6 drops Tabasco
  sauce

Trim any woody ends from mushroom stems. Wipe
trimmed mushrooms with a damp towel. Melt butter or
margarine in a heavy saucepan over medium heat. Add
mushrooms; toss to coat with butter or margarine. Stir in
Worcestershire sauce, pepper, salt and Tabasco sauce.
Increase heat to medium high. Cover pan; cook mushrooms, stirring frequently. Do not let mushrooms stick to
pan. Mushrooms are done when butter or margarine separates from Worcestershire sauce and mushrooms are
glazed with a heavy, dark caramel-colored sauce, about
20 minutes. Remove with a slotted spoon, discarding any
sauce. Serve hot. Makes about 8 servings.

Jezebel Sauce

This sauce is an institution in South Louisiana. No respectable home would be without a supply in the refrigerator for unexpected guests. Serve over cream cheese
to be spread on crackers.

1 (10-oz.) jar pineapple
  preserves (1 cup)
1 (10-oz.) jar apple jelly
  (1 cup)
¼ cup dry mustard

⅓ cup prepared
  horseradish
1½ teaspoons finely
  ground pepper

In a food processor fitted with the steel blade, process all
ingredients until blended. Spoon into jars. Cover and refrigerate until needed, up to 2 weeks. Makes about 2½
cups.

Vegetable & Cheese Pies Piquant

This is a fried version of meat pies, but vegetables and cheese replace the meat.

1 recipe Pastry from
    Baked Cajun Meat
    Pies, page 33
Filling, see below

1 egg, slightly beaten
2 tablespoons milk
Vegetable oil

Filling:
½ medium zucchini,
    finely chopped
1 medium onion, finely
    chopped
2 tablespoons minced
    parsley, preferably
    flat-leaf

1 large tomato, seeded,
    finely chopped
2 tablespoons chopped
    green bell pepper
¼ cup picante sauce
1 cup shredded Cheddar
    cheese (4 oz.)
Salt

To prepare Pastry, prepare pastry and chill as directed on page 33.

To prepare Filling, place all filling ingredients in a 4-quart bowl; stir until combined. Set aside.

To complete pies, on a floured surface, roll out 1 chilled pastry piece to a ¹⁄₁₆-inch-thick circle. Using a 4-inch-round cutter, cut circles from dough. Place a tablespoon of filling in center of each circle. In a small bowl, beat egg and milk until blended. Using a pastry brush, paint a ½-inch border of egg mixture around edge of each circle; fold dough in half, encasing filling. Seal edge with tines of a fork. Turn pie over; seal edge on opposite side. Repeat with remaining pastry piece, reserving dough scraps. Gather up dough scraps; gently press together. Roll out pastry; cut and fill as before. In a large saucepan, heat 3 inches oil to 350F (175C) or until a 1-inch bread cube turns golden brown in 65 seconds. Carefully place pies in hot oil, 3 at a time. Fry until golden brown

on both sides, about 4 minutes, turning once. Drain on
paper towels; serve hot. Makes 24 pies.

Patty Shells

In South Louisiana a hostess is judged by the patty shells
she serves! Patty shells filled with various things are required at a good party. This recipe is worth the price of
the book! It is shamefully simple, but you certainly do
not have to share your secret with your guests. Just ac-
cept their compliments on your wonderful pastry.

¼ cup unsalted butter or   **24 soft white-sandwich-**
**   margarine, melted**   **   bread slices**

Preheat oven to 400F (205C). Using a pastry brush, coat
inside of 24 miniature (2-inch diameter) muffin cups with
melted butter or margarine. Set aside. Using a 2½-inch
round cutter, cut a round from each slide of bread. Save
scraps from bread to dry for bread crumbs. Push each
round gently into buttered muffin cups, pressing snugly
against bottom and sides. If bread tears, patch with a
small piece of bread from scraps; pat patches in firmly.
Bake shells in preheated oven until lightly browned, 10
minutes. Remove from muffin pans; cool on wire racks.
When completely cooled, shells may be packed in plastic
freezer bags and frozen up to 3 months. Or fill for imme-
diate use. Makes 24 shells.

Home-Smoked Sausage

This complex and peppery-tasting sausage is probably
stored, at this moment, in half of the freezers in South
Louisiana! It is so simple to prepare that it is almost
magic. It cures overnight and needs no sausage casings.
The secret is the special salt, a fairly common item in
large grocery stores.

2 lbs. lean ground beef
1 cup water
1 teaspoon freshly ground
    black pepper
1 tablespoon peppercorns
1 tablespoon garlic
    powder

1 tablespoon liquid
    smoke
1 tablespoon onion
    powder
2 tablespoons Morton's
    Tender Quick Salt
2 teaspoons Tabasco
    sauce
Horseradish Sauce, see
    below

Horseradish Sauce:
1 (8-oz.) pkg. cream
    cheese, room
    temperature
1 tablespoon powdered
    sugar
1 tablespoon lemon juice

1 tablespoon
    Worcestershire sauce
3 tablespoons prepared
    horseradish
½ cup whipping cream,
    whipped to stiff peaks

In a 6-quart bowl, combine all sausage ingredients with a wooden spoon. Do not use your hands; curing salt is very irritating to any nicks or scratches you may have. Divide meat mixture into 4 equal portions; set aside. Cut 4 (15-inch-long) plastic-wrap pieces. Place 1 plastic-wrap piece on work surface; place 1 meat portion about 3 inches from long side. Fold over edge nearest sausage; use it to form sausage, packing it well to be sure there are no air pockets left within the mixture. Roll completed sausage tightly in plastic wrap; place on baking sheet. Repeat procedure with remaining sausage. Refrigerate sausages 36 hours. Preheat oven to 300F (150C). Carefully remove plastic wrap from refrigerated sausages. Place unwrapped sausages on a wire rack in a large ungreased baking pan. Bake in preheated oven 1 hour, turning after 30 minutes. Cool completely. Refrigerate until chilled or up to 2 days. To freeze sausage, bake before freezing. Refrigerate until chilled. Wrap first in plastic wrap, then in foil. Thaw frozen sausage in refrigerator before slicing and serving. To serve, prepare sauce. Slice sausage into rounds; serve with sauce. Makes 4 (8-ounce) sausages.

To prepare Horseradish Sauce, in a food processor fitted with the steel blade, process all ingredients except whipped cream until smooth. Using a rubber spatula, scrape mixture into a 2-quart bowl. Fold in whipped cream. Cover and refrigerate until needed or up to 2 days.

Oyster-Filled Patty Shells

Oyster lovers will rave about these bite-sized treats.

¼ cup unsalted butter or margarine
4 green onions, finely minced
1 small celery stalk, minced
½ small green or red bell pepper, minced
1 small onion, minced
¼ cup all-purpose flour
12 shucked oysters with their liquor (1 pint), finely chopped, liquor reserved

1 bay leaf, minced
¼ cup finely minced parsley, preferably flat-leaf
¼ teaspoon red (cayenne) pepper
¼ teaspoon freshly ground black pepper
Salt
24 baked Patty Shells, page 38
Thyme sprigs
Bell-pepper strips

Melt butter or margarine in a heavy 10-inch skillet over medium heat. Add green onions, celery, bell pepper and minced onion. Sauté until vegetables wilt, about 5 minutes. Stir in flour. Cook, stirring, over medium heat 2 to 3 minutes. Stir in oysters, oyster liquor and remaining ingredients except patty shells, combining well. Bring mixture to a boil, stirring. Reduce heat. Simmer until thickened, 3 to 4 minutes. If mixture is too thick, thin with a small amount of cream or milk. Preheat oven to 350F (175C). Place patty shells on an ungreased baking sheet; fill each patty shell with filling. Bake in preheated oven until filling bubbles, about 10 minutes. Decorate with thyme and bell-pepper strips. Serve at once. Makes 24 appetizers.

Mushroom-Cream-Filled Patty Shells

Rich and creamy, these are sure to be a hit!

¼ cup unsalted butter or margarine

4 green onions, finely chopped

2 tablespoons minced parsley, preferably flat-leaf

2 tablespoons finely minced chives

½ lb. mushrooms, finely chopped

3 tablespoons all-purpose flour

¾ cup whipping cream

¼ teaspoon dried leaf thyme or ¾ teaspoon chopped fresh thyme

¼ teaspoon red (cayenne) pepper

1½ teaspoons freshly ground black pepper

Salt

1 tablespoon fresh lemon juice

24 baked Patty Shells, page 38

Grated Parmesan cheese

2 tablespoons plus 2 teaspoons unsalted butter or margarine, room temperature

Melt ¼ cup butter or margarine in a heavy 10-inch skillet over medium heat. Add green onions, parsley and chives; cook over medium heat until vegetables are wilted, about 3 minutes. Stir in mushrooms. Cook 10 minutes or until liquid evaporates. Sprinkle flour over mixture; stir until blended. Cook 2 minutes, stirring. Mixture will be very dry. Stir in cream, thyme, cayenne, black pepper, salt and lemon juice, stirring to blend in all of flour. Reduce heat to low; cook 5 minutes or until thickened. Preheat oven to 350F (175C). Place patty shells on an ungreased baking sheet; fill each with mushroom filling. Top with a little Parmesan cheese and ¼ teaspoon butter or margarine. Bake in preheated oven until filling is bubbly, 10 minutes. Serve hot. Makes 24 appetizers.

Crawfish Beignets

One of the more trendy dishes developed from a traditional old recipe by New Orleans' innovative young chefs, this one, I believe, deserves immortality.

¾ cup water
1 teaspoon sugar
½ cup evaporated milk
1 (¼-oz.) pkg. active dry yeast (about 1 tablespoon)
3 to 3½ cups soft, southern wheat flour, page 290, or all-purpose flour
1 egg
2 tablespoons bacon drippings or vegetable shortening
3 medium garlic cloves

½ small green bell pepper, coarsely chopped
5 green onions, coarsely chopped
1 teaspoon salt
¼ teaspoon freshly ground black pepper
¼ teaspoon red (cayenne) pepper
1 teaspoon Creole mustard or other stone-ground mustard
½ lb. peeled boiled crawfish tails
Vegetable oil

In a medium saucepan over low heat, combine water, sugar and evaporated milk. Heat to 110F (45C). Pour hot mixture into a 2-cup measure. Stir in yeast until blended. Let stand 5 to 10 minutes or until foamy. Lightly oil a 6-quart bowl. In a food processor fitted with the steel blade, combine 3 cups flour and all remaining ingredients except oil and yeast mixture. Process until ingredients are chopped and blended. Add yeast mixture all at once. Process until blended. Dough should be smooth and nonsticky. If additional flour is needed, add 1 tablespoon at a time; process until blended after each addition. Process 15 seconds to knead dough. Oil a large bowl. Place dough in oiled bowl, turning to coat all surfaces of dough. Cover with plastic wrap. Let rise until doubled in bulk, about 1½ hours. Punch down dough. Turn out onto a lightly floured surface. Roll out dough into a rectangle about ½ inch thick. Working at a diagonal to rectangle, with a sharp knife, cut dough into 2-inch-wide strips, moving from left to right. Starting at top left and moving toward bottom of rectangle, cut dough diagonally into 2-inch-wide strips to form diamond shapes. See photos. Carefully place all completed diamonds ½ inch apart on ungreased baking sheets. Cover loosely with plastic wrap. Gather up remaining dough scraps; knead together. Cover loosely with plastic wrap; let rest 15 minutes to relax dough. Roll out and cut as before. Repeat until all dough has been used. Let rise 45 minutes. Do not double in bulk. Heat about 3 inches oil in a large saucepan to 350F (175C) or until a 1-inch bread cube turns golden brown in 65 seconds. Carefully slide raised beignets into oil, 3 or 4 at a time; do not crowd. Fry until puffy and golden brown on both sides, 2 to 3 minutes per side, turning once with tongs. Remove beignets with a slotted spoon; drain on paper towels. Serve hot. Makes about 36.

Paula's Dill Dip

This incredibly easy dip keeps well in the refrigerator and even improves with a day or two of aging. Serve with a selection of vegetable crudités.

⅔ cup mayonnaise
⅔ cup dairy sour cream
1 (¼-inch-thick) medium
    onion slice
4 parsley sprigs without
    stems

1 tablespoon dried dill
    weed or 3 tablespoons
    chopped fresh dill
1 teaspoon Beau Monde
    seasoning

In a blender or food processor fitted with the steel blade, process all ingredients until pureed. Place puree in a small bowl; cover and refrigerate until chilled or up to 2 days. Makes about 1½ cups.

Soups, Gumbos, Bisques & Breads

Supper for a Card Game

Green Salad with Garlic-Cream Dressing, page 86
Baked Cajun Meat Pies, page 33
Chicken & Andouille Sausage Gumbo
New Orleans French Loaves
Praline Cheesecake, page 202

If I were asked to name one dish that epitomizes Cajun or Creole food—worldwide—it would have to be gumbo. A simmering pot of gumbo embodies all of the rich and mysterious, complex and spicy tastes of the cuisine.

Gumbo, like so many of our wonderful dishes, can be created from whatever is available. This can vary from the most meager combination of greens, possibly with a tiny piece of pork; to tough and otherwise unusable cuts of beef; to the richest seafood-laden concoction affordable.

Gumbo is sublime. Indeed, one of my favorite meals is a spinach salad, a steaming bowl of gumbo, French bread and a glass of red wine. But we have much more than gumbo to offer for the soup course.

Turtle soup belongs in a class by itself. It is special. I have tasted turtle soup all over the country, but I have never tasted one that came even close to matching the complex taste of New Orleans-produced, roux-based turtle soup. The magic may be in the slightly soupy green bayou water in which our turtles live. But I really believe that the secret lies in the unique seasonings. As you read through the recipe you may think that you are going to make a pumpkin pie rather than a soup! But try it before you dismiss it. I guarantee you'll never again question anything that tastes that good!

The word bisque, in Cajun-Creole cookery, can refer to two entirely different dishes or variations of them. There are fine and delicate bisques derived from the cuisine's French heritage—cream-laden and pureed to velvet smoothness, finished perhaps, with a hint of liqueur. Many bisques are variations of this classic dish, with whole pieces or chunks of whole crab legs or lump crabmeat, chopped or whole shrimp or whole kernel corn added at the end and heated just to cook through. Or, as in Crawfish Bisque, it can be a smoky tasting, dark-roux-and-stock-based mixture served over rice and spicy enough to clear your sinus troubles.

Eating onion soup in South Louisiana is an experience not to be missed. It is one of those refreshing dishes composed of what I call honest tastes. That kind of flavor makes no pretenses. It simply says, "I'm good just like I come." New Orleans onion soup takes three of these tastes, onions, stock and cheese, and combines them in one soul-satisfying bowl of soup.

In short, we take the soup course very seriously. Sometimes we make it the whole meal.

A few words of advice before you tackle the recipes. Good stocks are the basis for soups. If you start with a weak stock, you will have a weak soup. Of course, a bad stock will produce nothing good. Master the three stocks, pages 18 to 22, and your soups, gumbos and bisques will have great foundations. Use canned stocks only if you must. Taste your soups carefully before salting, especially those made from canned stocks. Remember that the only way to duplicate the complex depth of taste so characteristic of Cajun-Creole soups, gumbos and bisques is to use good homemade stocks.

Okra and filé powder are added to gumbo both for their taste and for their inherent thickening qualities.

Both, however, break down with excessive cooking, resulting in a pot of stringy, viscous gumbo. Add sliced okra to the gumbo about 20 minutes before serving; cook just until tender. When reheating an okra gumbo, cook just to heat all of the ingredients thoroughly.

Filé powder should be added to the individual serving bowl, ¼ to ½ teaspoon each, depending on personal preference and bowl size. If you add it to the whole pot of gumbo, do not reboil.

So now you're ready to haul out the big pots and simmer away. But don't be surprised if the neighbors show up for supper, having been lured by the aromas wafting from your kitchen!

Chicken & Andouille-Sausage Gumbo

Gumbo may be fashioned from almost any ingredient on hand as evidenced by this popular chicken and andouille combination. Andouille is a hearty Cajun sausage somewhat on the spicy side.

Seasoning Mix, see below
8 boneless chicken-breast
   halves
1½ cups all-purpose flour
About 1 cup lard
2 cups chopped onion
1 cup chopped green bell
   pepper
1 cup chopped celery
3 qts. Louisiana Brown
   Poultry Stock, page
   19, or canned chicken
   broth
1 lb. andouille sausage or
   Polish kielbasa cut
   into bite-sized cubes

1½ teaspoons minced
   garlic
Salt
Freshly ground black
   pepper
Red (cayenne) pepper
2 cups sliced fresh okra or
   1 (10-oz.) pkg. frozen
   okra, thawed
1 cup sliced green onions
½ cup minced parsley,
   preferably flat-leaf
5 cups hot cooked rice

Seasoning Mix:
½ teaspoon each salt,
   freshly ground black
   pepper, red (cayenne)

pepper, paprika, onion
powder, garlic powder

Prepare Seasoning Mix. Remove skin from chicken, if necessary. Cut chicken into bite-sized pieces. Place pieces on a baking sheet; sprinkle liberally with seasoning. Let stand at room temperature 30 minutes. Place flour in a plastic bag; add seasoned chicken, shaking to coat all pieces thoroughly. Remove chicken; shake in a colander to remove all excess flour, reserving flour. Heat 1 cup lard in a large soup pot or Dutch oven over medium-high heat. When very hot, add chicken in batches; stir until browned and crisp on all sides. Remove from heat. Remove chicken with a slotted spoon; set aside. Loosen any browned bits from bottom of pan; strain fat to remove particles. Add enough lard to strained fat to equal 1 cup. Add fat back to pot over medium-low heat. Add reserved flour; whisk until a smooth mahogany-colored roux, about 45 minutes. Remove from heat; add onion, bell pepper and celery at once; stir to blend and prevent browning. Cook until vegetables are wilted and onion is transparent. *Slowly* stir in stock; stir until combined before adding more. When all stock has been added, bring to a full boil. Reduce heat; add sausage, garlic, salt, black pepper and cayenne. Add browned chicken; simmer 25 minutes, stirring often. Add okra; cook 20 minutes. To serve, remove from heat; stir in green onions and parsley. To serve, place ½ cup rice in each soup plate. Spoon gumbo over rice. Makes 8 to 10 servings.

To prepare Seasoning Mix, in a small bowl, combine all ingredients.

Gumbo Z'Herbes

Gumbo Z'Herbes is often referred to as *the king of gumbos* in New Orleans. In predominantly Catholic South Louisiana, it was traditionally served on Good Friday. The logic was that, after so many days of Lenten abstinence and fasting, the body needed the sort of revitalization provided by a combination of greens. The old

Creole women would rise early in the morning on Good Friday and head for the Vieux Carre's French Market to buy their greens for the day's Gumbo Z'Herbes. The vendors would have their bright, crisp greens temptingly arrayed. Stalls would be filled with the cries of "Get your twelve greens, lady," or "Get your seven greens, madame." Legend had it—and it is still nice to believe—that for every green added to the Gumbo Z'Herbes on this day, a new friend would be made during the following year!

10 oz. fresh spinach or 1 (10-oz.) pkg. frozen leaf spinach, thawed

10 oz. fresh mustard greens or 1 (10-oz.) pkg. frozen mustard greens, thawed

10 oz. fresh turnip greens or 1 (10-oz.) pkg. frozen turnip greens, thawed

10 oz. fresh collard greens or 1 (10-oz.) pkg. frozen collard greens, thawed

½ medium cabbage, shredded

2 bay leaves, minced

About 1 teaspoon each dried leaf basil, dried leaf thyme, dried leaf oregano

¼ teaspoon ground allspice

⅛ teaspoon ground cloves

¼ teaspoon freshly grated nutmeg

4 qts. Louisiana Brown Poultry Stock, page 18, or canned chicken stock

Seasoning Mix, see below

1 lb. lean boneless pork, cut into bite-sized pieces

1 lb. smoked ham, cut into bite-sized pieces

⅔ cup vegetable oil

2 large onions, chopped

4 celery stalks, chopped

1 large green bell pepper, chopped

4 large garlic cloves, chopped

2 tablespoons sugar

Salt

Freshly ground black pepper

Red (cayenne) pepper

24 shucked oysters with liquor (about 2 pints)

12 green onions, thinly sliced

½ cup minced fresh parsley, preferably flat-leaf

About 3½ tablespoons filé powder

5 cups hot cooked rice

Seasoning Mix:
½ teaspoon eash salt, **pepper, red (cayenne)**
    freshly ground black **pepper, paprika, onion**
    powder, garlic powder

Wash fresh greens; tear into small pieces. Remove large stalks and ribs. Place cleaned or frozen greens, cabbage, bay leaves, basil, thyme, oregano, allspice, cloves and nutmeg into a large soup pot. Add stock and enough water to cover greens by 3 inches. Bring to a boil. Reduce heat. Cover; simmer while preparing remaining ingredients. Prepare Seasoning Mix. Add pork and ham to Seasoning Mix. Shake to coat lightly. Set seasoned meat aside while oil heats. Heat oil in a large, heavy skillet over medium-high heat. When oil is very hot, add seasoned meat; stir until brown on all sides. Remove browned meat with a slotted spoon; add to simmering greens. Reduce heat to medium; add onions, celery, bell pepper and garlic to skillet. Cook until vegetables are wilted, about 5 minutes. Remove vegetables with a slotted spoon; add to simmering greens. Stir in sugar; simmer, uncovered, 1 hour. Season to taste with salt, black pepper and cayenne. Cover; simmer 2 hours. About 10 minutes before serving, gently stir in oysters with their liquor, green onions and parsley. Cook until edges of oysters curl. Spoon about ½ cup rice into each soup bowl. Spoon gumbo over rice; top with a pinch of filé powder. Makes 8 to 10 servings.

To prepare Seasoning Mix, place all ingredients in a large plastic bag. Shake to combine.

New Orleans Seafood Filé Gumbo

A unique and rich gumbo, this one is made with one of Louisiana's finest bayou delicacies—frog legs.

Seasoning Mix, see below
1½ recipes Cajun Roux, page 16
6 medium frog-leg pairs
1 large onion, chopped
1 medium, green bell pepper, chopped
½ cup chopped celery
4 medium garlic cloves, finely minced
4 qts. Seafood Stock, page 20, or 8 (8-oz.) bottles clam juice and 2 qts. water
2 lbs. uncooked heads-on shrimp, peeled, heads and shells reserved
2 bay leaves
½ of medium lemon
1 tablespoon minced parsley, preferably flat-leaf

1 teaspoon dried leaf thyme or 1 tablespoon chopped fresh thyme
1 teaspoon freshly ground black pepper
½ teaspoon red (cayenne) pepper
Salt to taste
1 lb. lump crabmeat
1 lb. skinned redfish fillets, or any mild, white-fleshed fish, cut into bite-sized chunks
½ lb. tiny bay scallops
5 cups hot cooked rice
About 3½ tablespoons filé powder
Chopped green onions
Minced parsley

Seasoning Mix:
½ teaspoon each salt, freshly ground black pepper, red (cayenne) pepper, paprika, onion powder, garlic powder

Prepare Seasoning Mix; set aside. Prepare roux as directed on page 16, cooking until mahogany-colored; set aside. Using your fingers, pull meat from frog legs; lay meat on a baking sheet. Sprinkle meat with Seasoning Mix. Add seasoned meat to hot roux. Cook, stirring, until lightly browned, about 5 minutes. Add onion, bell pepper, celery and garlic; cook until onion is wilted and transparent, about 5 minutes. Meanwhile, in a large saucepan, bring stock or clam juice and water to a boil. Tie reserved shrimp heads and shells and bay leaves in a cheesecloth bag. Add bag and lemon half to boiling stock. Slowly whisk roux into boiling stock until all has been added. Add parsley, thyme, black pepper, cayenne and salt. Reduce heat; simmer 1 hour. Remove and discard cheesecloth bag and lemon half. Add shrimp, crabmeat, fish and scallops. Cook over medium heat 15 minutes. Taste for seasoning; adjust if necessary. Spoon about ½ cup rice in each soup plate; spoon gumbo over top. Add about ¼ teaspoon filé powder to each bowl. Sprinkle each serving with chopped green onion and parsley. Makes 8 to 10 servings.

To prepare Seasoning Mix, in a small bowl, combine all ingredients.

Variation

Substitute 18 shucked oysters or ½ pound lump crabmeat for frog legs. Add with remaining seafood. Omit Seasoning Mix.

When purchased, greens are almost always sandy and dirty. It is very important to remove every trace of sandy material before cooking. To wash, fill sink with water; cut off and discard stem ends. Add trimmed greens to water, gently submerging them once or twice. Let stand in water a few minutes. With your hands, lift out washed greens; do not disturb sand that has accumulated in bottom. Place washed greens in a large colander to drain. Before cooking, rinse drained greens under running water two or three times.

Crawfish Bisque

If you visit the home of a Cajun and are served Crawfish Bisque, my friend, you are honored indeed. My opinion is very prejudiced, at best. I truly believe that this bisque, most regal of all bisques, is one of the finest concoctions ever put upon this earth. NOTHING can match the complexity of this smoky, spicy delicacy. Each Cajun household has its own recipe for Crawfish Bisque. A Cajun's Crawfish bisque is as unique as his signature.

It is always interesting to watch tourists eating real Crawfish Bisque for the first time. They stir it around, peering carefully into the bowl to see what lurks there in the dark liquid. And lo and behold—they scoop up these unidentified *things* from the bottom, down there with the rice. Dilemma number one is, of course, "What in the world are they?" Then the questions arise: "Do you really eat them?" and, if so, "*How* in the world do you eat them?" To answer the questions, we say: "Those are the thorax region, or body, of the crawfish shell. It is broken off right behind the beak and eyes, cleaned out and stuffed with a bread-and-crawfish-tail dressing. And good heavens, yes, you eat them. After you finish your bisque, just reach down there and hold onto them with one hand and scoop out the dressing with your spoon. That dressing has soaked up lots of the bisque liquid, and it is the best part of the meal!"

It is a very time-consuming process to make real Crawfish Bisque, but it is delicious to the very last drop you scrape out of the pot. The best way to make bisque is to make it a two-day project. If you are serving it on a weekend to guests, do a little each day during the week. Prepare ingredients for each step. Read directions carefully BEFORE you begin in order to avoid the frustration of leaving out a crucial step or ingredient. Crawfish Bisque is normally served in big soup plates as a full meal. Pass crisp French bread with lots of butter.

Boiled Crawfish, see
  below
Stuffed Crawfish Heads,
  see below
½ recipe Cajun Roux,
  page 16
1 large onion, chopped
2 medium garlic cloves,
  minced
1 medium, green bell
  pepper, chopped
2 celery stalks, chopped
2 medium tomatoes,
  peeled, chopped
¼ cup tomato paste
2 bay leaves, minced
½ teaspoon dried leaf
  thyme or 1½ teaspoons
  chopped fresh thyme

¼ teaspoon red (cayenne)
  pepper
½ teaspoon freshly
  ground black pepper
Salt to taste
1 tablespoon fresh lemon
  juice
2 teaspoons
  Worcestershire sauce
About 5 cups hot cooked
  rice
About 1 cup minced
  parsley, preferably
  flat-leaf
About 2 cups chopped
  green onions

Boiled Crawfish:
2 large onions, coarsely
  chopped
1 large lemon, sliced
3 garlic cloves, unpeeled,
  smashed
2 teaspoons red (cayenne)
  pepper

1 tablespoon freshly
  ground black pepper
2 tablespoons salt
1 (3-oz.) box crab and
  shrimp boil
10 lbs. live crawfish

Stuffed Crawfish Heads:
¼ cup unsalted butter or
  margarine
¼ cup vegetable oil
1 medium onion, finely
  chopped
⅓ cup minced green bell
  pepper
3 green onions, minced
2 medium garlic cloves,
  minced
1 tablespoon minced
  parsley, preferably
  flat-leaf

¼ teaspoon freshly
  ground black pepper
¼ teaspoon red (cayenne)
  pepper
Salt to taste
½ teaspoon dried leaf
  thyme
1 small bay leaf, minced
2 teaspoons fresh lemon
  juice
2 day-old bread slices
  soaked in ¼ cup milk
1 egg

Prepare Boiled Crawfish. Prepare Stuffed Crawfish Heads. In a heavy, deep 10-inch skillet, make roux as directed on page 16, cooking until mahogany colored. Add onion, garlic, bell pepper and celery to hot roux. Cook, stirring, until onion is wilted and transparent, about 5 minutes. Add tomatoes; cook 5 minutes. Add tomato paste, seasonings, remaining ½ of crawfish fat and remaining crawfish tails. Cook 5 minutes. Meanwhile, bring reserved 4 quarts stock to a rapid boil in an 8-quart soup pot. Add roux mixture to boiling stock, 1 large spoonful at a time until all has been added. Reduce heat. Add baked stuffed heads; simmer mixture 1 hour. Taste for seasoning; adjust if necessary. Spoon about ½ cup rice into each soup plate. Nest about 5 or 6 stuffed heads in rice. Ladle in bisque; sprinkle with parsley and green onions. Makes 8 to 10 servings.

To prepare Boiled Crawfish, place all ingredients except crawfish in a 20-quart stockpot; add 4 gallons water. Bring to a full rolling boil. Reduce heat; simmer, uncovered, 20 minutes to develop flavor. Bring back to a boil. Add live crawfish all at once; stir into water. Cook 20 minutes; drain, reserving 4 quarts cooking stock for bisque. Separate bodies from tails of crawfish. Using your little finger, reach into each body and scrape out yellow fat. This fat is a very important part of the taste of the bisque, so be sure to get it all. Set aside. Peel all tails; set aside. Holding body, break off and discard head with eyes and beak. Clean 40 to 50 heads; rinse under running water. Set aside while preparing stuffing.

To prepare Stuffed Crawfish Heads, preheat oven to 350F (175C). Heat butter or margarine and oil in a heavy 12-inch skillet over medium heat. Add onion, bell pepper, green onions, garlic and parsley; sauté until thoroughly wilted and transparent, about 8 minutes. Add 2 cups reserved crawfish tails, seasonings and lemon juice; cook 10 minutes, stirring often. Squeeze milk from bread. Tear bread into pieces. Add bread pieces, ½ reserved crawfish fat and egg to skillet. Stir until blended; remove from heat. Let mixture stand until cool enough to handle. Pack cooled mixture into reserved heads. Place on an ungreased baking sheet. Bake in preheated oven until stuffing is firm, about 10 minutes. Cool slightly; cover and refrigerate until needed.

Shrimp Bisque

This pureed bisque in classic Creole-French style is elegant enough for the most special occasion.

3½ lbs. uncooked heads-on shrimp
2 carrots, chopped
3 celery stalks, chopped
1 (3-oz.) pkg. crab and shrimp boil
2 onions, each stuck with 6 whole cloves
½ cup unsalted butter or margarine
5 green onions, chopped fine
¼ cup minced parsley, preferably flat-leaf
2 medium garlic cloves, minced
1 medium onion, chopped

½ lb. mushrooms, sliced
1 bay leaf
¾ cup all-purpose flour
1½ cups whipping cream
¼ teaspoon freshly ground black pepper
¼ teaspoon red (cayenne) pepper or to taste
Salt to taste
¼ cup dry sherry
Chopped chives, if desired

Peel shrimp, reserving shells and heads. Cover and refrigerate shrimp until ready to use. Place reserved shrimp heads and shells in a heavy 6-quart soup pot. Add carrots, celery, crab and shrimp boil and onions stuck with cloves. Add enough cold water to cover shells and vegetables by 5 inches. Bring shell mixture to a boil; skim grey foam from surface. Reduce heat to low; simmer, uncovered, 3 hours. Strain stock through a fine strainer; discard shells and vegetables. Reserve 2 quarts for bisque. Freeze extra stock for another use. Wash and dry soup pot. Melt butter or margarine in cleaned soup pot over medium heat. Add green onions, parsley, garlic, chopped onion, mushrooms and bay leaf. Sauté until vegetables are wilted, about 5 minutes. Do not brown. Stir in flour; cook 3 to 4 minutes, stirring. Slowly whisk in reserved shrimp stock. Bring to a boil to thicken; stir in refrigerated shrimp. Reduce heat; simmer 15 minutes. Discard bay leaf. Puree soup in small batches in a blender or food processor fitted with the steel blade. When all soup has been pureed, return to soup pot; reheat over low heat. Stir in cream; heat through. Add black pepper, cayenne, salt and sherry; heat through. Do not boil. Ladle soup into soup bowls; garnish with chives, if desired. Serve hot. Makes 8 to 10 servings.

Yellow-Squash Bisque

This recipe comes from the heart of Acadiana around Lafayette, Louisiana where both squash and potatoes grow in every rural backyard. It is simple, economical and really delicious.

6 tablespoons butter or margarine
1 large onion, chopped
2 medium baking potatoes, peeled, sliced
2 carrots, sliced
4 cups yellow crookneck squash (1½ lbs.), sliced
3 tablespoons all-purpose flour

1½ qts. Louisiana Brown Poultry Stock, page 19, or canned chicken broth
Salt to taste
¼ teaspoon red (cayenne) pepper
½ pint whipping cream (1 cup)
¼ teaspoon freshly grated nutmeg
About 2½ teaspoons Hungarian paprika

In a 4-quart heavy saucepan, melt butter or margarine. Add onion; sauté until wilted and transparent, about 5 minutes. Add potatoes, carrots and squash; toss to coat with butter or margarine. Add flour all at once; stir to combine. Cook over medium heat 3 to 4 minutes, stirring. Slowly stir in stock or broth. Puree soup in batches in blender or food processor fitted with a steel blade. When all soup has been pureed, return to soup pot. Stir in cream. Taste for seasoning; adjust if necessary. Heat through; do not boil. Stir in nutmeg; cook 3 to 4 minutes. Sprinkle ¼ teaspoon paprika into each soup bowl. Ladle hot soup over paprika. Stir soup in bowls; when soup is stirred, paprika will create an attractive marbled pattern. If desired, the soup base may be pureed, cooled and frozen up to 1 month. Thaw base in refrigerator; bring to a boil. Reduce heat; add cream. Makes 8 to 10 servings.

To reduce liquids, put liquid to be reduced into pan in which it will be cooked. Place handle of a wooden spoon on bottom of pan; use a small knife to mark a notch at level of liquid. Remove spoon; make a second notch at level of desired reduction, such as one-half or one-fourth. As liquid is reducing, use spoon handle as your measuring stick! If a recipe instructs you to reduce a liquid to one cup, or other measure, simply place one cup of water in pan in which you will reduce liquid; mark the one-cup level on your wooden spoon. Discard water. Add liquid; use spoon as your guide.

Turtle Soup with Madeira

Turtle Soup, or Terrapin Soup as it used to be called, is indeed one of the "grand old ladies" of classic Creole cuisine. Recipes for its preparation were closely guarded secrets which were written down in the "receipt books" of plantation cooks and passed down through generations. For the finest bowl of turtle soup in New Orleans, head for Commander's Palace. Or make the fascinating trip across Lake Ponchartrain Causeway to the sleepy little town of Mandeville, and sample Miss Jean's version at one of the area's best, and tiniest, seafood restaurants, Alnj's.

¾ cup unsalted butter or margarine
½ cup all-purpose flour
½ lb. smoked ham, cut into ½-inch cubes
2 lbs. boned turtle meat, trimmed, cut into ½-inch cubes
1 large onion, chopped
¼ cup chopped celery
3 tablespoons minced parsley, preferably flat-leaf
3 medium garlic cloves, minced
2 large tomatoes, peeled, chopped
1½ teaspoons salt
1 bay leaf, minced
1 teaspoon freshly ground black pepper

½ teaspoon ground cloves
½ teaspoon ground allspice
¼ teaspoon ground mace
¼ teaspoon freshly grated nutmeg
½ teaspoon dried leaf thyme or 1½ teaspoons chopped fresh thyme
3 cups Brown Veal & Pork Stock, page 21, or canned beef broth
2 cups Louisiana Brown Poultry Stock, page 19, or canned chicken broth
1 tablespoon Worcestershire sauce
1 tablespoon fresh lemon juice
½ cup Madeira, preferably Sercial
2 or 3 hard-cooked eggs, chopped

Melt butter or margarine in a heavy 4- to 5-quart soup pot over medium heat. Add flour all at once; stir until blended. Cook, stirring constantly, until peanut-butter colored, about 15 minutes. Add ham, turtle meat, onion, celery, parsley and garlic. Cook over medium heat, stirring, until vegetables are lightly browned, 6 to 7 minutes. Add tomatoes, salt, bay leaf, spices and thyme; cook 3 to 4 minutes. Slowly stir in stocks or broths; bring to a boil to thicken. Reduce heat. Partially cover; simmer 2 hours, stirring occasionally. About 10 minutes before serving, stir in Worcestershire sauce, lemon juice and Madeira. Ladle into individual soup plates; garnish with chopped eggs. Makes 8 to 10 servings.

When pureeing hot soups or sauces in a blender, start machine on low speed with container filled only half full. This prevents a splash-over of hot liquid.

Oyster-Artichoke Bisque

Delicate is the word to describe this classic New Orleans bisque. Even avowed oyster haters love this one because the oysters are pureed! The garnish of smoked oysters is the perfect touch.

3 bacon slices, finely chopped
¼ cup unsalted butter or margarine
4 green onions, chopped
1 (14-oz.) can artichoke hearts, drained, quartered
1 medium onion, chopped
½ cup all-purpose flour
18 shucked oysters (1½ pints), drained, liquor reserved
1 cup Seafood Stock, page 20, or 1 (8-oz.) bottle clam juice
1 cup Louisiana Brown Poultry Stock, page 19, or canned chicken broth

1 bay leaf, minced
1 tablespoon minced parsley, preferably flat-leaf
1 teaspoon dried leaf thyme or 1 tablespoon chopped fresh thyme
½ teaspoon freshly ground black pepper
Salt to taste
Red (cayenne) pepper to taste
1 pint whipping cream (2 cups)
⅓ cup dairy sour cream
1 (3⅔-oz.) can smoked oysters, drained, patted dry on paper towels
2 tablespoons butter or margarine, diced

In a 6-quart heavy soup pot over medium heat, sauté bacon until lightly browned. Add ¼ cup butter or margarine to bacon. Add green onions, artichoke hearts and onion; cook until onion is wilted and transparent, about 5 minutes. Do not brown. Stir in flour until combined; cook 4 to 5 minutes, stirring. Slowly stir in reserved oyster liquor and stocks or clam juice and broth. Bring to a boil to thicken. Reduce heat; add bay leaf, parsley, thyme, black pepper, salt and cayenne. Add oysters; simmer just until oysters begin to curl at edges. Puree soup in batches in blender or food processor fitted with a steel blade. When all soup has been pureed, return to soup pot over medium heat. Stir in whipping cream until blended. Stir in sour cream; whisk until combined. Heat through, about 6 minutes. Do not boil. Taste for seasoning; adjust if necessary. Stir in smoked oysters; heat through. Remove from heat; whisk in remaining 2 tablespoons butter or margarine. Spoon into bowls; place 1 to 2 smoked oysters in each bowl. Makes 8 to 10 servings.

Oysters-in-Cream Soup

Since I am a dedicated oyster lover, this very simple but delicious soup is one of my favorites.

36 shucked medium
   oysters (3 pints),
   drained, liquor
   reserved
3½ pints whipping cream
   (7 cups)
¼ cup unsalted butter or
   margarine
4 green onions, minced

2 tablespoons all-purpose
   flour
¼ teaspoon freshly
   ground white pepper
⅛ teaspoon red (cayenne)
   pepper
Salt to taste

Cover and refrigerate drained oysters until ready to use. Place oyster liquor and cream in a 4-quart saucepan over medium-high heat. Cook until reduced by ½, about 25 minutes. Set aside. In another 4-quart saucepan, melt butter or margarine over medium heat. Add green onions; cook until slightly wilted, about 2 minutes. Stir in flour; cook 3 to 4 minutes, stirring. Slowly whisk reduced cream mixture into flour mixture. Bring to a boil to thicken. Reduce heat; add oysters and seasonings. Simmer just until oysters begin to curl at edges, about 5 minutes. Ladle into soup plates, dividing oysters equally. Makes 6 servings.

Crab-Corn Soup

Many restaurants in South Louisiana serve their own version of this satisfying soup. To get the very best, you have to journey to the Inn at the Asphodel Plantation outside Jackson, Louisiana.

½ cup unsalted butter or margarine
1 medium onion, chopped
1 medium garlic clove, minced
¼ cup all-purpose flour
2 cups Seafood Stock, page 20, or 2 (8-oz.) bottles clam juice
2 cups Louisiana Brown Poultry Stock, page 19, or canned chicken broth
1 (17½-oz.) cans whole-kernel corn (1½ cups), drained

¼ teaspoon dried leaf thyme or ¾ teaspoon chopped fresh thyme
1 teaspoon salt
½ teaspoon freshly ground black pepper
¼ teaspoon red (cayenne) pepper
1 pint whipping cream (2 cups) 1 lb. lump crabmeat
4 green onions, chopped

Melt butter or margarine in a heavy 4- to 6-quart soup pot over medium heat. Add onion and garlic. Sauté until wilted and transparent, about 5 minutes. Add flour all at once; stir until blended. Cook 3 to 4 minutes, stirring. Slowly stir in stocks or clam juice and broth. Bring to a boil to thicken. Stir in corn, thyme, salt, black pepper and cayenne; reduce heat to medium. Cook, uncovered, 25 minutes. Stir in cream; cook 10 minutes. Taste for seasoning; adjust if necessary. Using your fingertips, carefully pick through crabmeat; remove any bits of shell or cartilage. Do not break up lumps of meat. Add crab-meat and green onions to soup; cook over medium heat just to heat through, 5 to 6 minutes. Serve hot. Makes 8 to 10 servings.

Creole Onion Soup

The combination of two stocks added to the lightly cara-melized onions creates a wonderful taste. Topped with garlic-bread rounds and lots of cheese, you have a New Orleans classic.

1½ cups unsalted butter
   or margarine
5 large onions, chopped
2 teaspoons sugar
½ cup all-purpose flour
6 cups Brown Veal &
   Pork Stock, page 21,
   or canned beef broth

6 cups Louisiana Brown
   Poultry Stock, page
   19, or canned chicken
   broth
Salt to taste
½ teaspoon freshly
   ground pepper
Garlic Bread, see below
10 (¼-inch-thick)
   Gruyère-cheese slices

Garlic Bread:
10 (½-inch-thick) French-
   bread slices
¼ cup olive oil

6 large garlic cloves
Salt

Melt butter or margarine in a heavy 5- to 6-quart soup pot over medium heat. Add onions; sauté, stirring often, until very limp and completely transparent, about 20 minutes. Sprinkle sugar over onions; stir to blend. In-crease heat to medium-high; cook, stirring, until onions are lightly browned and slightly crisp on edges, 5 to 6 minutes. Reduce heat to medium. Add flour all at once; stir until combined. Cook 3 to 4 minutes, stirring. Slowly stir in stocks or broths. Bring to a boil to thicken slightly. Reduce heat. Season with salt and pepper; simmer 1 hour, stirring occasionally. Taste for seasoning; adjust if necessary. Prepare Garlic Bread. When ready to serve, ladle soup into flameproof bowls. Place a garlic-bread slice on each bowl of soup. Top each bread slice with a cheese slice. Broil under preheated broiler until cheese melts, 1½ to 2 minutes. Serve hot. Makes 6 to 8 servings.

To prepare Garlic Bread, position oven rack 6 inches below heat. Preheat broiler. Using a pastry brush, brush both sides of bread lightly with olive oil. Place on an ungreased cookie sheet. Broil until crisp, turning once. Cool slightly. When toasts are cool enough to handle, rub garlic cloves on 1 side of each piece. Salt lightly; set aside.

Cold Cucumber Soup

In the hot summer, this soup is as refreshing as a dip in the pool.

2 large cucumbers
¼ cup minced parsley, preferably flat-leaf
4 green onions, chopped
2 cups buttermilk
1 cup Louisiana Brown Poultry Stock, page 19, or canned chicken stock
1 pint dairy sour cream (2 cups)

½ teaspoon freshly ground white pepper
Salt to taste
2 tablespoons fresh lemon juice
2 tablespoons minced fresh dill or
1½ teaspoons dried dill weed
Red caviar

Cut 6 to 8 thin slices from 1 unpeeled cucumber. Wrap in plastic wrap; refrigerate. Peel, seed and chop remaining cucumbers. In a blender or food processor fitted with the steel blade, puree chopped cucumbers, parsley, green onions and a small amount of buttermilk. Transfer puree to a 5-quart bowl. Whisk in remainder of buttermilk and all remaining ingredients except caviar. Cover with plastic wrap; refrigerate until chilled. To serve, taste soup for seasoning; adjust if necessary. Ladle into soup plates. Top each reserved cucumber slice with a red-caviar dollop. Place 1 caviar-topped slice on each serving. Makes 6 to 8 servings.

Duck & Artichoke Gumbo

This rich and hearty gumbo is a must for the duck lover. Even the roux is made with duck fat! It is served over wild rice for a perfect combination of flavors. For ease in preparation, make stock and roux one day; refrigerate overnight. Prepare gumbo the next day.

Duck Stock, see below
1 recipe Cajun Roux, page 16
¼ cup chopped shallots
1 large onion, chopped
3 celery stalks, chopped
1 medium carrot, chopped
1 medium, green bell pepper, chopped
1½ (14-oz.) cans artichoke hearts, drained, quartered
2 bay leaves, minced

2 teaspoons dried leaf chervil or 2 tablespoons chopped fresh chervil
⅛ teaspoon ground cloves
¼ teaspoon red (cayenne) pepper
1 teaspoon freshly ground black pepper
Salt to taste
1 cup dry vermouth
About 5 cups hot cooked wild rice
Minced parsley, preferably flat-leaf
Chopped green onions

Duck Stock:
2 (3- to 4-lb.) domestic ducks or 3 wild ducks
2 large onions, coarsely chopped
4 celery stalks, chopped
3 leeks, coarsely chopped
2 large carrots, chopped

5 parsley sprigs, preferably flat-leaf
2 teaspoons dried leaf thyme or 2 tablespoons chopped fresh thyme
1 tablespoon peppercorns
2 bay leaves

Make Duck Stock. Make roux as directed on page 16, using duck fat and enough lard to make 1 cup. Cook roux until mahogany-colored. Add shallots, onion, celery, carrot and bell pepper to hot roux. Cook, stirring, until vegetables are wilted and transparent, about 10 minutes. Meanwhile, bring reserved 4 quarts stock to a rapid boil in an 8-quart soup pot. Add reserved duck meat and artichoke hearts. Slowly stir roux mixture into boiling stock, 1 large spoonful at a time. Reduce heat. Add seasonings; simmer 1 hour. Stir in vermouth; heat through. Taste for seasoning; adjust if necessary. Spoon about ½ cup rice into each soup plate; spoon gumbo over rice. Sprinkle with parsley and green onions. Makes 8 to 10 servings.

To prepare Duck Stock, preheat oven to 400F (205C). Pull fat from inside of ducks; reserve. Using a cleaver or heavy chef's knife, quarter ducks; place pieces in 2 roasting pans. Roast in preheated oven until ducks are dark brown in color, 1 to 1½ hours. Turn pieces often. Place browned duck in a 10-quart stockpot; set aside. Carefully pour fat from roasting pans into a 2-cup pyrex measuring cup; set aside. Spread vegetables in roasting pans. Bake in preheated oven until vegetables are dark brown, about 30 minutes. Add browned vegetables to stockpot with duck. Place roasting pan over high heat; add 1 cup water. Using a metal spatula, scrape up all browned bits; add liquid to stockpot. Repeat with remaining pan. Add enough cold water to cover duck pieces and vegetables by 4 inches. Bring stock to a full boil; skim grey foam from surface. Reduce heat; stir in parsley, thyme, peppercorns and bay leaf. Barely simmer, uncovered, 6 hours. Strain stock through a fine strainer, pressing down on meat and vegetables to extract every drop of flavor. Discard vegetables; cool duck. Reserve 4 quarts stock for gumbo. Freeze any extra for another use. As soon as duck pieces are cool enough to handle, pull meat from bones; chop into bite-sized pieces for gumbo. Discard skin and bones.

Bread flour, milled especially for baking bread, is higher in gluten (a protein) than all-purpose flours. To determine gluten content of a flour, look at the panel on the side of the bag labeled "Nutritional Information." For bread baking you should use a flour with 14 percent protein. The higher this protein percentage, the greater volume in your bread loaf.

Cap Bread

This is a very traditional New Orleans bread with a wonderful texture. It is made from a rich yeast dough and is shaped to resemble a Bishop's cap!

¼ cup warm water (110F, 45C)	4 to 4¼ cups bread flour
	1½ teaspoons salt
1 cup milk, scalded, cooled to 110F, 45C	2 tablespoons unsalted butter or margarine, room temperature
1 tablespoon sugar	1 egg
1 (¼-oz.) pkg. active dry yeast (about 1 tablespoon)	

In a 2-cup liquid measuring cup, combine warm water, milk, sugar and yeast. Let stand until foamy, 5 to 10 minutes. In a food processor fitted with the steel blade, blend 4 cups flour, salt, butter or margarine and egg. Add dissolved yeast mixture all at once to flour mixture; process until blended, about 5 seconds. Stop machine to check consistency of dough. Dough should be slightly sticky but workable. If additional flour is needed, add 1 tablespoon at a time; process just until combined. If dough is too dry, add warm water 2 teaspoons at a time; process just until combined. Process 20 seconds to knead dough. Oil a 7- to 8-quart bowl. Turn out dough onto work surface. Knead 2 or 3 times by hand; place dough in oiled bowl. Turn dough to coat all surfaces with oil. Cover with plastic wrap; let rise in a warm, draft-free place, until doubled in bulk, about 1½ hours. Punch down dough completely. Turn out dough onto a lightly floured surface; form into a flattened circle, about 8 inches in diameter. With your hands, pull out 1 edge of circle to form a 4-inch rope on 1 side of circle. Grasp rope with your fingers; pull up over top of bread. Rope should reach center of circle. Seal rope edges securely to circle. Grease a baking sheet. Place loaf on greased baking sheet; cover loosely with plastic wrap. Let rise until doubled in bulk, about 1 hour. Preheat oven to 350F (175C). When loaf has doubled in bulk, remove plastic wrap. Bake in middle of preheated oven until golden brown, 35 to 40 minutes. Bread is done when loaf sounds hollow when tapped on bottom. Cool on rack before slicing. Makes 1 large loaf.

New Orleans Luncheon Biscuits

These are the perfect accompaniment to soups and salads. But make plenty—nobody can eat just one . . . or two . . .

About 3 cups soft,
    southern wheat flour,
    page 290, or all-
    purpose flour
2 teaspoons baking
    powder
1½ teaspoons salt

½ cup plus 1 tablespoon
    lard
1 to 1¼ cups milk
¾ teaspoon fresh lemon
    juice

Preheat oven to 400F (205C). Lightly grease 2 baking sheets. In a medium bowl, combine 3 cups flour, baking powder and salt with a fork. Cut lard into 1-inch cubes; add lard cubes to flour mixture. Using your fingertips, work lard into flour mixture until it resembles coarse cornmeal. Add 1 cup milk and lemon juice. Using a wooden spoon, gently stir mixture just until all flour is moist and dough is slightly sticky. If additional milk is necessary, stir in 1 tablespoon at a time. Turn out dough onto a heavily floured surface. Pat out dough into a flat circle about 8 inches in diameter. Flour surface of circle; roll out to a ½-inch thick rectangle. Fold pastry in half; line up corners. Reflour surface as necessary. With open edge to your right, roll out pastry and fold as before for a total of 4 times. When 4 folds have been completed, roll out pastry to ½ inch thick. Using a 1½-inch biscuit cutter, cut out biscuits. Place biscuits on greased baking sheets. Bake in middle of preheated oven until biscuits have risen and are light golden brown, 10 to 12 minutes. Serve hot. Makes about 36 (1½-inch) biscuits.

New Orleans French Loaves

French Bread—the kind with large, airy holes in the middle and a crispy crust that falls all over the table when you tear off a nice, big piece—can be created in the home kitchen. In fact, it is simple to prepare and bake. You don't need misters, steam, clay bricks or the complicated procedures often recommended in recipes for French bread. The following recipe was developed for the food processor. The loaves require no intricate rolling and measuring to shape them.

1½ cups warm water
   (110F, 45C)
1½ teaspoons sugar
1 (¼-oz.) pkg. active dry
   yeast (About
   1 tablespoon
About 3 cups bread flour
1½ teaspoons salt

1 teaspoon apple-cider
   vinegar or other mild
   fruit-flavored vinegar
¼ cup vegetable oil
¼ cup unsalted butter or
   margarine, melted
   with ½ teaspoon salt

In a 2-cup liquid measuring cup, combine water and sugar. Sprinkle in yeast; stir until blended. Let stand until foamy, 5 to 10 minutes. In a food processor fitted with the steel blade, blend 3 cups flour, salt and vinegar.

Add dissolved yeast mixture to flour mixture all at once. Process 3 to 4 seconds to combine. Stop machine to check consistency of dough. The dough should be wet and sticky with a slight degree of body. If it is too soupy, add additional bread flour, ONE TABLESPOON AT A TIME, processing to blend between each addition, until a wet, sticky dough is formed. Process no more than 15 seconds to knead dough. Pour vegetable oil into a large bowl; oil hands and fingers well. Remove blade from processor, placing any dough which clings to it in bowl. Remove rest of dough to oiled bowl, forming dough into a loose ball. Turn dough over several times to coat completely with oil. Cover bowl with plastic wrap; let rise in a warm place, free from drafts, until doubled in bulk, about 1½ hours. When dough has doubled in bulk, stir down dough, removing all air from first rising. Position oven rack in center of oven. Preheat oven to 400F (205C). Lightly grease 1 double-trough French-bread pan, or a triple baguette pan, using some of oil remaining in bottom of bowl. Thoroughly grease hands with some oil from bowl. To make 2 French loaves, pinch dough in half; lift out of bowl, 1 piece at a time. To make baguettes, divide dough into thirds. Lay dough in 1 trough of bread pan; repeat procedure with remaining dough. Because of its very wet and loose consistency, dough will shape itself. Brush dough surface thoroughly with some butter-and-salt mixture. Loosely cover loaves with plastic wrap. Let rise until double in bulk, about 1 hour. Reserve remaining butter-and-salt mixture. When loaves have doubled in bulk, carefully remove plastic wrap; brush loaves with remaining butter-salt mixture. Use very light pressure when applying butter mixture, taking care not to deflate loaves. Bake in center of preheated oven until golden brown on top, 25 minutes. Carefully turn loaves over in pan; bake about 10 minutes more to brown bottoms. Cool completely on cooling racks. To slice, cut a 45-degree angle using a serrated bread knife. Makes 2 French loaves or 3 baguette-size loaves.

A scientific discovery made by my good friend, Shirley Corriher, led to the addition of flavored vinegar to the French bread recipe. When testing breads prepared according to the age-old, long, slow-rising French method, it was discovered that the dough became acidic during extended and numerous risings. Her conclusion was simply to add acid at the beginning of the bread-making process. The resulting loaves had both the aroma and taste of the slightly soured and yeasty breads of Europe, without the long rising! Try this method with your favorite bread recipe, using as your guide one teaspoon of fruit-flavored vinegar for every three cups of flour. Don't be tempted to add more vinegar; excess acid can destroy the gluten in the flour.

Salads & Salad Dressings

Bridge-Club Luncheon

Minted Brandy Ices, page 280
Crabmeat & Vegetable Salad
New Orleans Luncheon Biscuits, page 67
Creamy Chocolate & Bourbon Pie, page 192

South Louisiana has a bounty of "salad makings." We were making gigantic salads from offbeat combinations of greens like roquette (rocket), dandelion and chicory long before they became trendy. But our salads are not limited to green things alone!

Often in the hot summer months it is too hot and humid, even in an air-conditioned kitchen, to get excited about any food that requires the use of heat in its preparation. So we put together a big bowl of seafood or vegetable salad, put some relishes on a plate and pass a loaf of crusty French bread or luncheon biscuits. Ah, just what the doctor ordered to satisfy the hunger, the temperament, and, most importantly, the cook!

Molded salads are very popular in South Louisiana. I've had some that were really inspired dishes. The two very best places to find the greatest salads in Cajun country are a big family reunion with a buffet supper and a church-sponsored covered-dish supper. There you'll find dozens and dozens of imaginative and delicious

71

salads of all varieties that will send you scrambling for
your paper and pencil to get the recipe. Now that's what
regional food is all about!

Fresh and cold are the key words to salad success.
When you shop for salad greens, look for freshness. If
the romaine looks as though it had been backed over by
the truck that delivered it, but the lowly iceberg lettuce
looks picture perfect, then by all means, select the iceberg. If the large tomatoes are pink at best and hard as
rocks, check out the cherry tomatoes. If they too are
unacceptable, throw in some sliced red bell pepper for
sharp color contrast. Let freshness guide your selections. All salad ingredients should be well chilled.

Texture and color are important in the composition of
a salad. In each salad you should have a variety of textures. Combine several varieties of greens for contrasts
in texture and color, with the bonus of an exciting flavor
combination. Garnishes are the cook's opportunity to
shine in salad making. With a little imagination in garnishing, you can create world-class salads.

Salad greens should be squeaky clean, but they must
also be bone dry. Damp greens will absolutely ruin your
finest homemade dressing.

Wash your greens thoroughly under running water to
remove dirt, grit and—yes, they can be there—critters.
Then either run them through a marvelous gadget called
a *salad spinner* or pat each leaf dry on paper towels. If
you would like a little exercise, put the greens in an open
mesh bag, step outside and swing them in wide circles 3
or 4 minutes!

Store salad greens dry. The fabric salad bags sold in
gourmet shops are very good. Or wrap the greens loosely
in paper towels; store in plastic bags in the vegetable
crisper.

Suggested Salad Garnishes

Tiny broccoli flowerets; cauliflowerets; grated or
paper-thin sliced carrots; shredded red cabbage; alfalfa
sprouts or mung-bean sprouts; bite-sized chunks of feta
cheese, blue cheeses or Cheddar cheese; grated Parme-

san or Romano cheese; whole anchovy fillets; sardines; chopped green olives with pimentos; chopped ripe olives; whole calamata or oil-cured black olives; sliced roasted red bell peppers; zucchini, yellow-squash or cucumber rounds; sliced green onions; thinly sliced purple onions; chopped hard-cooked egg; nuts and seeds, such as sliced almonds, sunflower seeds, toasted pine nuts; thinly sliced water chestnuts; canned crispy chow mein noodles; pepperoni or salami rounds; shredded prosciutto; REAL crumbled, crisp-cooked bacon; thinly sliced celery; tomato wedges; cherry-tomato halves; marinated artichoke hearts; canned hearts of palm; pickled baby eggplant; cocktail onions; croutons, especially if homemade.

Basil & Tomato Salad

In summer when big, scrumptious Creole tomatoes are in season and fresh basil is waist-high, this salad becomes a familiar item on my dinner table. It also makes a great buffet salad. Use the ripest home-grown tomatoes available in your area.

5 large, very ripe
    tomatoes, sliced
1 medium red onion,
    halved crosswise, then
    thinly sliced
Dressing, see below

Finely minced parsley,
    preferably flat-leaf
Parsley sprigs or basil
    sprigs

Dressing:
1 large garlic clove
¼ cup tomato sauce
⅓ cup red-wine vinegar
1 tablespoon sugar
½ teaspoon salt
1 tablespoon minced
    fresh basil or
    1 teaspoon dried
    leaf basil

1 teaspoon
    Worcestershire sauce
½ teaspoon Creole
    mustard or other
    stone-ground mustard
¼ teaspoon freshly
    ground pepper
¼ teaspoon Tabasco
    sauce
1 cup olive oil

Arrange tomato slices slightly overlapping on a large platter. Scatter onion over top. Cover and refrigerate until ready to serve. Prepare dressing. To serve, pour enough dressing over salad to coat well. Sprinkle with minced parsley; garnish with parsley or basil sprigs. Makes 6 to 8 servings.

To prepare Dressing, in a food processor fitted with the steel blade and motor running, drop garlic through feed tube to mince. Stop machine; add all remaining ingredients except olive oil. Process until blended. With motor running, add oil through feed tube in a slow, steady stream. When all has been added, process 10 seconds to form a smooth dressing.

Spinach Salad Vermillion

This tasty salad with a cooked dressing is elegant enough to serve at the finest dinner party. Serve on clear or smoked glass plates and get ready for the compliments.

1¼ lbs. spinach
½ lb. medium
  mushrooms, sliced
3 hard-cooked eggs,
  finely chopped
½ cup grated Parmesan
  cheese (1½ oz.)
6 bacon slices
2 teaspoons Dijon-style
  mustard

1 tablespoon sugar
½ cup sherry vinegar
½ teaspoon salt
½ teaspoon freshly
  ground pepper
½ cup olive oil
6 green onions, chopped

Remove large stems from spinach leaves; tear leaves into bite-sized pieces. Place in a large heatproof salad bowl. Add mushrooms, eggs, and cheese; set aside. In a heavy 10-inch skillet, cook bacon slices until crisp. Drain bacon on paper towels, reserving drippings in skillet. Crumble bacon when cool enough to handle; place crumbled bacon in bowl with spinach. Heat drippings over medium heat; whisk in mustard and sugar; whisk 1 minute. Pour in vinegar; whisk until sugar dissolves. Add salt and pepper. Add olive oil in a slow, steady stream, whisking constantly. Stir in green onions; immediately invert skillet over salad bowl. Leave in place 1 minute to slightly wilt greens. Remove skillet; toss salad well. Serve immediately. Makes 6 to 8 servings.

Spinach, Orange & Onion Salad with Poppy-Seed Dressing

This is a refreshing salad with beautiful color contrasts and a sublime taste. Serve with soup for lunch or a light supper.

10 oz. fresh spinach
1 (11-oz.) can mandarin-
    orange sections,
    drained
½ small red onion, halved
    crosswise, thinly sliced

2 tablespoons roasted
    sunflower kernels
Poppy-Seed Dressing,
    see below

Poppy-Seed Dressing:
¾ cup sugar
1 teaspoon dry mustard
1 teaspoon salt
⅓ cup raspberry-flavored
    vinegar

1 tablespoon grated onion
1 cup vegetable oil
1½ teaspoons poppy
    seeds

Remove large stems from spinach leaves; tear leaves into bite-sized pieces. Place in a large salad bowl; add orange sections, onion and sunflower kernels. Toss gently to combine. Cover and refrigerate until ready to serve. Prepare dressing. Remove salad from refrigerator; drizzle desired amount of dressing over top and toss well. Makes 6 to 8 servings.

To prepare Poppy-Seed Dressing, place all dressing ingredients except oil and poppy seeds in a food processor fitted with the steel blade. Process until combined, about

15 seconds. With motor running, add oil through feed tube in a slow, steady stream. Add poppy seeds; turn on and off 2 to 3 times. Makes 1½ cups.

Marinated Cole Slaw

Perfect for picnics, barbecues or do-ahead summer buffets, this cool and crisp salad actually improves if made two or three days ahead.

1 medium cabbage, cored, coarsely shredded
1 cup coarsely shredded red cabbage
6 green onions, chopped
3 medium carrots, shredded

2 medium, green bell peppers, quartered lengthwise, thinly sliced
Dressing, see below

Dressing:
1 cup red-wine vinegar
½ cup mayonnaise
¼ cup grated onion
1 teaspoon Tabasco sauce
2 teaspoons prepared horseradish

1½ tablespoons sugar
1 teaspoon freshly ground pepper
1½ teaspoons salt
1 cup vegetable oil

Toss all vegetables in a large bowl. Set aside. Prepare dressing. Pour dressing over vegetables; stir until coated well. Cover and refrigerate at least 24 hours or up to 3 days. Toss often. To serve, transfer slaw to a serving bowl with a slotted spoon; discard any excess dressing. Makes 6 to 8 servings.

To prepare Dressing, in a medium bowl, whisk all ingredients except oil until combined. Add oil in a slow, steady stream, whisking until combined.

Caribbean Cheese & Vegetable Salad

Caribbean cuisine had a great influence on the evolution of the Creole cuisine and vice versa. Ingredients and tastes were exchanged between large sugar and indigo plantations of the islands and the major port of New Orleans. This very satisfying salad reflects the cool, crunchy and subtly spicy taste that is a blend of these two cultures.

3 large, very ripe tomatoes, chopped
1 medium cucumber, peeled, seeded, chopped
1 medium, green bell pepper, chopped
⅔ cup chopped canned hearts of palm

1 medium red onion, finely chopped
1 cup shredded Monterey Jack cheese (4 oz.)
Dressing, see below
Red-leaf-lettuce leaves
Minced parsley, preferably flat-leaf

Dressing:
2 tablespoons fresh lemon juice
1 tablespoon red-wine vinegar
1 teaspoon minced fresh oregano or ¼ teaspoon dried leaf oregano
½ teaspoon sugar

½ teaspoon salt
¼ teaspoon freshly ground pepper
½ teaspoon Tabasco sauce
½ cup olive oil

In a 4-quart bowl, combine tomatoes, cucumber, bell pepper, hearts of palm, onion and cheese. Cover and refrigerate until ready to serve. Prepare dressing. Gently toss dressing with vegetable mixture. Line 4 to 6 individual plates with lettuce leaves. Spoon salad over lettuce. Garnish with parsley. Makes 4 to 6 servings.

To prepare Dressing, in a 3-quart bowl, whisk all dressing ingredients except olive oil until combined. Add olive oil in a slow, steady stream, whisking until slightly thickened.

Cajun Deviled Eggs

Everybody loves deviled eggs, and these have a nice
Cajun touch. I discovered them at a community supper
in Meaux (pronounced Moe), Louisiana and have loved
them ever since.

24 eggs
1 (4½-oz.) can deviled
  ham
2½ tablespoons sweet
  pickle relish
2 tablespoons cider
  vinegar
2 tablespoons sugar
2 tablespoons prepared
  yellow mustard
½ teaspoon Tabasco
  sauce
½ teaspoon freshly
  ground pepper
½ teaspoon salt
Paprika
Pimento-stuffed olives,
  sliced

Place eggs in a 10- to 12-quart Dutch oven. Add enough
cold water to completely cover eggs. Bring to a full boil
over high heat; immediately set a kitchen timer for 12
minutes. Reduce heat to maintain a low boil. Partially fill
a large bowl with water and ice cubes. When timer
sounds, drain eggs at once; place into iced water. Peel
eggs as soon as they are cool enough to handle. Slice
peeled eggs in half lengthwise; carefully scoop yolks into
a 2-quart bowl. Place whites on a serving platter; set
aside. Add all remaining ingredients except paprika and
olives to yolks. Using back of a fork, mash yolks until
blended. Using a spoon, fill each white with a portion of
filling, rounding off top. Or, for a more elegant presentation, spoon filling into a pastry bag fitted with a ½-inch
star tip. Pipe filling into whites. Sprinkle stuffed eggs
with paprika; place an olive slice in center of each.
Makes 48 stuffed egg halves.

Cajun Corn Salad

Vegetable salads are very popular in most of the South. It's probably because they meet so many requirements. They are simple, nutritious, filling, economical, tasty and attractive. The ingredients are also readily available, if not in the backyard, then certainly at a neighborhood market.

2 (17½-oz.) cans whole-kernel corn, well drained (3 cups)
1 large green bell pepper, chopped
1 cup hot pickled okra, sliced into thin rounds

6 green onions, sliced
½ cup minced parsley, preferably flat-leaf
1 cup cherry-tomato halves
Dressing, see below

Dressing:
1 teaspoon sugar
¼ cup herb-flavored white-wine vinegar
1 teaspoon Creole mustard or other stone-ground mustard
1 tablespoon dried leaf basil or 3 tablespoons minced fresh basil

2 tablespoons mayonnaise
½ teaspoon freshly ground pepper
½ teaspoon Tabasco sauce
½ teaspoon salt
½ cup olive oil

Toss all salad ingredients together in a serving bowl; set aside. Prepare dressing. Pour dressing over salad; toss gently to coat all ingredients. Cover and refrigerate overnight or up to 3 days before serving. Makes 6 to 8 servings.

To prepare Dressing, in a 2-quart bowl, whisk all dressing ingredients except olive oil until combined. Add olive oil in a slow, steady stream, whisking until slightly thickened.

Marinated Carrot Salad

This colorful and delicious vegetable salad is an old standby in Cajun country. Every lady has her own favorite seasonings. So the salad always tastes different in the many places that it shows up for dinner!

2 tablespoons sugar
1 tablespoon salt
2 lbs. carrots, sliced into
   thin rounds
1½ cups tomato juice
¾ cup tarragon-flavored
   white-wine vinegar
¾ cup sugar
1 tablespoon prepared
   yellow mustard

1 teaspoon salt
1 teaspoon freshly ground
   pepper
2 teaspoons dried leaf
   tarragon or 2
   tablespoons chopped
   fresh tarragon
¾ cup vegetable oil
2 medium, green bell
   peppers, sliced into
   thin strips
2 medium, red onions,
   halved lengthwise,
   thinly sliced

In a heavy 8-quart stockpot, combine 4 quarts water, 2 tablespoons sugar and 1 tablespoon salt. Bring to a rolling boil; add carrots. Cook until crisp-tender, about 10 minutes. Partially fill a large bowl with ice cubes and water. Drain carrots. Place into iced water; stir until cooled. Drain; set aside. In a 2-quart bowl, whisk tomato juice, vinegar, ¾ cup sugar, mustard, 1 teaspoon salt, pepper and tarragon until combined. Add oil in a slow, steady stream, whisking until combined. Toss drained carrots, bell peppers and onions in a 13″ × 9″ baking dish; pour dressing over vegetables. Toss gently to coat with dressing. Cover and refrigerate 24 hours or up to 3 days before serving. Makes 8 to 10 servings.

Crabmeat & Vegetable Salad

This is an attractive, pleasing, nutritious and positively delicious meal for summer lunches or dinners. Serve with French bread and a well-chilled white wine.

Boston-lettuce leaves
1 lb. lump crabmeat
1 avocado, sliced lengthwise into thin slices
12 large mushrooms, sliced
1 large ripe tomato, cut into wedges
1 (6 oz.) jar marinated artichoke hearts, drained, quartered

2 carrots, boiled until crisp-tender, cut into 2-inch-long julienne strips
6 small turnips, peeled, boiled until tender, sliced
3 hard-cooked eggs, halved
Salt to taste
Freshly ground pepper
Avocado Mayonnaise, see below
Paprika
Curly-parsley sprigs

Avocado Mayonnaise:
2 small, dark-skinned avocados, peeled, coarsely chopped
½ of a small onion, coarsely chopped
1 tablespoon capers, drained
1 tablespoon minced parsley, preferably flat-leaf
1 egg
2 teaspoons Creole mustard or other stone-ground mustard

1 teaspoon fresh lemon juice
2 teaspoons red-wine vinegar
½ teaspoon freshly ground pepper
½ teaspoon Tabasco sauce
1½ cups olive oil
Salt to taste

Place lettuce leaves on 4 to 6 individual serving plates. Using your fingertips, carefully pick through crabmeat; remove any bits of shell or cartilage. Arrange equal portions of crabmeat in center of each lettuce-lined plate;

arrange vegetables around crabmeat. Season with salt and pepper. Cover and refrigerate until served. Prepare mayonnaise. To serve, top salads with mayonnaise. Garnish plates with a dash of paprika and parsley. Makes 4 to 6 servings.

To prepare Avocado Mayonnaise, place all ingredients except olive oil and salt in a food processor fitted with the steel blade. Process until smooth and thick, stopping once or twice to scrape down side of bowl. With motor running, add olive oil through feed tube in a slow, steady stream. Season with salt.

Garlic Croutons

These crispy croutons will add a subtle hint of garlic to your favorite salad. For the garlic lover, they make great snacks for nibbling.

6 white-sandwich-bread   **6 medium garlic cloves**
  slices
¼ cup olive oil combined
  with ¼ teaspoon salt

Preheat oven to 375F (190C). Trim off crusts from bread; reserve for another use, if desired. Using a pastry brush, lightly brush both sides of bread with salted oil. Place on an ungreased baking sheet. Bake in preheated oven until golden brown and very crisp, about 15 minutes, turning once. Rub ends of garlic on 1 side of each browned bread slice. Cut browned slices into ½-inch cubes. Use at once or cool to room temperature on wire racks. Makes about 2 cups.

Creole Roquefort Dressing

Even if you are not a fan of blue cheeses, this could well be one of your favorite dressings. Decidedly Italian in nature, it is perfect for a lettuce-and-tomato salad.

1 small garlic clove
¼ cup white-wine vinegar
1 tablespoon fresh lemon juice
4 anchovy fillets, drained
1 teaspoon dried leaf oregano or 2½ teaspoons minced fresh oregano
1 teaspoon celery salt

¼ teaspoon salt
1 egg
¼ cup coarsely crumbled Roquefort cheese or other blue cheese (1 oz.)
½ teaspoon Dijon-style mustard
½ teaspoon sugar
¾ cup olive oil

In a food processor fitted with the steel blade and with motor running, drop garlic through feed tube to mince. Add all ingredients except olive oil. Process until blended, about 5 seconds. Stop machine; scrape down side of bowl. With motor running, pour oil through feed tube in a slow, steady stream. Process until combined. Pour into a bowl; cover and refrigerate until chilled or up to 3 days before serving. Whisk briefly if dressing separates. Makes about 1 cup.

Tomato Aspic with Cheese

Tomato aspic is a dish born of the South and reminiscent of grand meals in elegant plantation dining rooms. Making GOOD tomato aspic is an art. Thankfully, there are a few restaurants keeping the tradition and fine old recipes alive. If you find yourself in Natchez, Mississippi, have lunch or dinner at the Carriage House and enjoy true southern tomato aspic as your salad course.

4 (¼-oz.) envelopes
    unflavored gelatin
    (about 3¼
    tablespoons)
⅔ cup dry white wine
5 cups tomato juice
2 medium onions,
    coarsely chopped
1 jalapeño pepper,
    coarsely chopped
6 green onions, chopped
3 celery stalks, coarsely
    chopped

⅔ cup Brown Veal &
    Pork Stock, page 21,
    or canned beef broth
2 tablespoons
    Worcestershire sauce
Juice of 2 lemons
2 bay leaves
1½ teaspoons celery salt
8 chopped basil leaves or
    ½ teaspoon dried leaf
    basil
Cheese Centers, see
    below
Boston-lettuce leaves
Mayonnaise
Curly-parsley sprigs

Cheese Centers:
2 (3-oz.) pkgs. cream
    cheese, room
    temperature
1 tablespoon grated onion
1 tablespoon prepared
    horseradish

2 tablespoons mayonnaise
1 tablespoon chili sauce
¼ teaspoon Tabasco
    sauce
2 teaspoons powdered
    sugar

In a small bowl, combine gelatin and wine. Stir well; let
stand 5 minutes. Meanwhile, combine tomato juice,
green onions, jalapeño pepper, green onions, celery,
stock or broth, Worcestershire sauce, lemon juice, bay
leaves, celery salt and basil in a heavy 4-quart saucepan.
Bring to a boil over high heat. Reduce heat. Cover; simmer 30 minutes. Stir gelatin-wine mixture into hot mixture; heat until gelatin dissolves, stirring often. Strain
mixture through a fine strainer, pressing down on vegetables to extract all liquid. Lightly oil 8 (¾-cup) molds.
Pour aspic liquid into oiled molds. Cover and refrigerate.
Prepare Cheese Centers. When aspics have thickened
slightly, but are not set, drop 1 cheese ball into center of
each aspic. Refrigerate until set, about 6 hours. Line 8
individual plates with lettuce leaves. Run tip of a knife
around each aspic to loosen. Dip each mold into warm

water a few seconds. Immediately invert on lettuce-lined plates. Remove molds. Top each aspic with a dollop of mayonnaise; garnish with parsley. Makes 8 servings.

To prepare Cheese Centers, place all ingredients in a food processor fitted with the steel blade. Process until smooth, stopping once to scrape side of bowl. Form mixture into 8 balls.

Blueberry-Flavored Vinegar

The old Creole cooks were making fruit-flavored vinegars from native fruits before the turn of the century.

1 cup fresh or frozen blueberries	1 qt. white-wine or champagne vinegar

Combine blueberries and vinegar in a glass container with a tight-fitting lid. Seal. Let steep at least 2 weeks before using. To use, strain through a fine sieve as needed. Makes 1 quart.

When cooking alone and you need to pour one liquid into another while whisking, do not despair! To keep the bowl from sliding, roll up a very damp kitchen towel lengthwise; wrap it into a ring large enough to fit around bottom of bowl. Nest bowl into towel ring and whisk away. The bowl will now stay put.

Blueberry-Cream Dressing

This tasty dressing does justice to the noble blueberry. Blueberry-flavored vinegar may be purchased at specialty food stores or in the gourmet section of many grocery stores—or you can make your own from the recipe, opposite.

½ pint dairy sour cream
  (1 cup)
¼ cup whipping cream
½ teaspoon salt

1 tablespoon powdered
  sugar
¼ cup blueberry-flavored
  vinegar
¼ cup vegetable oil

In a 2-quart bowl, whisk all ingredients except oil until combined. Add oil in a slow, steady stream, whisking constantly until blended. Pour into a jar with a tight-fitting lid; refrigerate until chilled or up to 3 days. Serve dressing over a salad of fresh spinach leaves and sliced cucumber. Makes 1¾ cups.

Garlic-Cream Dressing

South Louisianians take their garlic very seriously. Many house dressings found in restaurants are quite redolent of this not-so-delicate member of the lily family. This creamy dressing is my house version. Serve over a mixed green salad.

3 large garlic cloves
⅓ teaspoon dried leaf
  basil or 1 teaspoon
  minced fresh basil
½ teaspoon salt
¼ teaspoon freshly
  ground pepper

6 tablespoons red-wine
  vinegar
6 tablespoons whipping
  cream
3 tablespoons dairy sour
  cream
3 tablespoons mayonnaise
⅓ cup vegetable oil

In a food processor fitted with the steel blade and with motor running, add garlic through feed tube to mince. Add all ingredients except oil. Process until combined. Stop machine; scrape side of bowl. With motor running, add oil through feed tube in a slow, steady stream. Process until combined. Pour dressing into a jar with a tight-fitting lid. Refrigerate until chilled or up to 3 days. Makes about 1¼ cups.

Pecan-Garlic Dressing

South Louisiana is blessed with a bountiful pecan crop. Ancient pecan groves line the bottom land along the Mississippi. We use pecans in any course of the meal. This uniquely different salad dressing is one of my favorite uses for this delicious nut.

3 large garlic cloves	**½ teaspoon sugar**
¼ cup coarsely chopped pecans	**¼ cup red-wine vinegar**
	¾ cup olive oil
½ teaspoon salt	
¼ teaspoon freshly ground pepper	

In a food processor fitted with the steel blade and with motor running, drop garlic through feed tube to mince. Add pecans, salt, pepper and sugar. Stop machine; scrape side of bowl. Add vinegar; process until blended, turning on and off 3 or 4 times. With motor running, add olive oil through feed tube in a slow, steady stream. Process until combined. Toss dressing with your favorite combination of greens. Makes about 1 cup.

Strawberry-Cream Dressing

This versatile dressing can even be served as a cold soup garnished with strawberry halves or as a dip with a platter of fresh fruit tidbits!

½ cup mayonnaise
1 (8-oz.) pkg. cream
  cheese, room
  temperature
1 (3-oz.) pkg. cream
  cheese, room
  temperature

½ pint dairy sour cream
  (1 cup)
1 cup fresh strawberries
½ cup powdered sugar

Place all ingredients in a food processor fitted with the steel blade. Process until smooth and creamy. Serve over fresh fruit. Thin slightly with milk to use as a soup. Covered and refrigerated, dressing will keep up to 3 days. Makes 2½ cups dressing.

Variation

Substitute 1 (10-oz.) pkg. frozen sweetened strawberries that have been thawed and well drained for fresh strawberries. Decrease sugar, if desired.

Poultry & Meat

Dinner for a Winter Night

Oysters Rousseau, page 143
Spinach, Orange & Onion Salad, page 75
Boned Duck Stuffed with Sausage Paté
Embellished Pecan Rice, page 105–8
Spinach & Artichoke Stuffed Tomatoes, page 173
Cap Bread, page 66
Cajun-Country Bread Pudding, page 180

The time is not long past when every respectable rural Cajun home would have its supply of chickens and three or four pigs. These animals made a large contribution to the family's diet. Many Cajun men remember the childhood chore of wringing chicken's necks and dressing them out for mama to work her magic for supper.

Both chickens and pigs were fairly self-sufficient animals and kept things going nicely for the Cajun families. Chickens and pigs lived on the family's scraps, and the family lived on the chickens and pigs! Hog-butchering was a time for celebration. Called a *boucherie*, it started early in the morning with the killing and butchering of the pig. Sausages of several varieties were made and stuffed into the cleaned intestines or wrapped in the caul fat from the stomach area. Lard was rendered. Feet were pickled. The poor-quality spare parts such as shoulder meat were rubbed with a mixture of spicy seasonings and put in the smokehouse to slowly smoke down into *tasso*, the delicious Cajun seasoning meat still in use today. It is said that the Cajuns use every part of the pig but the squeal!

Chicken in the hands of a Cajun cook can become a magnificent work of art. Good South Louisiana Chicken Fricassee is so sublime that it is difficult to perceive that intensity of flavor stemming from the barnyard clucker! In the United States we are blessed with a bounty of excellent quality chickens. They are raised on large chicken farms all over the country and are, for the most part, plump, juicy and quite flavorful. Chickens are also inexpensive, nutritious, low in fat and readily available. Now don't get me wrong—NOTHING will replace the taste of yard chickens that feed on whole corn and peck around the family garden. If you're blessed with a farmer or market that supplies fresh-killed chickens, it will be worth the time and the extra money to purchase them.

Ducks are staple fare in South Louisiana. Any person who is not a hunter probably lives next door to one, which means that both houses have freezers full of ducks. I don't think I've ever met a Cajun who, when the subject of food was mentioned, didn't want to give me his or her recipe for duck. There are certainly as many recipes for duck as there are Cajuns. Being an ardent lover of duck, I have tried every recipe shared with me. I can't recall that I've ever had a bad one! When preparing wild duck for cooking, it is important that you remove the small bony "nub" at the tail. At the base of this appendage, there are ducts which secrete oil with which the duck preens or lubricates its feathers. If the ducts are not removed, the meat will acquire an unpleasant musky taste from the oil. If you do not have a duck hunter in your house, you may substitute domestic ducks in any of the recipes and obtain admirable results. Keep in mind, however, that domestic ducks, especially young ducklings, are very fatty. A single domestic duckling can easily render 1½ cups fat during roasting.

Stuffed meats are very popular in South Louisiana; some of the most memorable Cajun and Creole dishes are stuffed, roasted meats. One word of caution is in order when stuffing meats: Be certain that the stuffing is thoroughly cooled before using. Do not allow it to sit at room temperature for an extended period of time.

Veal has been an important part of the haute-Creole cuisine of New Orleans throughout the city's history. Local chefs have always seemed to possess a natural penchant for creating combinations of veal with seafood, such as Veal with Crabmeat, or veal with veal, such as Veal Scallops with Sweetbread Sauce. When selecting veal, look for meat that is a very pale pinkish-white color with no visible marbling of fat.

Sweetbreads were very popular in New Orleans fine cuisine in the mid-1800s and continued to be used extensively until well after the turn of the century. Today the delectable Ris de Veau are featured on only a few of the city's finest restaurant menus. To clear the air about sweetbreads once and for all, let me give a quick course on sweetbread-ology! True sweetbreads are the thymus gland of young calves. The gland lies in the neck of the animal and consists of two lobes, one slightly rounded, the other elongated. As the animal matures, the thymus decreases in size until it finally disappears. The pancreas is often referred to as the "stomach sweetbread". It bears no resemblance in taste to the thymus, which is the sweetbread most often available in the market and always used in restaurants featuring sweetbread dishes.

Beef is not as popular as other meats or fish in South Louisiana. Little beef is produced in the area. When beef is eaten, however, it is serious business. Second-best beef simply will not do. Steaks are the most popular cut of beef, and the rib-eye reigns as the number-one steak. Locals like them cut into 1½- to 2-inch-thick slabs and charcoal grilled or pan broiled.

When selecting steaks, look for a good marbling of white fat throughout the meat. Each of these little veins of fat will melt into the meat, adding juicy flavor to the steak.

Rib-Eye Steak with Garlic-Mushroom Sauce

Among beef-eaters in South Louisiana, rib-eye reigns as the "king of steaks." Well-marbled beef is cut into slabs 1½- to 2-inches thick. Grill, broil or pan-grill to individual perfection. Pan-grilling is a favored method of cooking meats in Cajun-Creole country. This is probably due, in part, to the fact that we do wonderful things with the browned bits of meat glaze left in the bottom of the pan. Here two Cajun-Creole favorites, mushrooms and garlic, are added. The whole garlic cloves acquire a mild, nut-like taste during cooking that gives a delightful flavor bonus. Serve steaks with a green salad and potatoes for a sample of Cajun-Creole Saturday-night supper fare.

4 (15-oz.) beef rib-eye steaks, about 1-inch thick
Salt to taste
Freshly ground pepper

1 tablespoon unsalted butter or margarine
3 tablespoons vegetable oil
Garlic-Mushroom Sauce, see below

Garlic-Mushroom Sauce:
1 lb. small button mushrooms
6 tablespoons unsalted butter or margarine
16 medium garlic cloves, peeled
Salt to taste
½ teaspoon freshly ground pepper

2 teaspoons Worcestershire sauce
½ cup Burgundy wine
2 cups Brown Veal & Pork Stock, page 21, or canned beef broth

Pat steaks dry on paper towels; season both sides with salt and pepper. In a heavy 12-inch skillet over medium-high heat, heat 1 tablespoon butter or margarine and oil. When oil mixture is very hot, add 2 steaks; cook to desired degree of doneness. Using tongs, turn steaks every minute during cooking. For rare steaks, cook a total of 5 to 6 minutes. For medium steaks, cook 7 to 8 minutes. For well-done steaks, cook 9 to 10 minutes. Repeat with 2 remaining steaks; keep warm. Prepare sauce. Spoon sauce over steaks. Serve hot. Makes 4 to 8 servings.

To prepare Garlic-Mushroom Sauce, using a damp paper towel, wipe mushrooms; set aside. Working quickly, pour oil from skillet; place skillet over medium-high heat. Melt butter or margarine in skillet. Add mushrooms, garlic, salt, pepper and Worcestershire sauce; stir to blend. Sauté, tossing mushrooms and garlic constantly, until well browned, about 4 minutes. Add wine; swirl pan. Scrape up browned bits from bottom. Cook, stirring, quickly until wine is reduced to a glaze, about 5 minutes. Stir in stock; reduce to a glaze, about 10 minutes.

Boiled Beef with Parsnips

Boiled beef and lunch time go hand-in-hand in New Orleans. No respectable luncheon restaurant in town would dare run out of it! The vegetables literally cook away to nothing and become part of the stock. Parsnips were popular in New Orleans in the late 1800s but are seldom cooked today. This is unfortunate because they are very good indeed.

10 to 12 (14-inch-long) salt pork strips
Red-wine vinegar
2 large onions, coarsely chopped
4 carrots, coarsely chopped
6 garlic cloves, mashed
4 celery stalks, with leafy tops, coarsely chopped
1 (5- to 6-lb.) boneless beef brisket

4 parsley sprigs
3 bay leaves
1 tablespoon peppercorns
1 teaspoon whole cloves
2 teaspoons salt
12 parsnips, peeled, cut into 2-inch lengths
Horseradish Sauce, see below
Curly-parsley sprigs

Horseradish Sauce:
1 (8-oz.) cream cheese, room temperature, cut into 1-inch cubes
2 teaspoons powdered sugar
1 tablespoon fresh lemon juice

1 tablespoon Worcestershire sauce
1 teaspoon liquid beef extract
¼ cup prepared horseradish
½ cup whipping cream, whipped

In a shallow bowl, soak salt-pork strips in enough vinegar to cover 15 to 20 minutes. Place onions, carrots, garlic and celery in bottom of a heavy 6- to 8-quart soup pot. Drain salt-pork strips. Use strips to lard brisket using a larding needle. Add larded brisket to soup pot. Add enough cold water to cover meat by 2 inches. Bring to a rapid boil. Skim foam from surface. Add parsley, bay leaves, peppercorns, cloves and salt. Reduce heat. Cover and simmer 2¼ hours. Add parsnips; cook until parsnips are very tender, 45 minutes. While beef is cooking, prepare sauce. Remove beef from cooking liquid, reserving cooking liquid for another use. Place cooked beef on a cutting board. Slice into ½-inch-thick slices; arrange on a platter. Remove parsnips; arrange around sliced beef. Garnish platter with parsley sprigs. Pass Horseradish Sauce separately. Makes 6 servings.

To prepare Horseradish Sauce, combine all ingredients except whipped cream in a food processor fitted with the steel blade; process until smooth. Spoon into a medium bowl; fold in whipped cream. Cover tightly; refrigerate until ready to serve. Makes about 1½ cups.

A larding needle is a tool used for larding, or adding fat to, large, lean cuts of meat. A good larding needle has a handle large enough for a firm grip and a blade at least 15 inches long. The tip should have a sharp point for piercing raw meats. To use, run blade through meat; lay a strip of larding fat in the trough that runs the length of needle. Slowly withdraw needle from meat, twisting handle as you do, depositing fat inside meat.

Orange-Glazed Pork Roast

This dish, an elegant and flavorful presentation for a humble pork roast, provides an exciting contrast of tastes and features a seldom-talked-about Louisiana crop—oranges.

1 (3½- to 4-lb.) boneless
    pork loin top loin roast
4 large garlic cloves, cut
    into slivers
1 tablespoon dried
    rosemary or 2
    tablespoons minced
    fresh rosemary
2 teaspoons rubbed sage
    or 2 tablespoons
    minced fresh sage

1 teaspoon salt
1 teaspoon freshly ground
    pepper
Orange Glaze, see below
Pan Sauce, see below
2 navel oranges, thinly
    sliced
Curly-parsley sprigs

Orange Glaze:
¼ cup orange marmalade
¼ cup orange juice

¼ cup Creole mustard or
    other stone-ground
    mustard
2 tablespoons light-brown
    sugar

Pan Sauce:
¼ cup Grand Marnier or
    other orange-flavored
    liqueur

1 cup orange juice

Preheat oven to 350F (175C). Place roast on a cutting board, fat-side up; make small slits in fat with a paring knife. Insert garlic slivers in slits. In a small bowl, combine rosemary, sage, salt and pepper; pat onto roast. Place meat in a large roasting pan. Roast in preheated oven to an internal temperature of 165F (75C) or until juices run clear when pierced, about 1 hour. Meanwhile prepare glaze. About 15 minutes before meat is done, brush glaze over roast; roast 15 minutes more. Place roast on a carving board while preparing Pan Sauce. Prepare sauce. Slice roast into ½-inch-thick slices; arrange, slightly overlapping, on a platter. Drizzle sauce over slices; garnish platter with orange slices and parsley sprigs. Makes 6 to 8 servings.

To prepare Orange Glaze, in a small bowl, combine glaze ingredients.

To prepare Pan Sauce, skim all fat from roasting pan; place pan over medium-high heat. Add Grand Marnier and orange juice; scrape up browned bits from bottom of pan. Cook 5 minutes.

> **Zest is the colored part of citrus-fruit peels. It contains the rich, full-flavored oils. It is a very thin layer that is joined to the white bitter pith. When a recipe calls for grated citrus peel or zest, grate only deep enough to remove the colored outer skin.**

Veal Scallops with Sweetbread Sauce

Sweetbreads, prepared in a variety of ways, were very popular in both Creole homes and restaurants in the late 19th and early 20th centuries. However, they have become a much-maligned and misunderstood variety meat among present-day diners. Little do they know what they are missing. This recipe combines sweetbreads with veal scallops, Marsala wine and mushrooms in a dish of memorable delight.

1 lb. veal sweetbreads
4 cups Brown Veal &
    Pork Stock, page 21,
    or canned beef broth
1 lb. veal scallops
Salt to taste
Freshly ground pepper
About 1 cup all-purpose
    flour
¼ cup unsalted butter or
    margarine

3 garlic cloves, minced
¼ lb. mushrooms, sliced
2 teaspoons dried leaf
    basil or 2 tablespoons
    minced fresh basil
¼ cup all-purpose flour
⅔ cup dry Marsala
4 green onions, chopped
¼ cup unsalted butter or
    margarine
Curly-parsley sprigs

Place sweetbreads in a medium bowl; add cold water to cover. Refrigerate 1 hour. Drain sweetbreads; set aside.

In a heavy 4-quart saucepan, bring stock or broth to a boil; add sweetbreads. Reduce heat. Simmer sweetbreads 10 minutes. Remove sweetbreads with a slotted spoon. Place on a plate; cover with a second plate. Place a heavy object such as a pitcher of water on top of the second plate; set aside until sweetbreads are cool. Return cooking stock to heat; cook until reduced by ½. Trim veal scallops to remove any tendons from edges. Using a meat mallet, pound veal until very thin and almost doubled in size. Salt and pepper both sides of scallops; dredge in about 1 cup flour to coat, shaking off excess. Set aside. When sweetbreads are cool, remove and discard all large membranes; slice meat into thin slices. Melt ¼ cup butter or margarine in a heavy 10-inch skillet over medium heat. Add sliced sweetbreads; cook until lightly browned, about 5 minutes, stirring often. Stir in garlic, mushrooms and basil; cook 4 minutes Add ¼ cup flour all at once; stir until combined, 3 to 4 minutes. Slowly stir in Marsala. Add reduced cooking stock; bring to a boil. Reduce heat. Add green onions, salt and pepper to taste. Simmer sauce while cooking veal. In a heavy 12-inch skillet over medium heat, melt ¼ cup butter or margarine; quickly sauté floured veal scallops 2 minutes per side, turning once with tongs. To serve, place veal scallops on individual plates; top with sauce. Garnish with parsley sprigs. Makes 4 servings.

Breaded Veal Panné

Pannéed veal is one of the most popular of all veal dishes served in major New Orleans restaurants. The dish is a combination of three simple ingredients—veal, a light breading and white wine. The results are delicious and refreshingly satisfying. Serve with your choice of pasta and a green salad.

1 lb. veal scallops
About 1½ cups dry bread
    crumbs
2 teaspoons salt
2 teaspoons freshly
    ground pepper
2 tablespoons unsalted
    butter or margarine
⅓ cup vegetable oil

About 1½ cups all-
    purpose flour
1 egg beaten with 1 cup
    milk
½ cup dry white wine
6 tablespoons unsalted
    butter or margarine
Minced parsley,
    preferably flat-leaf

Trim veal scallops to remove any tendons from edges. Using a flat veal pounder or meat mallet, pound veal until very thin and almost doubled in size. Pat dry with paper towels; set aside. In a medium bowl, combine bread crumbs, salt and pepper; set aside. In a heavy 12-inch skillet over medium heat, melt 2 tablespoons butter or margarine and oil. When oil is hot, dredge veal scallops in flour to coat; shake off excess. Dip floured veal in egg-and-milk mixture, coating well. Dredge in bread-crumb mixture to coat well; shake off excess bread crumbs. Place coated veal in hot oil. Sauté quickly about 2 minutes per side, turning once with tongs. Drain on paper towels; keep warm. Discard oil from skillet, leaving browned bits at bottom. Return skillet to medium heat; add white wine. Cook 3 to 4 minutes to deglaze pan, scraping up browned bits from bottom. Add 6 tablespoons butter or margarine; swirl to melt. To serve, place sautéed veal on individual plates; drizzle with butter sauce. Sprinkle with parsley. Makes 4 to 6 servings.

Oyster-Stuffed Beef Fillet

Even steaks get stuffed in South Louisiana. This is one of my favorites—with a rich surprise of cheese and the silky smoothness of hidden oysters.

4 (8-oz.) beef loin
   tenderloin steaks, 1½
   inches thick
4 large oysters or 8 small
   to medium oysters,
   shucked, liquor
   reserved
⅓ cup crumbled
   Roquefort cheese
   (about 1¾ oz.)
Salt to taste
Freshly ground pepper

1 tablespoon unsalted
   butter or margarine
3 tablespoons vegetable
   oil
¼ cup brandy
½ cup Brown Veal &
   Pork Stock, page 21,
   or canned beef broth
½ pint whipping cream
   (1 cup)
8 smoked oysters,
   drained, patted dry
Minced parsley,
   preferably flat-leaf

Using a sharp knife, cut a 2-inch slit into side of each steak. Carefully extend cut about three-fourths of way through steaks. Gently make opening within steak large enough for an oyster and cheese. Do not cut through sides at any other point. Stuff each steak with ¼ of cheese and 1 large oyster or 2 smaller ones. Pat steaks dry on paper towels. Salt and pepper both sides. Heat butter or margarine and oil in a heavy 12-inch skillet over medium-high heat. When oil mixture is hot, add steaks; cook to desired doneness, using tongs to turn every minute during cooking. For a rare steak, cook a total of 7 to 8 minutes. For a medium steak, cook 10 to 11 minutes. For a well-done steak, cook 13 to 14 minutes. Place steaks on individual plates; keep warm. Pour off oil from skillet; place skillet over medium-high heat. Add brandy; flame, gently swirling pan until flame goes out. Cook, scraping up browned bits from bottom of pan, until brandy has evaporated to a thin film. Add oyster liquor and stock or broth; cook until reduced to a thick glaze, 4 to 5 minutes. Add cream; cook until slightly thickened, 3 to 4 minutes. Add smoked oysters; stir to heat through. To serve, spoon sauce over each steak; top each steak with 2 smoked oysters. Sprinkle with minced parsley. Makes 4 servings.

Veal, Crabmeat & Artichoke Hearts with Mustard Hollandaise Sauce

This is one dish that is worthy of a special occasion. Once you've tasted it, you'll find yourself inventing occasions! Serve with a green salad and dry white wine.

Mustard Hollandaise
    Sauce, see below
4 veal cutlets, about 1¼
    lbs. total
1 cup all-purpose flour
½ teaspoon salt
½ teaspoon freshly
    ground pepper
2 tablespoons unsalted
    butter or margarine
¼ cup vegetable oil

¾ lb. backfin lump
    crabmeat
¼ cup unsalted butter or
    margarine
1 (14-oz.) can artichoke
    hearts, drained,
    quartered
6 green onions, chopped
Hungarian paprika
Curly-parsley sprigs

Mustard Hollandaise Sauce:
5 egg yolks
1 tablespoon water
1 tablespoon fresh lemon
    juice
½ teaspoon salt

¼ teaspoon red (cayenne)
    pepper
1 cup unsalted butter or
    margarine, melted
1 tablespoon Creole
    mustard or other
    stone-ground mustard

Prepare Mustard Hollandaise Sauce; keep warm. Pat veal cutlets dry on paper towels. In a medium bowl, combine flour, salt and pepper. Heat 2 tablespoons butter or margarine and oil in a heavy 12-inch skillet over medium heat. When oil mixture is hot, dredge cutlets in seasoned flour; shake off excess. Sauté until golden brown on both sides, turning once, about 8 minutes. Set aside to keep warm. Using your fingertips, carefully pick through crabmeat; remove and discard any bits of shell or cartilage. Do not break up lumps. Melt ¼ cup butter or margarine in a heavy 10-inch skillet over medium heat; add crabmeat, artichoke hearts and green onions. Cook just to heat through, stirring gently, about 5 minutes. To serve, place sautéed cutlets on individual plates; top cutlets with crabmeat-artichoke mixture. Spoon sauce over top. Garnish with a sprinkling of paprika and parsley sprigs. Serve hot. Makes 4 servings.

To prepare Mustard Hollandaise Sauce, place bottom of a double boiler containing water over medium-low heat. Bring water to a simmer. Reduce heat to low. Water should be hot, never simmering. Combine egg yolks, water, lemon juice, salt and cayenne in top of double boiler. Place over almost simmering water. Whisk constantly until mixture thickens and yolks are lemon-colored, 5 to 6 minutes. Remove entire pan from heat; whisk melted butter or margarine into yolks in a slow, steady stream, almost drop-by-drop. After all butter has been whisked into sauce, add mustard; whisk until smooth, 2 to 3 minutes. Set aside. Makes about 2 cups.

Hearty Poultry Stuffing

Hearty is the word for this corn-bread-based, rich dressing which contains almost everything but the kitchen sink. Double recipe for a turkey.

½ cup unsalted butter or margarine
1 medium onion, chopped
1 large green bell pepper, chopped
¼ cup chopped celery
4 bacon slices, diced
1 teaspoon rubbed sage or 1 tablespoon fresh chopped sage
1 teaspoon dried leaf thyme or 1 tablespoon fresh chopped thyme
1 teaspoon minced dried rosemary or 1 tablespoon fresh minced rosemary

1 teaspoon dried leaf oregano or 1 tablespoon fresh chopped oregano
1 teaspoon salt
½ teaspoon freshly ground pepper
¼ lb. smoked ham, coarsely ground
4 cups crumbled corn bread, lightly packed (4 oz.)
6 cups French-bread cubes, lightly packed (6 oz.)
2 eggs, slightly beaten
About 1¼ cups Louisiana Brown Poultry Stock, page 19, or canned chicken stock

Melt butter or margarine in a heavy 10-inch skillet over medium heat. Add onion, bell pepper, celery, bacon, seasonings and ham. Sauté, stirring often, until vegetables are wilted and bacon is cooked, but not browned, about 10 minutes. Place corn bread and French bread in a large bowl. Pour vegetable mixture over bread; toss to combine. Stir in eggs. Add enough stock or broth to make a moist dressing, stirring to break up corn bread and French bread. Makes about 1 pound or 8 cups.

Creole Oyster Stuffing

In South Louisiana, oyster-dressing devotees will argue its merits to the death. Indeed it is hard to dispute its one-of-a-kind taste. For the most delicious results, start with genuine French bread.

9 cups French-bread cubes, lightly packed (½ lb.)
¼ cup unsalted butter or margarine
Heart, gizzard and liver from 1 chicken, minced
1 small onion, chopped
¼ cup celery, chopped
4 green onions, chopped
3 garlic cloves, minced
¼ cup minced parsley, preferably flat-leaf
½ teaspoon dried leaf thyme or 1½ teaspoons chopped fresh thyme
½ teaspoon rubbed sage or 1½ teaspoons chopped fresh sage
¼ teaspoon dried leaf marjoram or ¾ teaspoon chopped fresh marjoram
¼ teaspoon red (cayenne) pepper
1 teaspoon salt
½ teaspoon freshly ground black pepper
12 small to medium oysters and their liquor (about 1 pint)
2 eggs, slightly beaten
About 1 cup Louisiana Brown Poultry Stock, page 19, or canned chicken broth

Preheat oven to 350F (175C). Spread French bread on a baking sheet. Dry in preheated oven 10 minutes. Place dried bread cubes in a large bowl; set aside. Melt butter or margarine in a heavy 10-inch skillet over medium heat. Add heart, liver, gizzard, onion, celery, green onions, garlic, parsley and seasonings. Sauté until wilted, about 5 minutes. Pour cooked vegetables over bread cubes; toss until combined. Add oysters, their liquor and eggs; stir until blended. Add enough stock or broth to make a moist dressing, stirring to break up French bread. Makes about 1 pound or 8 cups.

Chicken Fricassee

Chicken Fricassee is one of those subjects that can incite people to ugly behavior in our part of the country. When conversations turn to food, as they invariably do among Cajuns and Creoles, the subject of fricassee is bound to come up, and battle lines are drawn with one utterance: "But you should taste MY fricassee..." Chicken Fricassee is traditional fare among Cajuns—an economical meal that cooks with little supervision. It is a good example of the Cajun *cooking-down* method of food preparation. Serve with rice for a simple and delicious meal.

1 cup lard or vegetable oil
2 (1½- to 2-lb.) broiler-fryer chickens, cut up
Salt to taste
Freshly ground black pepper
Red (cayenne) pepper
1 cup all-purpose flour
5 medium onions, halved lengthwise, sliced
3 celery stalks, chopped
3 large garlic cloves, minced
2 bay leaves, minced

½ teaspoon red (cayenne) pepper
1 teaspoon freshly ground black pepper
½ teaspoon dried leaf thyme or 1½ teaspoons chopped fresh thyme
3 cups Louisiana Brown Poultry Stock, page 19, or canned chicken broth
6 green onions, chopped

Heat lard or vegetable oil in a heavy 14-inch skillet over medium heat. Season chicken pieces with salt, black pepper and cayenne. When fat is hot, add seasoned chicken. Quickly brown chicken on both sides. Drain on paper towels. Add flour to fat in skillet; whisk until combined. Cook, whisking constantly, until peanut-butter-colored, about 25 minutes. Stir in onions, celery, garlic, bay leaves, ½ teaspoon cayenne, 1 teaspoon black pepper and thyme. Cook, stirring, until onions are wilted and transparent, about 10 minutes. Slowly stir in stock or broth. Return chicken to skillet; season with salt. Reduce heat. Simmer 1 hour. To serve, place chicken on a large platter; stir green onions into sauce. Serve vegetables and sauce in a separate bowl. Makes 4 to 6 servings.

Boned & Stuffed Chicken

The procedure for boning a chicken is exactly the same as for boning a duck, page 107.

1 (5-lb.) baking chicken	1 recipe Wine Sauce,
1 recipe Hearty Poultry	from Boned Stuffed
Stuffing, page 102, or	Duck with Wine
1 recipe Creole Oyster	Sauce, page 105
Stuffing, page 103	Sautéed vegetables

Bone, stuff and bake chicken following directions for Boned Stuffed Duck with Wine Sauce, page 106, leaving in leg and wing bones. Substitute 1 of the above stuffings from page 102–3 for pâté and duxelles. Prepare Wine Sauce from pan drippings. Serve with sautéed vegetables. Makes 4 to 6 servings.

Variation

You may use boning instructions to bone a turkey; leave wing and leg bones for a nicer presentation. Increase quantity of stuffing in relation to size of turkey. Spread softened butter or margarine over surface of stuffed turkey. Roast boned, stuffed turkey, covered, in a preheated 325F (165C) 20 minutes per pound. Remove cover during last 45 minutes to brown turkey.

Boned Stuffed Duck with Wine Sauce

Duck and pork just seem to have a natural affinity for each other. The combination is a taste favorite in Cajun country, where both are treasured foods. This dish is impressive for a special occasion.

Sausage Pâté, see below
Duxelles, see below
1 (4- to 5-lb.) domestic
   duck
Olive oil

2 cups Louisiana Brown
   Poultry Stock, page
   19, or canned chicken
   broth
Wine Sauce, see below

Sausage Pâté:

6 oz. chicken livers
6 oz. bulk pork sausage
8 juniper berries, mashed
4 green onions, coarsely
   chopped
¼ cup Madiera
⅔ cup cognac or other
   brandy
1 teaspoon salt
½ teaspoon freshly
   ground pepper
¼ teaspoon dried leaf
   thyme or ¾ teaspoon
   chopped fresh thyme

1 bay leaf, crushed
¼ teaspoon dried leaf
   basil or ¾ teaspoon
   chopped fresh basil
½ teaspoon rubbed sage
   or 1½ teaspoons
   chopped fresh sage
¼ teaspoon ground
   coriander
¼ teaspoon ground mace

Duxelles:

3 tablespoons unsalted
   butter or margarine
½ lb. mushrooms, minced
4 green onions, minced
2 garlic cloves, minced

½ teaspoon salt
1 teaspoon freshly ground
   pepper
1 tablespoon all-purpose
   flour
½ cup dry white wine

Wine Sauce:

1½ cups dry white wine
2 garlic cloves, mashed
3 green onions, minced
2½ cups Louisiana Brown
   Poultry Stock, page
   19, or canned chicken
   broth

Salt to taste
Freshly ground pepper
½ cup unsalted butter or
   margarine, cut into
   1-inch cubes

To prepare Sausage Pâté, combine all pâté ingredients in a medium bowl, adding liver and fat from duck. Cover with plastic wrap; refrigerate 24 hours. Drain marinated pâté ingredients, pressing down to remove moisture.

Place drained ingredients in a food processor fitted with the steel blade; process until smooth.

To prepare Duxelles, melt butter or margarine in a heavy 10-inch skillet over medium heat. Add mushrooms, green onions, garlic, salt and pepper. Sauté until mixture is dry and starting to stick to pan slightly, 10 minutes. Stir in flour; cook 3 to 4 minutes. Stir in wine; cook, stirring often, until wine evaporates, 7 to 8 minutes. Stir in flour; cook 3 to 4 minutes. Stir in wine; cook, stirring often, until wine evaporates, 7 to 8 minutes. Refrigerate until chilled.

To bone duck, place duck on a cutting board, breast-side-down. Using a sharp, thin-bladed knife or boning knife, cut down length of backbone, cutting all the way to bone. Working down right side first, carefully cut your way toward breast, always keeping knife against bone and taking care not to puncture skin. When you get to thigh joint, use tip of knife to expose ball-and-socket joint. Cut meat away from it, leaving meat attached to skin. Lay knife down; using your right hand, get a good grip on thigh bone. Twist thigh and leg free from carcass. Now, take knife and begin to scrape meat away from thigh bone toward leg. Carefully cut around leg joint; scrape meat off leg toward end of leg. Cut to within 1 inch of end, grasp leg bone with a paper towel; pull hard until bone pulls free. Feel end of leg skin and cut off hard, cartilaginous knob on end. The leg will now be turned completely inside-out. Carefully turn it back right-side-out, leaving some of end of leg skin tucked in to seal end opening. Now carefully cut meat away from ribs, always keeping knife against bones, until you reach breast meat. Be sure to sever membranous-appearing meat, which will be attached to ribs, toward tail end. This is meat and should stay with skin. When you reach wing joint, follow same procedure as for disjointing thigh bone. When wing has been broken free, carefully cut meat away from ribs toward middle of breast bone. Continue toward tail, removing all breast meat from bones, until you reach middle of breast bone. Now remove all meat from first bone of wing. Disjoint bone; discard. Leave remaining wing bones attached. You are now half-way through! Place duck back on its breast. Go back to backbone where you started, working to left this time and following same procedure. When you reach middle of breast bone, very carefully sever meat from cartilage; remove entire carcass. Reserve carcass for making stock. Spread now flattened duck on cutting board, skin-side-down. Feel carefully over meat and remove any small fragments of bone or cartilage.

To assemble and cook, preheat oven to 400F (205C). Spread out duck on a flat surface; spread with a layer of pâté, leaving a border of 1½ inches. Spread a layer of duxelles over pâté. Fold skin from neck down over stuffings; fold bottom skin up. Bring sides of duck together, overlapping 1 side. Starting at top of duck and using a large trussing needle and kitchen twine, sew duck back together using over and under stitches. Draw seam together tightly as you sew, using your hands to reshape duck. Truss duck. Heat ¼ inch of olive oil in a heavy 12-inch skillet over medium heat. When oil is hot, add duck; quickly brown on all sides. Remove browned duck; place in a roasting pan. Add stock. Roast in pre-heated oven until juices run clear when duck is pierced, about 1 hour, basting often. Carefully remove twine. Place roasted duck on a platter. Reserve pan drippings for sauce. Cover; keep warm while preparing sauce. Prepare sauce. To serve, slice duck into ½-inch-thick slices using a serrated knife. Pass sauce separately. Makes 4 to 6 servings.

To prepare Wine Sauce, skim and discard fat from surface of pan drippings. Place pan over medium-high heat. When pan drippings are hot, add wine. Scrape up all browned bits from bottom of pan; add garlic and green onions. Cook until reduced by ½, about 15 minutes. Add stock; reduce again by ½. Strain mixture into a 2-quart saucepan. Season with salt and pepper. Over low heat, whisk butter or margarine cubes into sauce, 1 or 2 at a time, until each is blended before adding more.

Mesquite-Smoked Duck

If you are a lover of duck, you will find true happiness in the taste of this sausage-stuffed, slowly-smoked version prepared in a home smoker.

2 (4- to 5-lb.) domestic ducks or 6 wild ducks
1 lb. sage-flavored bulk sausage
1 celery stalk, chopped
1 medium onion, chopped
¼ cup minced parsley, preferably flat-leaf
Salt to taste
Freshly ground black pepper

12 bacon slices
1 gallon jug-wine-quality Burgundy wine
2 tablespoons peppercorns
2 large onions, coarsely chopped
5 to 6 mesquite-wood pieces, soaked in water 30 minutes, patted dry

Prepare a charcoal fire in bottom pan of a home smoker; place racks in proper position. Remove and discard tails from ducks. In a medium bowl, combine sausage, celery, 1 chopped onion and parsley. Stuff body cavity of each duck with sausage mixture. Salt and pepper skin. Wrap ducks in bacon slices; tie securely, using kitchen twine. In drip pan of smoker, combine part of wine and all of peppercorns and coarsely chopped onions. Place mesquite wood in charcoal fire; place ducks on upper grill racks. Smoke 6 hours. Alternately add remaining wine and water to drip pan throughout smoking period. The pan should never be allowed to cook dry. The moisture is necessary to insure a juicy and tender finished product. The combined tastes of the ever-concentrating wine mixture are an integral part of this dish. The duck should be

well done. Remove kitchen string; carve. Serve hot.
Makes 4 to 6 servings.

Barbecued Pork Spareribs

There are few taste experiences more soul-satisfying
than juicy, falling-off-the-bone tender spareribs dripping
with barbecue sauce. The Cajun method of parboiling
ribs and allowing them to cool in the liquid before grilling
insures ribs that are crisp-grilled on the outside and
moist and succulent on the inside. This barbecue sauce is
a staple item around my house. The recipe makes a large
quantity, so you'll have plenty on hand to share with
good friends.

**About 1 qt. Louisiana
  Barbecue Sauce, see
  below**
**2 racks pork spareribs,
  about 7 lbs. total**
**2 large onions, coarsely
  chopped**

**2 celery stalks, coarsely
  chopped**
**3 tablespoons
  peppercorns**
4 bay leaves

Louisiana Barbecue Sauce:
**¼ cup unsalted butter or
  margarine**
**6 green onions, finely
  minced**
¼ cup garlic salt
**1 (1½-oz.) can chili
  powder**
**3 tablespoons finely
  ground black pepper**
2 (32-oz.) bottles ketchup
2 qts. water

¼ cup Tabasco Sauce
¾ cup prepared mustard
1 cup granulated sugar
**½ cup firmly packed
  light-brown sugar**
**2 cups herb-flavored
  white-wine vinegar**
1 (12-oz.) can beer
½ cup Burgundy wine

Prepare sauce. Let stand several hours before using.
To prepare ribs, cut ribs into 4 to 6 rib sections. Place
rib sections in a heavy 10-quart stockpot or Dutch
oven. Add remaining ingredients. Add water to cover
meat; bring to a boil over medium-high heat. Reduce
heat. Simmer 45 minutes. Let ribs cool in liquid. Drain

ribs; pat dry on paper towels. The cooking liquid is a delicately-flavored pork stock; reserve for other use, if desired. Prepare a charcoal fire in an outdoor grill; position grill 6 inches above coals. When coals are evenly burning and glowing red, place ribs on grill. Cook 30 minutes, turning often and basting each time with barbecue sauce. Remove ribs from grill; cut into individual riblets. Serve hot. Pass additional sauce at table, if desired. Makes 4 to 6 servings.

To prepare Louisiana Barbecue Sauce, in a heavy 6-quart saucepan over medium heat, melt butter or margarine; add remaining ingredients. Cook, stirring occasionally, 30 minutes. Cool; pour into jars. Seal tightly. Store in refrigerator up to 2 weeks. Discard bay leaves before serving. Makes about 5 quarts.

Lee Hebert's Orange-Roasted Duck

Lee Hebert is a Cajun hunter and fisherman extraordinaire. In South Louisiana it is an accepted fact that such a person invariably works magic in the kitchen, turning hunting bounty into irresistible and mouth-watering dishes fit for royalty. Lee is no exception, and I am forever in his debt for sharing this recipe with me. This dish embodies the Cajun philosophy on eating: "Things just can't get no better."

6 wild ducks or 2 (4- to 5 lb.)domestic ducks
Salt to taste
Freshly ground pepper
2 tablespoons unsalted butter or margarine
⅓ cup vegetable oil
2 medium onions, halved lengthwise, sliced
6 garlic cloves

½ cup brandy
10 small oranges
1 teaspoon dried leaf thyme or 1 tablespoon chopped fresh thyme
2 bay leaves
1 cup Louisiana Brown Poultry Stock, page 19, or canned chicken broth
Orange slices
Curly-parsley sprigs

Preheat oven to 300F (150C). Remove and discard tail from ducks. Salt and pepper ducks; set aside. In a heavy 10-quart roaster over medium heat, heat butter or margarine and oil. When oil is hot, brown ducks quickly on all sides; remove from pan. Add onions and garlic; brown quickly, stirring often. Return ducks to pan; remove pan from heat. Add brandy; immediately ignite. Baste ducks constantly until flame goes out. Pour orange juice into pan to a depth of about ¼ inch. Add thyme and bay leaves. Cover pan. Bake in preheated oven, basting often with pan juices, until drumsticks move loosely at joints, 2 hours. During cooking, let level of juice cook down almost to a glaze; add another ¼ inch of juice. Repeat as necessary. When all juice has been used, begin adding stock or broth in same way as juice. At end of cooking time, place ducks on a platter; keep warm. Skim any accumulated fat from roasting pan; place pan over medium-high heat. Add remaining stock; quickly reduce to a glaze. Discard bay leaves. Taste for seasoning; adjust if necessary. Garnish ducks with orange slices and parsley sprigs. Serve hot. Pass sauce separately. Makes 4 to 6 servings.

Braised Wild Duck

This is a very old duck-and-fishing-camp recipe. It is a sublime dish. The gravy alone is worth the trouble.

4 large wild ducks, such
    as mallards
1 large onion, quartered
8 large garlic cloves
¾ lb. andouille sausage
    or kielbasa, cut into 4
    pieces
3 medium onions,
    chopped
4 large garlic cloves,
    minced
1 medium, green bell
    pepper, chopped
3 celery stalks, chopped
¼ cup minced parsley,
    preferably flat-leaf
½ lb. andouille sausage
    or kielbasa, sliced into
    rounds

1 lb. mushrooms, sliced
1½ teaspoons red
    (cayenne) pepper
⅓ cup Worcestershire
    sauce
3 bay leaves
1 teaspoon dried leaf
    thyme or 1 tablespoon
    chopped fresh thyme
1 teaspoon rubbed sage or
    1 tablespoon chopped
    fresh sage
½ cup dry vermouth
1 (14-oz.) can artichoke
    hearts, quartered
Salt to taste
Hot cooked white rice

Remove and discard tails from ducks. Stuff each duck with 1 onion quarter, 2 garlic cloves and 1 sausage piece. To truss, place ducks on a surface with legs pointing toward you. Thread a trussing needle with kitchen string; thrust needle through lower part of carcass—the area where tail was removed. Bring twine back over 1 leg through tip of breast bone. Stretch twine over second leg; tie with other end of string. Thread needle again; thrust needle completely through carcass where thigh joins legs, coming out at same spot on other side. Turn ducks breast-side down. Fold wings against body; push needle through closest wing. Pull neck skin up over backbone; secure by passing needle through it, into skin of back and out same spot on other wing. Pull twine taut; tie securely. Place ducks, breast-side down, in a flameproof 13-quart Dutch oven or roasting pan. Add all ingredients except artichoke hearts and rice. Add enough cold water to cover ducks. Place pan on medium-high heat; bring to a boil. Reduce heat. Simmer until liquid is reduced by ¾, about 1 hour and 15 minutes. Add water to cover again; repeat reduction. Check often to prevent sticking. Carefully turn ducks onto their backs; add enough water to come halfway up side of ducks. Add artichoke hearts and salt to taste. Cook until liquid is reduced by ½, 30 to 45 minutes. Place ducks on a carving board; remove trussing strings. Carve ducks. Serve on individual plates with rice. Skim any fat from surface of liquid; discard bay leaves. Spoon liquid and artichoke hearts over rice. Serve hot. Makes 4 servings.

Fish & Shellfish

Birthday Dinner

Acadian Crabmeat Tarts
Spinach Salad Vermillion, page 74
Shrimp Bisque, page 55
Pompano en Papillote with Champagne Sauce
Creole Spinach Mousse, page 168
New Orleans French Loaves, page 68
Bittersweet Chocolate Cake, page 196
Cafe Brulot, page 285

Shellfish are an integral part of the lifestyle in South Louisiana. Some of the oldest and most deeply rooted social customs center around the eating of different varieties of shellfish. The crab, shrimp or crawfish boil, for instance, has become an institution reaching every level of society. It is served by the bayou-dwelling Cajun who caught the crawfish himself and cooked them over a butane burner on his back porch to the New Orleans Garden District gentleman who had the whole affair catered. No matter how it's done, everyone gets good and messy and shares some of the best food to be had anywhere on this earth.

"If it swims, we'll eat it" is the Cajun policy concerning fish. But then anyone living in South Louisiana who doesn't like fish is in a serious dilemma, because we are

115

literally surrounded by them! Our bayous, marshlands, rivers, lakes, streams and the Gulf of Mexico are teeming with hundreds of species of fresh and saltwater fish. Many species are held in great esteem by gourmets the world over.

Fish and fishing are the basis for a unique South Louisiana social institution known as the *fishing camp*. Many families of avid fishermen own one somewhere. It's usually a dilapidated little house on pilings, sitting on the banks of a bayou, lake, river, brackish marshland or gulf inlet.

Come Friday afternoon when work is done and the fish are biting, the car is loaded and the family heads for the camp. Perhaps on Saturday, friends and relatives come, and the weekend is spent fishing, fellowshipping, swatting horseflies and mosquitoes and telling tales. But, most importantly, the weekend is actively dedicated to cooking and eating the catch of the day. I wish to tell you, fishing-camp cooking has produced some of the finest food you could ever aspire to eat. Fish recipes that could make a food writer rich and bring tears of joy to the eyes of a gourmet have been passed down through generations of fishing-camp cooks.

If you catch your own fish, gut them as soon as possible after taking them off the hook and store on ice until they can be refrigerated. Use fresh fish within two days or freeze immediately.

If you buy your fish at the market, select a reputable market that is clean and pleasant-smelling. You should not have to hold your nose inside a fish market! Whenever possible, make your selections from whole, uncut fish and have the market fillet and skin them, if desired.

When purchasing whole fish to fillet, you will lose about 70 to 75 percent of the weight in the head and bones, depending on the species. The average serving of filleted fish is 6 to 8 ounces per person. When serving whole fish, allow 12 to 16 ounces per person. When selecting a fresh fish, look at it closely. The eyes should be clear and protruding from the sockets, not clouded and sunken. The flesh should be firm to the touch and never "mushy." It should not be slimy feeling. It should be moist with no signs of dryness. The gills should be bright red in color. Be sure to get the carcasses to use in making stock. After all, if you buy a whole fish, you have paid for those bones! If your market has only filleted fish or steaks from which to choose, select those fillets which have moist translucent flesh, and let your nose be your guide.

If fresh Gulf fish is not available, I urge you to experiment with the recipes, substituting your local fresh fish. If you live in the Pacific Northwest, but you are literally dying to try Blackened Redfish, let me say that one of the best dishes I have ever cooked was Blackened Salmon. Use fresh Pacific salmon and substitute dill for the thyme in the Blackened Redfish recipe.

Even if you live in the Midwest, you needn't despair. If the selection of fresh fish is limited, select frozen fish fillets. Most major supermarket chains carry a selection of unbreaded frozen fish fillets, such as ocean perch, halibut, catfish and haddock. I have had great success in preparing many of the recipes in this chapter using frozen fish fillets from local supermarkets.

Ideally, fish should never be cooked to an internal temperature over 131F (55C). There is a very simple formula that will insure perfectly cooked fish every time: Fish should be cooked at 375F (190C) 10 MINUTES PER INCH OF THICKNESS. This rule applies to fillets, whole fish, steaks, stuffed fish, fish with toppings or fish any way. Stand a ruler on end next to the fish to be cooked; measure its height. If it's 3 inches thick, it cooks 30 minutes. If it's 1 inch thick, it cooks 10 minutes. If it's ½ inch thick, it cooks 5 minutes.

Please don't overcook fish. You will be doing yourself a great favor. Throughout my years of teaching cooking, I have found countless students who are amazed and delighted when they taste properly cooked fish.

Boiled Shrimp

Boiled shellfish is probably the number one company dish in South Louisiana, and what could be easier? No need to set a table. Just cover the kitchen table or backyard picnic table with several layers of newspaper. Spread the boiled seafood out along the length of the table directly on the newspaper. When dinner is over, simply roll up the newspaper with the peeled shells, and toss it all away! To make a real meal out of boiled seafood, drop whole ears of shucked corn, whole new potatoes and whole onions into the water 20 minutes before adding shellfish. The vegetables soak up the seasonings and are almost as good as the shellfish!

1 (3-oz.) pkg. crab and
   shrimp boil
3 lemons, cut into
   quarters
3 bay leaves
1½ teaspoons red
   (cayenne) pepper

3 tablespoons salt
2 tablespoons
   peppercorns
3 lbs. uncooked heads-on
   shrimp
2 tablespoons salt
2 qts. ice cubes

In a heavy 12- to 15-quart stockpot, combine crab and shrimp boil, lemons, bay leaves, cayenne, 3 tablespoons salt, peppercorns and 2 gallons water. Bring to a boil over high heat. Reduce heat to low. Simmer 20 minutes to develop flavor. Bring back to a boil. Add shrimp; stir in quickly. Cook just until all shrimp turn coral pink, 3 to 4 minutes. Drain immediately. While shrimp are cooking, combine 2 gallons water and 2 tablespoons salt in sink with stopper in place. Stir to dissolve salt; add ice cubes. Place drained shrimp in ice bath; let stand until shrimp are well chilled, about 10 minutes. Drain and refrigerate if not using at once. Makes 2 to 3 servings.

Boiled Blue Crabs

Pack live crabs on ice in a cooler 2 to 3 hours before cooking. This will make them sluggish and easy to handle. And they will not lose their claws during cooking!

2 (3-oz.) pkgs. crab and
  shrimp boil
½ cup seasoned salt
4 bay leaves
4 lemons, cut into
  quarters

¼ cup red (cayenne)
  pepper
1 tablespoon peppercorns
24 live blue crabs

In a heavy 25- to 30-quart stockpot, combine crab and
shrimp boil, seasoned salt, bay leaves, lemons, cayenne
and peppercorns. Add 3 gallons water; bring to a boil
over high heat. Reduce heat to low. Simmer 20 minutes
to develop flavor. Bring back to a boil; add live crabs,
pushing them into water with a large spoon. Boil 15 minutes. Drain crabs. Serve hot. To serve chilled, cool in ice
baths as for Boiled Shrimp, above, then refrigerate until
chilled. Makes 4 servings.

Boiled Crawfish

In Cajun Country during crawfish season, the restaurants serve up plastic trays piled high with steaming, hot
and spicy boiled crawfish. Serve these boiled "mudbugs"
this way at your house for a great casual dinner.

2 (3-oz.) pkgs. crab and
  shrimp boil
½ cup seasoned salt
4 bay leaves
4 lemons, cut into
  quarters

½ cup red (cayenne)
  pepper
1 tablespoon peppercorns
2 tablespoons whole
  cloves
20 lbs. live crawfish

In a heavy 35- to 40-quart stockpot over high heat, combine crab and shrimp boil and all seasonings. Add 5 gallons water; bring to a boil over high heat. Reduce heat to
low; simmer 20 minutes to develop flavor. Sort through
crawfish; remove and discard any dead ones. Bring
water back to a boil; add crawfish. Boil 10 minutes.
Drain; serve hot. Makes 4 servings.

Red Cocktail Sauce

Serve this piquant red sauce with boiled shellfish cocktails. Or for a tasty finger food, use it as a dip with chilled, boiled shrimp.

1½ cups ketchup
½ cup chili sauce
½ teaspoon garlic powder
½ teaspoon onion powder
2 tablespoons prepared
   horseradish

1 tablespoon lemon juice
2 teaspoons
   Worcestershire sauce
¼ teaspoon Tabasco
   sauce
¼ teaspoon freshly
   ground pepper
Salt to taste

In a small bowl, whisk all ingredients until combined. Cover and refrigerate until chilled before serving. Makes about 2 cups.

Mustard Sauce

This tasty sauce is an alternative to the traditional red sauce for seafood. Or serve both kinds!

1¼ cups Creole mustard
   or other stone-ground
   mustard
⅔ cup mayonnaise

4 teaspoons prepared
   horseradish
¼ teaspoon red (cayenne)
   pepper

In a small bowl, whisk all ingredients until combined. Cover and refrigerate until chilled before serving. Makes about 2 cups.

Crawfish Dauphine

If you could taste this dish, you would never guess it was the easiest recipe in the book. It's one of the best!

6 to 12 frozen puff-pastry
   patty shells
¼ cup unsalted butter or
   margarine
1 lb. peeled crawfish tails
½ lb. (1-inch) mushrooms
1 cup Seafood Stock,
   page 20, or 1 (8-oz.)
   bottle clam juice
½ pint whipping cream
   (1 cup)

Salt to taste
Finely ground black
   pepper
Red (cayenne) pepper to
   taste
Dash each of onion
   powder and garlic
   powder
1½ tablespoons minced
   parsley
3 green onions, chopped
Curly-parsley sprigs

Bake patty shells according to package directions; keep warm. Melt butter or margarine in a heavy 10-inch skillet. Add crawfish; sauté 5 minutes, stirring. Remove crawfish with a slotted spoon; set aside. Add mushrooms to skillet; sauté until liquid is reduced to a glaze and mushrooms are caramelized. Add stock or clam juice to deglaze pan, scraping up all browned bits from pan. Cook over medium heat until liquid is reduced by ½. Add cream, seasonings and minced parsley. Again, reduce by ½. Stir in green onions. Return crawfish to sauce; cook just to heat through. Serve in patty shells. Garnish with parsley. Makes 6 to 12 servings.

Acadian Crabmeat Tarts

This dish pairs two Creole favorites—lump crabmeat and Bérnaise Sauce.

1½ recipes Flaky Pie
    Pastry, page 183
¼ cup unsalted butter
6 green onions, chopped

½ green bell pepper,
    chopped
1 lb. backfin lump
    crabmeat

Creole Béarnaise Sauce:
2 tablespoons minced
    green onions
1½ teaspoons dried leaf
    tarragon
1½ teaspoons dried leaf
    chervil
1 tablespoon minced
    shallots
¼ teaspoon salt
¼ teaspoon freshly
    ground black pepper
3 garlic cloves, minced
¼ cup fresh lemon juice

¼ cup dry white wine
1 teaspoon Tabasco sauce
3 egg yolks
¼ teaspoon red (cayenne)
    pepper
1 teaspoon Creole
    mustard or other
    stone-ground mustard
¾ cup unsalted butter,
    melted
Minced fresh parsley,
    preferably flat-leaf

Preheat oven to 375F (190C). Place 10 (3-inch) tart pans on baking sheet. On a lightly floured surface, roll out pastry to a ¹⁄₁₆-inch-thick circle. Cut 10 (6-inch) circles from dough, rerolling scraps. Carefully fit circles into tart pans. Trim pastry even with edges of pans. Prick pastry with a fork. Bake in preheated oven until golden brown, 15 minutes. Remove from pans; cool on a wire rack. Prepare sauce. Place a tart shell on each of 10 individual plates. In a heavy 12-inch skillet, melt butter. Add onions and bell pepper; sauté until slightly wilted, 5 minutes. Add crabmeat; toss quickly, but gently. Heat through. Place warm crabmeat mixture in tart shells. Spoon sauce over crabmeat. Sprinkle with parsley. Makes 10 first-course servings.

To prepare Creole Béarnaise Sauce, in a heavy medium saucepan over medium-high heat, combine ingredients through Tabasco sauce; cook until about 1 tablespoon liquid remains, about 15 minutes. Set aside. Combine egg yolks, cayenne and mustard in top of a double boiler. Cook over hot, never simmering water. Whisk constantly until mixture thickens and lightens in color, about 10 minutes. Remove from heat; whisk in reduced wine mixture. Whisking constantly, add melted butter very slowly, almost a drop at a time, until all has been added. Whisk sauce 1 to 2 minutes more; remove top of double boiler from hot water.

Crabmeat au Gratin

This traditional dish never seems to lose its popularity in South Louisiana. It's an easy-to-prepare and delicious one-dish meal. Serve with a salad and French bread.

1 lb. lump crabmeat
¼ cup unsalted butter or
  margarine
1 medium onion,
  chopped
1 large celery stalk,
  chopped
1 small green bell pepper,
  chopped
2 medium garlic cloves,
  minced
4 green onions chopped
¼ cup all-purpose flour

2 cups milk
¼ cup dry bread crumbs
1 teaspoon salt
¼ teaspoon red (cayenne)
  pepper
¼ teaspoon freshly
  ground black pepper
2 egg yolks, well beaten
¾ cup shredded Cheddar
  cheese (3 oz.)

Preheat oven to 375F (190C). Lightly grease a 13″ × 9″ baking dish or 4 to 6 individual au gratin dishes. With your fingertips, carefully pick through crabmeat; remove and discard any bits of shell or cartilage. Do not break up lumps of meat. Set aside. In a heavy 12-inch skillet over medium heat, melt butter or margarine. Add onion, celery, bell pepper, garlic and green onions. Sauté until onions are wilted and transparent, about 5 minutes. Stir in flour. Cook, stirring, 3 to 4 minutes. Slowly stir in milk. Cook, stirring constantly, until thickened, 5 minutes. Stir in bread crumbs, salt, cayenne and black pepper until moist. Stir in egg yolks; cook 5 minutes, stirring. Remove pan from heat; gently fold in crabmeat; do not break up lumps. Spoon mixture into greased baking dish or au gratin dishes. Sprinkle cheese over top. Bake in preheated oven until cheese is light golden brown and bubbly, 15 to 20 minutes. Serve hot. Makes 4 to 6 servings.

Shrimp Creole

Shrimp Creole is probably one of the most widespread of the old Creole classics, and rightfully so, because it's certainly one of the best. This spicy version gains extra richness from the addition of Burgundy wine.

⅓ cup vegetable oil
6 green onions, chopped
1 large onion, chopped
2 medium, green bell
    peppers, chopped
4 garlic cloves, minced
3 celery stalks, chopped
6 large tomatoes, peeled,
    chopped
1½ cups Burgundy wine
1 cup Seafood Stock,
    page 20, or 1 (8-oz.)
    bottle clam juice
1 large bay leaf, minced
1 tablespoon minced
    fresh thyme or ¾
    teaspoon dried leaf
    thyme

1 tablespoon minced
    parsley, preferably
    flat-leaf
½ teaspoon freshly
    ground black pepper
½ teaspoon red (cayenne)
    pepper
Salt to taste
Juice of 1 lemon
3 lbs. uncooked medium
    shrimp, peeled,
    deveined
Hot cooked rice
Chopped green onions
Minced parsley,
    preferably flat-leaf

In a heavy 12-inch skillet, heat oil over medium heat. Add 6 green onions, onion, bell peppers, garlic and celery; sauté until vegetables are thoroughly wilted, about 10 minutes. Stir in tomatoes and wine. Cook, stirring often, until liquid is reduced by ½. Stir in stock or clam juice, seasonings and lemon juice. Cover; cook over medium-low heat 30 minutes, stirring occasionally. Stir in shrimp. Cook just until shrimp are coral pink, 7 to 8 minutes. Taste for seasonings; adjust if necessary. To serve, spoon rice onto each plate; top with sauce and shrimp. Sprinkle green onions and parsley over top; serve hot. Makes 4 to 6 servings.

Stuffed Crabs Lafitte

Knowing that I have a dozen stuffed crabs in the freezer brings me inner peace. I am assured that as long as I have a supply, a rave-review meal is only 15 minutes from the table. A meal of stuffed crab, green salad and French bread is very hard to beat. The crabmeat mixture may be served in real crab shells which have been well scrubbed, in ceramic crab shells, in scallop shells, or if you prefer, in individual au gratin dishes.

1 lb. backfin lump crabmeat
3 eggs, well beaten
1 cup evaporated milk
6 (1-inch-thick) French-bread slices
½ cup unsalted butter or margarine
1 large onion, chopped
2 large celery stalks, chopped
1 small green bell pepper, chopped
2 medium garlic cloves, minced

1½ teaspoons Worcestershire sauce
3 tablespoons dry sherry
½ teaspoon freshly ground black pepper
½ teaspoon red (cayenne) pepper
Salt to taste
5 green onions, finely chopped
¼ cup minced fresh parsley, prefereably flat-leaf
About ¾ cup dry bread crumbs

Preheat oven to 375F (190C). Using your fingers, carefully pick through crabmeat; remove and discard any bits of shell and cartilage. Do not break up lumps of meat; set aside. In a flat baking dish, whisk eggs and milk until blended; place bread slices in mixture, breaking up slices. Set aside. In a heavy 12-inch skillet over medium heat, melt butter or margarine. Add onion, celery, bell pepper and garlic; cook, stirring often, until vegetables are wilted, about 5 minutes. Add Worcestershire sauce, sherry, black pepper, cayenne, salt and crabmeat to skillet. Stir gently to combine; simmer mixture 10 minutes. Add green onions and parsley; cook 5 minutes. Add bread-and-egg mixture, completely breaking up bread and combining thoroughly with crab mixture. Grease 12 baking dishes if using. Use crab mixture to stuff 12 individual crab shells or greased baking dishes. Sprinkle tops of stuffed shells with bread crumbs; place on a baking sheet. Bake in preheated oven until golden brown on top, 10 minutes. Serve hot. To make ahead, wrap stuffed crab shells individually in a double layer of plastic wrap, then foil. Freeze up to 3 months. Bake in preheated oven, frozen, 15 to 20 minutes. Makes 12 stuffed crab shells or 6 to 12 servings.

Garlic-Broiled Shrimp

A garlic-lover's delight, this dish is so easy to prepare you can serve it to company after a full day's work!

4 lbs. uncooked large
   shrimp, peeled,
   deveined, leaving
   shells on tails
½ cup unsalted butter or
   margarine
½ cup olive oil
4 green onions, chopped
4 large garlic cloves,
   minced
1½ tablespoons fresh
   lemon juice

1½ teaspoons
   Worcestershire sauce
½ teaspoon Tabasco
   sauce
1 teaspoon salt
2 tablespoons minced
   fresh parsley,
   preferably flat-leaf
Grated Parmesan cheese
Curly-parsley sprigs

Divide shrimp equally among 4 small au gratin dishes; set aside. In a heavy 2-quart saucepan, heat butter or margarine with olive oil. Add remaining ingredients except cheese and parsley sprigs; cook 5 minutes over medium heat. Position oven rack 4 inches below heat source. Preheat broiler. Pour garlic-butter sauce equally over shrimp; top with a generous sprinkling of cheese. Place au gratin dishes on a large baking sheet. Broil under preheated broiler until shrimp are coral pink and sauce is bubbly and lightly browned, about 5 minutes. Garnish with parsley sprigs. Serve hot. Makes 4 servings.

Peppered Shrimp

Every South Louisiana cook has a recipe for barbecued shrimp which never see a grill! These tasty concoctions are based on butter and perhaps stock, but always have enough seasoning to bring tears to the eyes of mere mortals. People ask "Why on earth do I keep eating these things?" as they reach for another.

3 cups unsalted butter or
   margarine
1 cup Seafood Stock,
   page 20, or 1 (8-oz.)
   bottle clam juice
5 garlic cloves, minced
4 bay leaves, minced
4 teaspoons minced dried
   rosemary or 1
   tablespoon minced
   fresh rosemary
1 teaspoon dried leaf
   basil or 4 teaspoons
   chopped fresh basil

1 teaspoon dried leaf
   oregano or 4 teaspoons
   chopped fresh oregano
1 teaspoon salt
1 teaspoon red (cayenne)
   pepper
1 teaspoon freshly grated
   nutmeg
1 tablespoon Hungarian
   paprika
½ cup very finely ground
   black pepper
¼ cup fresh lemon juice
6 lbs. uncooked,
   unpeeled shrimp

In a heavy 10-quart Dutch oven, melt butter or margarine over medium heat. Add all remaining ingredients
except shrimp. Cook, uncovered, stirring occasionally,
until butter or margarine is a rich hazelnut brown, about
20 minutes. Add shrimp to sauce; stir gently to coat well.
Cook over medium heat just until all shrimp are coral
pink, 10 to 12 minutes. Ladle shrimp into soup plates;
spoon a liberal amount of buttery sauce over each portion. Serve with plenty of French bread for the sauce and
lots of napkins. Makes 6 servings.

Trout Marguery

The origin of this dish is often mistakenly attributed to
New Orleans, where it has long been popular. The dish
actually originated in France and is believed to have
been introduced to New Orleans by Jean Galatoire when
he came from France around the turn of the century.
Today, the dish remains on the menu of his famous Galatoire's restaurant. Two schools of thought exist regard-
ing the sauce for this dish. One sauce is based on a basic
bechamel, or cream sauce, with fish stock and shrimp
added. The other is based on a hollandaise sauce with

seafood stock, white wine and shrimp added. I prefer the rich latter version.

6 (6- to 8-oz.) Gulf-speckled-trout fillets, skinned
3 cups Seafood Stock, page 20, or 3 (8-oz.) bottles clam juice
1 cup dry white wine
1 teaspoon salt
½ teaspoon freshly ground white pepper
1 large bay leaf, minced

2 parsley sprigs, preferably flat-leaf, coarsely chopped
4 green onions, coarsely chopped
2 teaspoons fresh lemon juice
¼ teaspoon red (cayenne) pepper
Marguery Sauce, see below
Curly-parsley sprigs
Hungarian paprika

Marguery Sauce:
3 egg yolks, room temperature
½ teaspoon Dijon-style mustard
¼ teaspoon red (cayenne) pepper
2 teaspoons fresh lemon juice

½ cup unsalted butter or margarine, melted
1 lb. small cooked shrimp, peeled, deveined
Salt to taste

Preheat oven to 375F (190C). Place fish fillets in a 13″ × 9″ baking dish; set aside. Combine stock or clam juice, wine, salt, white pepper, bay leaf, parsley, green onions, lemon juice and cayenne in a 2-quart saucepan over medium heat; bring to a boil. Pour boiling liquid over fish fillets. Bake in preheated oven until fish turns from transparent to opaque, 10 minutes. Place fillets on a platter. Cover; keep warm. Strain poaching broth; reserve 1 cup for sauce. Prepare sauce. To serve, place a poached fillet on each plate; cover with sauce. Garnish with parsley sprigs and a light dusting of paprika. Makes 4 to 6 servings.

To prepare Marguery Sauce, in top of a double boiler over hot, not boiling, water, combine egg yolks, mustard, cayenne and lemon juice. Cook, whisking constantly, until thickened and lemon-colored, about 10 minutes. Very slowly add melted butter or margarine, almost drop-by-drop, whisking constantly, until all has been added. Slowly whisk in reserved 1 cup poaching liquid. Stir in shrimp and salt; remove from heat.

Creole Trout Amandine

Trout Amandine is one of the most popular of all New Orleans seafood dishes—and deservedly so. It is important that you use SLICED rather than slivered almonds. I prefer unblanched ones.

6 (6- to 8-oz.) Gulf speckled-trout fillets, skinned
Milk
About 2 cups all-purpose flour
1½ teaspoons salt
2 teaspoons freshly ground black pepper
2 teaspoons red (cayenne) pepper
2 tablespoons unsalted butter or margarine
⅓ cup vegetable oil

1 cup unsalted butter or margarine, melted
1 cup sliced almonds
2 teaspoons Worcestershire sauce
2 tablespoons fresh lemon juice
¼ teaspoon Tabasco sauce
6 green onions, chopped
¼ cup minced parsley, preferably flat-leaf
Lemon wedges

Place fillets in a 13″ × 9″ baking dish; add enough milk to cover. Cover and refrigerate 1 hour. Drain, discarding milk. Pat dry with paper towels; set aside. In a medium bowl, combine flour, salt, black pepper and cayenne. In a heavy 12-inch skillet over medium heat, heat 2 tablespoons butter or margarine and oil. When oil mixture is hot, dredge fish fillets in seasoned flour; shake to remove excess. Gently lower fillets into hot oil in batches. Sauté until fish turns from transparent to opaque, about 4 minutes on each side, turning once. Place on individual serving plates; keep warm. Pour oil from skillet, leaving browned bits in pan. Add 1 cup butter or margarine; scrape up browned bits from bottom of pan. Add almonds; cook, stirring, until almonds are light golden brown. Stir in Worcestershire sauce, lemon juice and Tabasco sauce. Remove from heat; stir in green onions and parsley. To serve, spoon almond-butter sauce over each fillet; garnish with lemon wedges. Makes 4 to 6 servings.

Trout with Roasted-Pecan Sauce

This innovative dish, made popular in New Orleans by the Commander's Palace Restaurant, is a delicious combination of two native favorites, Gulf speckled trout and pecans toasted to deep-brown perfection.

Roasted-Pecan Sauce,
  see below
Pecan Garnish, see below
6 (6- to 8-oz.) Gulf
  speckled-trout fillets,
  skinned
About 2 cups all-purpose
  flour
2 teaspoons salt

2 teaspoons freshly
  ground black pepper
2 teaspoons red (cayenne)
  pepper
2 tablespoons unsalted
  butter or margarine
⅓ cup vegetable oil
2 eggs beaten with 1 cup
  milk
Curly-parsley sprigs

Roasted-Pecan Sauce:
1¼ cups chopped pecans
½ cup unsalted butter or
  margarine, cut into
  1-inch chunks
2 teaspoons
  Worcestershire sauce

½ teaspoon Tabasco
  sauce
1 tablespoon fresh lemon
  juice
½ teaspoon salt
3 medium garlic cloves

Pecan Garnish:
2 tablespoons unsalted
  butter or margarine

1½ teaspoons
  Worcestershire sauce

Prepare sauce. Prepare garnish. Position oven rack 6 inches below heat source. Preheat broiler. Pat fish fillets dry with paper towels; set aside. In a medium bowl, combine flour, salt, black pepper and cayenne with a fork. In a heavy 12-inch skillet over medium heat, heat 2 tablespoons butter or margarine and oil. When oil is hot, dredge fillets in seasoned flour; shake to remove excess. Dip into egg-and-milk mixture. Then dredge again in seasoned flour to coat well; shake off excess. Gently lower coated fillets into hot oil in batches. Sauté about 4 minutes on each side, turning once. Drain on paper towels; lay in an ungreased baking pan. Top each fish fillet with 3 tablespoons pecan sauce; broil under preheated broiler until sauce is slightly softened, about 30 seconds. To serve, place fillets on individual plates. Top with Pecan Garnish. Garnish with parsley sprigs. Makes 4 to 6 servings.

To prepare Roasted-Pecan Sauce, preheat oven to 350F (175C). Spread pecans in a single layer on an ungreased baking sheet. Roast in preheated oven until a deep golden brown, about 10 minutes. Cool to room temperature. Place ¾ cup roasted pecans in a food processor fitted with the steel blade; reserve remaining ½ cup pecans for garnish. Add butter or margarine, Worcestershire sauce, Tabasco sauce, lemon juice and salt. With motor running, add garlic through feed tube to mince. Stop machine; scrape down side of bowl. Process to a smooth paste.

To prepare Pecan Garnish, in an 8-inch skillet over medium heat, melt butter or margarine. Stir in Worcestershire sauce. Add reserved ½ cup toasted pecans. Sauté 2 minutes, shaking pan back and forth.

Trout with Crabmeat & Artichoke Hearts

Pairing the delicate taste of Gulf speckled trout with the succulent sweetness of lump crabmeat results in a taste that is hard to beat—and it's so easy to prepare!

6 (6-to 8-oz.) Gulf
  speckled-trout fillets,
  skinned
Salt to taste
Freshly ground pepper
¾ lb. backfin lump
  crabmeat
¼ cup unsalted butter or
  margarine
⅓ cup vegetable oil
About 2 cups all-purpose
  flour

¾ cup unsalted butter or
  margarine, melted
6 canned artichoke
  hearts, drained,
  quartered
1 tablespoon fresh lemon
  juice
6 green onions, chopped
¼ teaspoon Tabasco
  sauce
1 tablespoon minced
  parsley, preferably
  flat-leaf

Pat fish fillets dry with paper towels. Season with salt
and pepper; set aside. Using your fingertips, carefully
pick through crabmeat; remove and discard any bits of
shell or cartilage; set aside. In a heavy 12-inch skillet
over medium heat, heat ¼ cup butter or margarine and
oil. When oil is hot, dredge fillets in flour, coating both
sides well; shake off excess flour. Add fillets to hot oil
mixture in batches; sauté over medium heat until light
golden brown, about 4 minutes per side, turning once.
Remove fillets; keep warm. Drain oil mixture from skillet, leaving any browned bits in pan. Return to heat; add
¾ cup butter or margarine; scrape up any browned bits
from bottom of pan. Add artichoke hearts; sauté until
butter is light golden brown, about 3 minutes. Whisk in
lemon juice. Add crabmeat, green onions, salt, pepper,
Tabasco sauce and parsley, stir until heated through. Do
not break up lumps of crabmeat; set aside. Place fillets
on individual plates; top with crab mixture, making sure
that each fillet gets plenty of the buttery liquid. Serve
hot. Makes 4 to 6 servings.

Barbecued Red Snapper

In South Louisiana we barbecue practically anything that will fit on the grill. During the summer months, fish is one of the favorites. Serve these succulent fillets with cole slaw and potato salad for a crowd-pleasing backyard cookout.

½ cup unsalted butter or margarine
1 small onion, chopped
3 green onions, minced
3 medium garlic cloves, minced
1 cup ketchup
1 cup water
¼ cup Burgundy wine
2 tablespoons red-wine vinegar

2 tablespoons fresh lemon juice
¼ cup firmly packed light-brown sugar
1½ teaspoons dry mustard
¼ teaspoon red (cayenne) pepper
1 teaspoon chili powder
2 teaspoons Worcestershire sauce
6 (6- to 8 oz.) red snapper fillets, skinned

Light a charcoal fire in an outdoor grill; position grill rack 6 inches above coals. Spray a hinged fish basket with nonstick vegetable spray; set aside. In a heavy 3-quart saucepan over medium heat, melt butter or margarine. Add onions, green onions and garlic. Sauté until wilted and transparent, about 5 minutes. Stir in all remaining ingredients except fish. Reduce heat; simmer 15 minutes, stirring occasionally. Set aside. When coals are evenly hot, pat fillets dry with paper towels; place in sprayed basket. Baste both sides of fish with sauce, coating well. Place on grill over coals. Cook until fish turns from transparent to opaque, 4 minutes per side, turning once. Remove from basket; serve hot. Pass remaining sauce, if desired. Makes 4 to 6 servings.

Red Snapper a la Creole

This dish is probably more representative of the type of food that would be served in a Creole home than any other dish. It is impressive when served on an attractively garnished platter and placed in the center of the table with pride.

1 (5-lb.) whole red
  snapper, cleaned
½ cup vegetable oil
2 large onions, quartered,
  thinly sliced
2 medium, green bell
  peppers, chopped
4 celery stalks, chopped
4 garlic cloves, minced
2 bay leaves, minced
½ teaspoon dried leaf
  thyme or 1½ teaspoons
  chopped fresh thyme
½ teaspoon dried leaf
  oregano or 1½
  teaspoons chopped
  fresh oregano
½ teaspoon freshly
  ground black pepper
½ teaspoon red (cayenne)
  pepper

1 tablespoon brown sugar
5 large tomatoes, peeled,
  chopped
1 (6-oz.) can tomato paste
¼ cup fresh lemon juice
2 cups Seafood Stock,
  page 20, or 2 (8-oz.)
  bottles clam juice
¼ cup minced parsley,
  preferably flat-leaf
6 green onions, chopped
2 lbs. small uncooked
  shrimp, peeled,
  deveined
Salt to taste
Lemon slices
Curly-parsley sprigs

Place red snapper in a large baking dish or roasting pan. Cover and refrigerate while preparing sauce. In a heavy 12-inch skillet over medium heat, heat oil until hot. Add onions, bell peppers, celery and garlic. Cook until vegetables are wilted and transparent, about 8 minutes. Stir in seasonings, sugar and tomatoes. Cook 10 minutes. Stir in tomato paste, lemon juice and stock or clam juice. Reduce heat. Simmer, partially covered, 45 minutes. Add parsley and green onions; stir until distributed. Add shrimp and salt; cook 5 minutes. Preheat oven to 375F (190C). Pour sauce over fish. Bake in preheated oven until fish turns from transparent to opaque, 40 minutes. To serve, place fish in center of a large platter; spoon sauce around fish. Place lemon slices and parsley sprigs around edge of platter. Makes 6 to 8 servings.

Grilled Shark Steak

Shark meat has a truly delicate flavor and it's inexpensive.

1½ cups unsalted butter
   or margarine
½ cup fresh lime juice
¼ cup minced capers
¼ teaspoon red (cayenne)
   pepper

6 (8-oz.) shark steaks
Salt to taste
Freshly ground black
   pepper

Light a charcoal fire in an outdoor grill; position grill 6 inches above coals. Spray a hinged fish basket with non-stick vegetable spray; set aside. In a 2-quart saucepan over medium heat, melt butter or margarine. Cook, stirring occasionally, until butter is a light hazelnut color, about 10 minutes. Stir in lime juice, capers and cayenne; remove from heat. When coals are evenly hot, pat steaks dry with paper towels. Season both sides with salt and pepper. Place on grill in sprayed basket. Baste both sides with butter sauce. Place on grill over coals. Cook until shark turns from transparent to opaque, about 5 minutes per side, turning once and basting often. Place on a serving platter. Serve hot. Pass remaining butter sauce separately. Makes 6 servings.

New Orleans Oyster Loaf

No visit to New Orleans would ever be complete without at least one oyster loaf. It's a 6-inch length of crusty French bread stacked with oysters fried just long enough to be crispy on the outside but still almost liquidy-smooth on the inside. An oyster loaf is some of the best eating New Orleans has to offer. To be native, have yours "dressed" with all the toppings.

Tartar Sauce, see below
Vegetable oil
8 shucked medium oysters, well drained
3 cups yellow cornmeal
1½ teaspoons salt
1½ teaspoons freshly ground black pepper
1 teaspoon red (cayenne) pepper

2 cups all-purpose flour
2 eggs beaten with 2 cups milk
1 (6-inch-section) toasted French bread
4 pickled okra pods, sliced into thin rounds
Shredded lettuce
3 tomato slices

Tartar Sauce:
1¼ cups mayonnaise
⅓ cup chopped dill pickles
¼ cup chopped pimento-stuffed olives
½ small onion, minced

1 tablespoon fresh lemon juice
½ teaspoon salt
½ teaspoon freshly ground pepper
½ teaspoon sugar

Prepare Tartar Sauce; cover and refrigerate until served. Heat 3 inches oil in a large saucepan to 365F (185C) or until a 1-inch bread cube turns golden brown in 60 seconds. Pat oysters dry on paper towels. In a shallow bowl, combine cornmeal, salt, black pepper and cayenne. Place flour in a shallow bowl. Dredge dried oysters in flour; shake off excess. Dip each floured oyster into egg-and-milk mixture. Then dredge in seasoned cornmeal to coat well; shake off excess. Fry oysters in hot oil, 2 or 3 at a time, just until crust is golden brown and crisp, 3 to 4 minutes. Drain on paper towels. Using a serrated knife, slice bread in half lengthwise. Generously coat inside of top and bottom of bread with Tartar Sauce.

Arrange oysters on bottom; top with okra rounds. Sprinkle with shredded lettuce; add tomato slices. Replace top. Makes 1 serving.

To prepare Tartar Sauce, combine all ingredients in a 2-quart bowl. Cover with plastic wrap, refrigerate until ready to serve or up to 2 days. Makes 2 cups.

Oysters en Brochette

This is one of the very best oyster dishes. It is so easy to prepare that you can have dinner for company in the time it takes to cook the rice!

8 bacon slices
½ cup unsalted butter or margarine
1 tablespoon Worcestershire sauce
⅛ teaspoon liquid smoke
1 tablespoon fresh lemon juice
½ teaspoon garlic powder
½ teaspoon salt
¼ teaspoon red (cayenne) pepper

½ teaspoon freshly ground black pepper
24 shucked oysters (about 2 pints), well drained, liquor reserved
16 medium mushrooms
16 cherry tomatoes
1 green bell pepper, cut into 1-inch pieces
About 2 cups hot cooked rice
Minced fresh parsley, preferably flat-leaf

In a medium skillet over medium heat, cook bacon until half cooked. Cut each slice into 8 pieces; set aside. In a heavy 2-quart saucepan, melt butter or margarine. Add Worcestershire sauce, liquid smoke, lemon juice, garlic powder, salt, cayenne, black pepper and reserved oyster liquor. Cook over medium heat 5 minutes. Cool slightly. Position oven rack 4 inches from heat source; preheat broiler. Place oysters in butter mixture, turning gently to coat well. Using 6 oysters per skewer, thread vegetables and oysters on 4 skewers, alternating vegetables and oysters with a bacon piece between each item. Lay skewers across top of a baking pan with ends of skewers resting on sides of pan. Drizzle remaining butter mixture over top of vegetables and oysters. Broil under pre-heated broiler 3 minutes per side, turning once. To serve, place a mound of rice in center of each plate; slide oysters and vegetables from skewers onto rice. Drizzle each serving with buttery drippings from baking pan. Sprinkle with minced parsley. Makes 4 servings.

Broiled-Stuffed Shrimp

This spicy broiled shrimp dish with its piquant mayonnaise may become a permanent part of your culinary repertoire.

Creole Mayonnaise, see
   below
¾ cup unsalted butter or
   margarine
2 medium onions, finely
   minced
4 medium garlic cloves,
   finely minced
2 tablespoons minced
   parsley, preferably
   flat-leaf
2 teaspoons dried leaf
   oregano or 2
   tablespoons chopped
   fresh oregano
1 teaspoon salt

½ teaspoon freshly
   ground black pepper
2 teaspoons red (cayenne)
   pepper
1½ cups finely crushed
   butter-flavored
   crackers
½ cup dry white wine
3 lbs. large uncooked
   shrimp, peeled,
   deveined, leaving
   shells on tails
Curly-parsley sprigs
Lemon wedges

Creole Mayonnaise:
1 large clove garlic
1 egg
1 tablespoon Creole
   mustard or other
   stone-ground mustard

1 teaspoon salt
½ teaspoon red (cayenne)
   pepper
2 tablespoons red-wine
   vinegar
1½ cups vegetable oil

Prepare mayonnaise. Melt butter or margarine in a heavy 12-inch skillet over medium heat. Add onions and garlic.

Sauté until wilted and transparent, about 5 minutes. Stir
in parsley, oregano, salt, pepper and cayenne. Cook 2
minutes. Remove skillet from heat; stir in cracker
crumbs until moistened. Stir in wine. Mixture should
have consistency of cookie dough and form a ball when
squeezed in your hand. If mixture is too dry, add additional wine. Set aside. Position oven rack 6 inches below
heat source. Preheat broiler. Using a small sharp knife,
start at tail end of shrimp and split through vein line on
outside of curve, cutting almost completely through to
butterfly shrimp. Lay butterflied shrimp on ungreased
baking sheets with tail section curving upward. Press
about 1 tablespoon cracker mixture on each shrimp. Pat
down firmly with your fingertips. Broil under preheated
broiler until topping is firm and golden brown and shrimp
are coral pink, about 8 minutes. Place shrimp on a platter. Garnish with parsley sprigs and lemon wedges.
Serve hot with Creole Mayonnaise. Makes 4 to 6 servings.

To prepare Creole Mayonnaise, in a food processor fitted
with the steel blade and motor running, drop garlic
through feed tube to mince. Stop machine; add all remaining ingredients except oil. Start and stop 3 to 4
times or until blended. With motor running, add oil
through feed tube in a slow, steady stream to form a
smooth mayonnaise. Spoon mayonnaise into a bowl.
Cover and refrigerate until ready to serve. Makes about
1½ cups.

Oysters Bienville

This egg-rich shrimp topping is named for the city's founder, Jean Baptiste le Moyne, Sieur de Bienville.

¼ cup unsalted butter or
   margarine
4 green onions, minced
2 tablespoons minced
   parsley, preferably
   flat-leaf
2 garlic cloves, minced
⅓ cup minced
   mushrooms
½ lb. deveined, peeled
   boiled shrimp, minced
¼ cup all-purpose flour
½ pint whipping cream
   (1 cup)
2 egg yolks, beaten until
   frothy

¼ cup dry sherry
½ teaspoon freshly
   ground black pepper
½ teaspoon red (cayenne)
   pepper
Salt to taste
⅓ cup grated Parmesan
   cheese (1 oz.)
¼ cup dry bread crumbs
½ teaspoon salt
24 shucked oysters, well
   drained
24 well-scrubbed oyster
   shells
Rock salt

In a heavy 10-inch skillet over medium heat, melt butter or margarine. Add green onions, parsley, garlic, mushrooms and shrimp. Cook until vegetables are wilted and transparent and liquid has evaporated, 8 to 10 minutes. Stir in flour until blended; cook 3 to 4 minutes, stirring. Slowly stir in cream; stir until combined. Stir in egg yolks, sherry, black pepper, cayenne and salt until combined. Cook until mixture thickens, 5 to 6 minutes. Set aside. In a small bowl, combine cheese, bread crumbs and ½ teaspoon salt; set aside. Preheat oven to 400F (205C). Line a large baking pan with rock salt. Pat oysters dry on paper towels. Place a dried oyster in each shell; nest shells into rock salt. Spoon a portion of shrimp mixture over each oyster; sprinkle with cheese mixture. Bake in preheated oven until bubbly and browned on top, 10 to 15 minutes. Serve hot. Makes 6 to 8 first-course servings or 4 light entrees.

Oysters Rockefeller

This classic oyster dish has become one of New Orleans' signature dishes.

1 (10-oz.) pkg. frozen
  chopped spinach,
  cooked
6 tablespoons unsalted
  butter or margarine
1 bunch watercress, finely
  chopped
¼ cup minced parsley,
  preferably flat-leaf
6 green onions, minced
2 teaspoons finely minced
  green bell pepper
½ teaspoon freshly
  ground black pepper
½ teaspoon dried leaf
  marjoram

½ teaspoon dried leaf
  basil
½ teaspoon red (cayenne)
  pepper
Salt to taste
1 tablespoon Herbsaint
About ½ cup whipping
  cream
Rock salt
24 shucked oysters, well
  drained
24 well-scrubbed oyster
  shells

Press spinach until very dry; set aside. Melt butter or margarine in a heavy 10-inch skillet over medium heat. Add spinach, watercress, parsley, green onions and bell pepper; sauté until vegetables are slightly wilted, about 5 minutes. Stir in black pepper, marjoram, basil, cayenne, salt, Herbsaint and ½ cup whipping cream. Cook, stirring, until mixture is thick and creamy, 5 minutes. Add additional cream if mixture is too thick to spoon easily. Set aside. Preheat oven to 400F (205C). Line a large baking pan with rock salt. Pat oysters dry on paper towels; place 1 dried oyster in each shell. Nest shells into rock salt. Divide topping among oysters, placing an even layer on top of each. Bake in preheated oven until bubbly and lightly browned on top, 10 to 15 minutes. Makes 6 to 8 first-course servings or 4 light entrees.

Oysters Rousseau

A light and zesty oyster dish perfect for the cocktail hour, this one is easy to prepare. The sauce can be made ahead and stored in the refrigerator up to 24 hours.

3 large tomatoes, peeled, seeded
¼ cup olive oil
½ medium onion, finely chopped
3 medium garlic cloves, minced
½ green bell pepper, finely chopped
¾ teaspoon dried leaf basil or 1 tablespoon minced fresh basil
¾ teaspoon dried leaf savory or 1 tablespoon minced fresh savory
¾ teaspoon dried leaf oregano or 1 tablespoon minced fresh oregano
1 tablespoon minced parsley, preferably flat-leaf

½ small bay leaf, minced
2 teaspoons fresh lemon juice
1 teaspoon Worcestershire sauce
½ teaspoon salt
½ teaspoon freshly ground black pepper
¼ teaspoon red (cayenne) pepper
8 bacon slices
Grated Parmesan cheese
Rock salt
24 shucked oysters, well drained
24 well-scrubbed oyster shells

In a food processor fitted with the steel blade, puree tomatoes; set aside. Heat olive oil in a heavy 10-inch skillet over medium heat. Add onion, garlic, bell pepper and herbs. Sauté until onion is wilted and transparent, about 5 minutes. Stir in tomato puree. Add lemon juice, Worcestershire sauce, salt, black pepper and cayenne; cook over medium heat until mixture has thickened slightly, 15 to 20 minutes. Taste for seasonings; adjust if necessary. Sauce should be piquant. Set aside. Preheat oven to 400F (205C). Cut bacon slices into thirds; lay pieces in a baking pan. Bake in preheated oven until half cooked, 4 to 5 minutes. Remove from pan; drain on paper towels.

Line a large baking pan with rock salt. Pat oysters dry on paper towels. Place 1 dried oyster in each half-shell; nest shells into salt. Divide tomato sauce among oysters. Place a bacon strip on each oyster. Top with grated Parmesan cheese. Bake in preheated oven until bacon is crisp and cheese is bubbly and light golden brown, 10 minutes. Serve hot. Makes 6 to 8 first-course servings or 4 light entrees.

Fried Crawfish Tails

This is one of the best ways to eat crawfish—it's no wonder that these tasty little tidbits have become popular snacks all over the country. We call them "Cajun popcorn."

Vegetable oil
2 cups yellow cornmeal
2 cups corn flour, page
   290, or very finely
   ground cornmeal
2 tablespoons red
   (cayenne) pepper

1 tablespoon finely
   ground black pepper
1 tablespoon salt
4 cups all-purpose flour
3 lbs. peeled crawfish tails
4 eggs beaten with
   3 cups milk

In a heavy large saucepan, heat 3 inches oil to 365F (185C) or until a 1-inch bread cube turns golden brown in 60 seconds. In a large bowl, whisk eggs and milk until blended. In a medium bowl, combine cornmeal, corn flour or very finely ground cornmeal and seasonings with a fork. Place all-purpose flour in a third bowl. Dredge crawfish tails in flour; shake off excess. Dip into egg-and-milk mixture. Then dredge in cornmeal mixture; shake off excess. Place a fry basket in hot oil. Carefully place coated crawfish in batches into preheated oil. Do not crowd pan or tails will stick together and crust will not be crispy. Fry until crust is crisp, 4 minutes. Drain on paper towels. Repeat until all crawfish have been fried. Serve hot. Makes 4 to 6 servings.

Pan-Fried Catfish with Tartar Sauce

Deep down, every Louisianian adores cornmeal-battered catfish fried to golden perfection. Middendorf's Restaurant in Pass Manchac, Louisiana is the home of the best fried catfish ANYWHERE—bar none. Their secret for getting it nice and crispy is to use thin fillets. Serve catfish with cole slaw, potato salad and a bowl of greens for a real "down-home" meal. And don't forget Sweet Hush Puppies, below!

2 lbs. thin catfish fillets, skinned
1 cup yellow cornmeal
1 cup corn flour, page 290, or very finely ground cornmeal
½ cup all-purpose flour
1½ teaspoons salt
2 teaspoons freshly ground black pepper

2 teaspoons red (cayenne) pepper
1½ teaspoons garlic powder
Vegetable oil
3 eggs beaten with 1½ cups milk
Lemon wedges
1 recipe Tartar Sauce, from New Orleans Oyster Loaf, page 137

Pat fish fillets dry on paper towels; set aside. In a medium bowl, combine cornmeal, corn flour or very finely ground cornmeal, all-purpose flour and seasonings with a fork. Heat ½ inch oil in a heavy 12-inch skillet over medium heat. When oil is hot, dredge fillets in cornmeal mixture; shake off excess. Dip into egg-and-milk mixture. Then dredge in cornmeal mixture to coat well; shake off excess. Carefully lower coated fillets into hot oil in batches. Do not crowd pan. Fry on both sides until golden brown and crispy, about 4 minutes per side, turning once. Drain on paper towels; serve hot with lemon wedges and Tartar Sauce. Makes 4 to 6 servings.

Sweet Hush Puppies

No meal of fried fish and tartar sauce is complete without hush puppies, and every Louisiana cook thinks he or she makes the best. Each one is probably right! I never tire of the story of the origin of hush puppies. It so fits the slow way of life we enjoy. South Louisiana has always had an over-abundance of yapping, precious little yellow mongrel dogs. Because kitchens on big plantations did not have doors, dogs would come begging when dinner preparation started. There was always more than enough corn bread batter waiting to be baked and always a great pot of hot lard hanging in the fire. The cook would take several handfuls of batter and throw them into the hot fat. When they floated to the top, she would fish them out and toss them to the dogs with the stern admonishment "Hush, puppy!"

1½ cups water
¾ cup unsalted butter or
  margarine
2 cups plus 2 tablespoons
  white cornmeal,
  preferably stone
  ground
½ cup sugar

1 tablespoon salt
1½ teaspoons baking
  powder
⅓ cup finely chopped
  green onions
Vegetable oil

In a heavy 2-quart saucepan over medium heat, combine water and butter or margarine. Bring to a full boil. Meanwhile, blend cornmeal, sugar, salt, baking powder and green onions in a large bowl. Stir boiling water mixture into cornmeal mixture until all dry ingredients are moist. Let mixture stand until cool enough to handle. Heat 3 inches oil to 350F (175C) or until a 1-inch bread cube turns golden brown in 65 seconds. Form dough into 2-inch long ovals by rolling between palms of your hands. Add 3 or 4 at a time to hot oil; do not crowd. Cook, turning once, until deep golden brown, about 2 minutes per side. Drain on paper towels. Repeat until all batter has been used, making sure that oil maintains a constant temperature. Serve hot. Makes about 32 hush puppies.

Mustard-Fried Catfish

Mustard-battered catfish is very popular in Cajun country. Some of the best catfish I've ever had was cooked by this method at a fishing camp deep in the Atchafalaya Basin, a tranquil and primeval marshland wilderness outside of Henderson, Louisiana.

6 (10- to 12-oz.) catfish, cleaned, beheaded, skinned
Vegetable oil
2 cups prepared yellow mustard
3 eggs, well beaten
1 teaspoon Tabasco sauce
1 cup corn flour, page 290, or very finely ground cornmeal
1 cup yellow cornmeal

1 cup all-purpose flour
1 cup Italian-seasoned bread crumbs
2 teaspoons salt
1 teaspoon garlic powder
1 teaspoon freshly ground pepper
1 teaspoon Hungarian paprika
Lemon wedges
Green onions

Pat fish dry with paper towels; set aside. In a heavy 12-inch skillet, heat 1 inch of oil to 350F (175C) or until a 1-inch bread cube turns golden brown in 65 seconds. In a medium bowl, combine mustard, eggs and Tabasco sauce. Pour mixture into a 13″ × 9″ baking dish. In a medium bowl, combine all remaining ingredients except lemon wedges; pour into another 13″ × 9″ baking dish. Dredge fish in mustard mixture, turning to coat all surfaces. Dip fish in cornmeal mixture, turning to coat well. Shake off excess. Gently place fish, 2 or 3 at a time, in preheated oil. Fry until golden brown and crispy, 6 to 7 minutes on each side, turning once. Drain on paper towels. Serve hot with lemon wedges. Makes 4 to 6 servings.

Baked Flounder & Tomatoes

In summer, when tomatoes reach ripe perfection in the garden next to the basil, and flounder are plentiful, this dish can't be beat for taste and ease of preparation.

1 (3- to 3½-lb.) whole flounder, head removed, cleaned
½ cup unsalted butter or margarine, melted
Salt to taste
Freshly ground black pepper
1 medium onion, halved lengthwise, sliced
3 tablespoons minced fresh basil or 1 tablespoon dried leaf basil

2 large ripe tomatoes, sliced
1 tablespoon Creole mustard or other stone-ground mustard
¼ teaspoon red (cayenne) pepper
2 cups dry white wine
Lemon slices
Basil sprigs or curly-parsley sprigs

Preheat oven to 375F (190C). Lightly butter bottom of a 13″ × 9″ baking pan. Place flounder in buttered baking pan; drizzle melted butter or margarine over surface. Season with salt and pepper. Spread onion over fish; scatter basil over onions. Top with sliced tomatoes. In a small bowl, combine mustard, cayenne and wine; pour into baking pan. Bake in preheated oven until fish turns from transparent to opaque, 20 minutes. Using 2 long spatulas, place fish on a serving platter; keep warm. Place baking pan over high heat; rapidly reduce pan juices by ½. Pour reduced sauce over fish; serve hot. Garnish with lemon slices and basil or parsley sprigs. Makes 4 to 6 servings.

Flounder Rockefeller with Crawfish-Buttercream Sauce

The rich and delicate taste combinations in this dish make it simply divine. The sauce, made from butter ground with whole boiled crawfish—shells, heads and all—is so delicious you'll want to use it with other fish dishes too.

6 (6- to 8-oz.) flounder
    fillets, skinned
Rockefeller Filling, see
    below
2 tablespoons fresh lemon
    juice

3 tablespoons unsalted
    butter or margarine,
    melted
Crawfish-Buttercream
    Sauce, see below
Spinach leaves
Lemon slices

Rockefeller Filling:
2 (10-oz.) pkgs. frozen
    chopped spinach,
    thawed
2 tablespoons unsalted
    butter or margarine
3 large garlic cloves,
    minced
1 tablespoon all-purpose
    flour
½ cup whipping cream

1 teaspoon Herbsaint or
    other anise-flavored
    liqueur
¼ teaspoon red (cayenne)
    pepper
½ teaspoon freshly
    ground black pepper
Salt to taste
2 eggs, slightly beaten

Crawfish-Buttercream Sauce:
½ pound cooked crawfish
    in shells
½ cup unsalted butter or
    margarine, cut into
    1-inch cubes
½ pint whipping cream
    (1 cup)
½ cup Seafood Stock,
    page 20, or bottled
    clam juice

1 teaspoon
    Worcestershire sauce
¼ teaspoon freshly
    ground black pepper
¼ teaspoon red (cayenne)
    pepper
Salt to taste

Pat flounder fillets dry with paper towels; set aside. Make Rockefeller Filling. Lay fillets on a work surface;

place equal amounts of filling in center of each fillet. Fold both ends of fish over filling, overlapping at center. Lift carefully; place, seam-sides-down, in an ungreased 13″ × 9″ baking pan. Drizzle fish bundles with lemon juice, then with melted butter or margarine. Refrigerate until ready to bake, if making ahead. Preheat oven to 275F (190C). Bake in preheated oven until fish turns from transparent to opaque, 15 minutes. Meanwhile, prepare Crawfish-Buttercream Sauce. Carefully place cooked fish on individual plates. Top with sauce; serve hot. Garnish plates with fresh spinach leaves and lemon slices. Makes 4 to 6 servings.

To prepare Rockefeller Filling, press out all moisture from spinach. In a heavy 10-inch skillet over medium heat, melt butter or margarine. Add drained spinach and garlic; saute 2 minutes over medium heat, stirring often. Sprinkle with flour; stir in flour. Stir in whipping cream, liqueur, cayenne and black pepper. Season with salt. Cook 3 to 4 minutes, stirring. Cool spinach mixture slightly. Stir eggs into warm filling mixture; set aside.

To prepare Crawfish-Buttercream Sauce, in a food processor fitted with the steel blade, combine crawfish in shells and butter or margarine. Process until pureed, stopping to scrape down side of bowl often. Set aside. In a heavy 2-quart saucepan over medium-high heat, reduce whipping cream by ½. Add Seafood Stock or clam juice; reduce by ½. While cream and stock are reducing, press crawfish butter through a very fine strainer or tamis, using a rubber spatula or the palm of your hand. Extract as much pure butter as possible, leaving minute particles of shell behind in strainer. Reduce heat; whisk strained crawfish butter into reduced mixture, a spoonful at a time, continuing until all butter has been added. Remove from heat; whisk in Worcestershire sauce. Season with black pepper, cayenne and salt. Makes about 3 cups.

Pompano en Papillote with Champagne Sauce

Pompano was elevated to regal status with the creation of this impressive dish at the turn of the century by Jules Alciatore, then proprietor of Antoine's Restaurant. Ask the fish market to save you the pompano carcasses for the sauce.

Unsalted butter or
    margarine, room
    temperature
6 (5- to 6-oz.) pompano
    fillets, skinned
14 oz. backfin lump
    crabmeat
6 tablespoons unsalted
    butter or margarine
Juice of 1 lemon

½ lb. mushrooms, sliced
6 green onions, chopped
¼ cup minced parsley,
    preferably flat-leaf
Salt to taste
2 egg whites, slightly
    beaten
Champagne Sauce, see
    below

Champagne Sauce:
Pompano carcasses
2 oz. backfin lump
    crabmeat
5 green onions, roughly
    chopped
3 parsley sprigs,
    preferably flat-leaf,
    roughly chopped
1 fifth dry Champagne
1 pint whipping cream
    (2 cups)

¼ cup fresh lemon juice
4 garlic cloves, unpeeled,
    mashed
½ cup unsalted butter or
    margarine, cut into
    1-inch cubes
½ teaspoon Tabasco
    sauce
Salt to taste

Assemble papillotes. They can be completely assembled ahead of time and stored in refrigerator up to 12 hours before baking. Cut 6 (15″ × 12″) parchment-paper sheets. Fold parchment sheets in half on 15-inch side. Using a pencil, draw half-heart shapes starting at folds. The hearts should extend from top to bottom and side to side of folded sheets. Using scissors, cut out hearts; lay open on work surface. Spread right half of each papillote with butter or margarine, leaving a 1-inch unbuttered border at outside edge. Place a pompano fillet in center of each buttered papillote section; set aside. With your fingers, carefully pick through crabmeat; remove and discard any bits of shell or cartilage. Melt 6 tablespoons butter or margarine in a heavy 10-inch skillet over medium heat; cook until lightly browned, about 5 minutes. Rapidly whisk in lemon juice. Add mushrooms, green onions, parsley and crabmeat, tossing gently just to coat with browned butter. Remove from heat; salt to taste. Spoon equal amounts of crabmeat mixture over each fish fillet. Using a pastry brush, paint unbuttered edges of papillotes with egg white. Fold left half of heart over, sealing 2 halves at egg-white border. Starting at center of heart, on fold, seal papillotes using overlapping pleats, continuing to bottom tip of heart. Paint folds with egg white; repeat pleating a second time. When you reach bottom tip of heart, twist paper 3 or 4 times, corkscrew fashion. Give pleats a final coat of egg white to form a tight seal. Lay sealed papillotes in a single layer on 2 baking sheets. Refrigerate while preparing sauce. Prepare sauce. Place baking sheet containing papillotes in preheated oven; bake 15 minutes. Place on individual plates. At the table, split papillotes open down the middle using a small, very sharp knife. Spoon sauce inside. Makes 6 servings.

To prepare Champagne Sauce, preheat oven to 375F (190C). Remove heads from fish carcasses and discard. Wash remaining bones under running water to remove all traces of blood. Place washed bones, crabmeat, green onions and parsley in a 13″ × 9″ baking pan; add champagne. Bake in preheated oven 15 minutes. Remove and discard bones from baking pan. Place baking pan on burner over high heat; cook to reduce liquid by ½, about

10 minutes. Add whipping cream, lemon juice and garlic. Cook again to reduce by ½, 10 to 15 minutes. Strain sauce into a heavy 2-quart saucepan. Over medium heat, whisk butter or margarine into reduced champagne mixture, 1 or 2 chunks at a time, making sure each piece is incorporated before adding next. When all butter has been added, remove from heat; whisk in Tabasco sauce. Salt to taste.

Blackened Redfish

This now-famous dish certainly needs no introduction, but a few pointers are in order for the home cook. If redfish are unavailable, you must use a fish with strong connective tissue, such as red snapper, grouper or tilefish. Fillets must be no thicker than ¾-inch thick. You MUST use a solid cast-iron frying pan to cook this dish. Do not attempt to use any other type of skillet or you will ruin the skillet and possibly create a serious fire hazard. The best way to blacken redfish is on an open-flame butane burner outside. If this is not possible, be forewarned that the cooking process will create great clouds of smoke. Two precautions: (1) If you have smoke detectors, disarm them before proceeding; (2) if you have a cooktop with a "space-saver" microwave overhead, do not attempt to prepare this dish. The butter sauce from the fish may ignite because of intense heat—it almost always does when using electric heat. The flames, of course, would ruin the microwave. Keep a snug-fitting lid for your skillet close at hand. Should flaming occur, do not panic! Merely place lid on the skillet momentarily to smother the flames and proceed with cooking. Even if you are ardently devoted to using fresh herbs, it is important to use dried thyme in this recipe. The minced particles of fresh thyme char and burn immediately in the intense heat involved, giving fish an acrid and bitter taste.

6 redfish fillets, about ½-
   to ¾-inch thick,
   skinned
2-½ cups unsalted butter
   or margarine
½ cup fresh lemon juice
1½ teaspoons red
   (cayenne) pepper

1 teaspoon salt
2 teaspoons freshly
   ground black pepper
1 tablespoon dried leaf
   thyme
Curly-parsley sprigs
Lemon wedges

Place fish fillets on a cutting board; trim off any thin
edges and very thin tip of tail. If left on, these thin areas
will char and break away. Pat fillets dry with paper
towels; cover and refrigerate until ready to cook. The
butter sauce adheres better to cold fillets. In a heavy
3-quart saucepan over medium heat, melt butter; add
lemon juice, cayenne, salt, black pepper and thyme. Stir
to blend seasonings; cool to lukewarm. Place an EMPTY
10-inch cast-iron skillet over HIGH heat until bottom has
a definite white haze and begins to smoke slightly. Remove fish from refrigerator; dip 1 fillet in warm butter
sauce, coating well. Place fish in hot skillet, taking care
that spits and spatters do not burn you. The fish will sear
and cook almost immediately. Turn fillet over; blacken
other side. Repeat with remaining fillets, cooking no
more than 2 at a time. Reserve remaining butter sauce.
As fillets are cooked, place them on individual plates;
keep warm. Remove and discard any accumulated butter
sauce and charred bits between batches. When all fish
have been cooked, quickly remove skillet from heat; discard any accumulated butter sauce and charred bits. Immediately place empty skillet back on heat. Add
reserved butter sauce; carefully swirl skillet 5 or 6 times
to blacken butter. Remove pan from heat; drizzle butter
over each fillet. Garnish with parsley sprigs and lemon
wedges. Serve hot. Makes 4 to 6 servings.

Stuffed Flounder

Stuffed flounder has long been a popular dish on New Orleans restaurant menus. The fish may be completely assembled ahead, refrigerated and baked when ready to serve.

1 (2½- to 3-lb.) flounder, head removed, cleaned
¾ lb. backfin lump crabmeat
¼ lb. mushrooms, chopped
¾ cup dry bread crumbs
6 green onions, chopped
¼ cup minced parsley, preferably flat-leaf
1 teaspoon salt

1 teaspoon red (cayenne) pepper
1¾ cups shredded Monterey Jack cheese (7 oz.)
1 cup unsalted butter or margarine
Juice of 1 lemon
12 lemon slices
Hungarian paprika
Curly-parsley sprigs

Preheat oven to 350F (175C). Lightly grease a baking sheet; set aside. Lay flounder, dark-side up, on a cutting board with tail nearest to you. Using a sharp, thin-bladed knife or boning knife, start about ¾-inch from head, make a slit down midline to one-half inch from where tail begins. Cut into fish until you feel knife touch bone in middle. Now, starting at top, carefully work knife into slit, keeping knife against bones and working toward outside edge. Separate flesh from bones all way to outside fins on both sides of center slit, taking care not to pierce skin. Turn fish over so that white side is facing up. Starting at head end, carefully slip knife between bones and bottom fillet of fish. Working toward tail and both sides with knife always against bones, separate fillet from bones. The bones should now be completely separated from meat on both sides. Working from slit on top and from head end, use your fingers to gently tear bones loose from side fins. When you reach tail end, snip bones free using kitchen shears. Use tweezers or small pliers to remove any bones remaining at side edges. Place fish on greased baking sheet; refrigerate while preparing stuffing. Place crabmeat in a medium bowl. With your fingers, carefully pick through crabmeat; remove and discard any bits of shell or cartilage. Do not break up lumps of crabmeat. Add mushrooms, bread crumbs, green onions, parsley, salt, cayenne and cheese. Toss gently to combine ingredients. Melt butter or margarine in a small saucepan; set aside ⅓ cup. Add remaining melted butter or margarine to crabmeat mixture; toss gently to blend. Carefully stuff crabmeat mixture into boned flounder, mounding it toward middle. Pat top down over filling. Drizzle lemon juice over fish and exposed stuffing. Using a pastry brush, brush fish with reserved butter or margarine. Place lemon slices, slightly overlapping, down center of fish; lightly dust top with paprika. Bake in preheated oven until stuffing is light golden brown and fish turns from transparent to opaque, 25 minutes. Using 2 long spatulas, carefully place fish on a serving platter. Garnish with parsley sprigs. Makes 4 to 6 servings.

If fish smells a little *fishy*, try this. Place fish in a shallow dish; add enough milk to cover. Cover tightly; refrigerate 3 to 4 hours. Drain, pat dry and use as desired.

Vegetables & Rice

South Louisiana is richly blessed with a growing season that extends throughout most of the year. What a treat it is to wander through the stalls at the French market and see the colorful patterns formed by the bins of fresh vegetables. There are golden yellow kernels of corn peeking out of fresh green husks, brilliant, scarlet-red Creole tomatoes lined up in row after row, shiny green bell peppers piled precariously high—all just waiting to be chopped and tossed into a big pot.

Cajun-Creole vegetable-cooking methods have really "taken it on the chin" from the nutrition-conscious, al dente-vegetable advocates. It is quite true that most Cajun-Creole home-cooked vegetables are overcooked and that they are cooked in large quantities of water into which all of their nutrients leach. Ah, but the taste of those vegetables will provide the victor's edge in any such discussion. It is that magical and complex taste created by combinations of vegetables and seasonings cooking down for hours that forms an integral part of *la bouche Creole*, or the Creole mouth.

In defense of the Cajun-Creole method of overcooking vegetables, let me say that even though most of the vitamins and minerals do leach out into the excessive liquid during the long cooking times, they are not completely lost. In fact, that excessive liquid, which becomes a rich and flavor-packed broth, is one of the most important taste aspects of the dish. In South Louisiana it is called *pot likker*, and is usually served in bowls with the vegetable.

When cooking any type of dried beans, the Cajuns and Creoles like to cook them until they start to break down to a pulpy consistency. What a delicious and smooth gravy-like sauce they make. Some of us believe that the bean gravy is the best part, especially when combined with rice.

All members of the onion family are aromatic vegetables. The leek, like the true shallot, is rarely used in Cajun-Creole cooking. The yellow onion is the most bold-flavored member of the family and should be used in dishes that will be cooked. In uncooked dishes such as potato salad or sandwiches, use either white onions or red onions.

Greens are a mainstay of the Cajun-Creole diet. The most commonly used varieties are spinach, turnip, mustard and collard greens. Often supper consists of a big pot of mixed greens with onions, turnips and a bit of seasoning meat, cooked for several hours and served in a big bowl with corn bread on the side. The most important thing to remember in preparing greens is that they are generally grown in slightly sandy soil and must be washed thoroughly.

South Louisianians eat a great many of the old-fashioned, or non-trendy vegetables, transforming the dull tastes of strange-looking things, such as turnips, rutabagas and kohlrabi, into something mighty good, using a pinch of this and a dab of that.

The Cajuns and Creoles prepare dishes from the lowly

sweet potato that are so delicious that they must be divinely inspired. Louisiana is second only to North Carolina in sweet-potato production. There's even a Yamboree each year in Opelousas to celebrate the harvest and give an opportunity to sample sweet potatoes prepared by every method under the sun.

One of the best-kept vegetable-seasoning secrets is the pinch of sugar that the Cajuns add to their vegetables! Sugar acts as a marvelous flavor enhancer, adding a definite flavor perk. There is never enough sugar to make the vegetables taste sweet, but enough to let you know that there is something very unique about those vegetables!

The Cajuns and Creoles use herbs extensively to flavor vegetables. If you have fresh herbs available, all the better! If you gain nothing else from this chapter, I hope that you will be inspired to experiment with vegetables. Who knows, you may gain so much love for down-home vegetables that you will feel compelled to serve Mixed Greens with Turnips & Tasso at your next sit-down dinner for 12. Just discreetly tuck a bib under the edge of the bowl and tell your guests that greens are "in" this year.

Mixed Greens with Turnips & Tasso

Greens are good for you, everybody's heard that one. But not everybody knows that greens are just plain good, too. They're an institution in Cajun country. The best way to enjoy them is to serve them on the side in a bowl with lots of juice. The Cajuns call this juice *pot likker*. It is the custom to pick up the bowl and drink the likker after the greens have been eaten. For a real down-home meal, serve a large soup plate of greens and pot likker with Cajun Corn Bread, page 212. Be sure each bowl gets some tasso or ham.

10 oz. fresh collard greens
10 oz. fresh mustard
   greens
10 oz. fresh turnip greens
2 medium onions, halved
   lengthwise, sliced
3 medium turnips, halved
   lengthwise, sliced
¾ lb. tasso, below, or
   smoked ham, cut into
   bite-sized chunks

1½ tablespoons sugar
½ cup picante sauce
1 tablespoon salt
1 tablespoon freshly
   ground pepper

Place all greens in sink or a large pot; fill to brim with lukewarm water. Let greens stand 15 minutes. Carefully remove greens from water without disturbing sandy silt which has settled to bottom. Wash leaves under running water; tear leaves into small pieces, removing tough ribs. Place torn greens, onions, turnips and tasso or ham in a 10- to 12-quart soup pot; fill to top with water. Add sugar, picante sauce, salt and pepper. Bring to a boil over medium-high heat; boil 5 minutes. Reduce heat. Barely simmer, stirring occasionally, 3 hours. Taste for seasoning; adjust if necessary. Greens should have lots of liquid left; add more water if necessary. Serve hot; enjoy one of the greatest Cajun treats. Makes 8 to 10 servings.

Artichoke-Heart Casserole

This rich and flavorful dish offers a delightful alternative to everyday vegetable dishes. It can't be beaten for ease in preparation.

1 (14-oz.) can artichoke
  hearts, drained
¼ cup unsalted butter or
  margarine
1 medium onion, halved
  lengthwise, sliced
4 green onions, chopped
3 medium garlic cloves,
  minced
1 tablespoon minced
  parsley, preferably
  flat-leaf
1 teaspoon dried leaf
  basil or 1 tablespoon
  chopped fresh basil

1 teaspoon salt
¼ teaspoon freshly
  ground pepper
½ cup mayonnaise
2 tablespoons dairy sour
  cream
¼ cup whipping cream
1 tablespoon Creole
  mustard or other
  stone-ground mustard
½ cup Italian-seasoned
  bread crumbs
½ cup grated Parmesan
  cheese (1½ oz.)

Preheat oven to 350F (175C). Lightly butter an 8-inch au
gratin dish; set aside. Cut artichoke hearts into quarters;
set aside. Melt butter or margarine in a heavy 10-inch
skillet over medium heat. Add onion slices; cook until
slightly wilted and transparent, about 5 minutes. Add
artichoke-heart quarters, green onions, garlic, parsley,
basil, salt and pepper; cook 5 minutes. Meanwhile, in a
small bowl, whisk together mayonnaise, sour cream,
whipping cream and mustard. In another small bowl,
combine bread crumbs and cheese with a fork. Place
artichoke-heart mixture in buttered dish; pour cream-
mixture over top, spreading evenly. Sprinkle bread-
crumb mixture over top. Bake in preheated oven until
golden brown and bubbly, 25 minutes. Serve hot. Makes
4 to 6 servings.

Tasso is a smoked pork or beef seasoning meat
made from poor-quality meat cuts. The meat is
coated with a very spicy seasoning mixture and slow
smoked until hard and very flavorful.

Rosemary Potatoes

This delicious dish, which makes use of leftover baked potatoes, is sure to become a house favorite. Fresh rosemary, if available, is an added enhancement. The dish is great with steaks, or serve with any grilled or broiled meats, fish or poultry.

4 medium baking
  potatoes, baked,
  chilled
2 tablespoons unsalted
  butter or margarine
½ cup vegetable oil
1 large onion, halved
  lengthwise, sliced

1½ teaspoons minced
  dried rosemary or 1½
  tablespoons minced
  fresh rosemary
1 tablespoon sugar
½ teaspoon salt
1½ teaspoons freshly
  ground pepper

Halve unpeeled potatoes lengthwise; slice into thin slices. In a heavy 12-inch skillet over medium-high heat, heat butter or margarine and oil. Add sliced potatoes and onion; toss to coat with oil. Add rosemary, sugar, salt and pepper; stir until combined. Cook, tossing often, until onion is thoroughly wilted and both potatoes and onions are caramelized, 10 to 15 minutes. Serve hot. Makes 4 to 6 servings.

Creole Stewed Okra & Tomatoes

In South Louisiana, stewed okra with tomatoes is like an old shoe—good and comfortable. Serve with grilled, broiled or roasted meats, poultry or fish.

½ cup bacon drippings
1 medium onion, chopped
1 small green bell pepper, chopped
2 large garlic cloves, minced
3 medium tomatoes, peeled, chopped
1 teaspoon salt
½ teaspoon freshly ground black pepper

½ teaspoon red (cayenne) pepper
1 teaspoon sugar
1 tablespoon minced parsley, preferably flat-leaf
35 medium okra pods, sliced into ½-inch-thick slices
1½ cups Louisiana Brown Poultry Stock, page 19, or canned chicken broth

Heat bacon drippings in a deep 12-inch skillet over medium heat. Add onion, bell pepper and garlic; cook until onion is thoroughly wilted and transparent, about 10 minutes. Add tomatoes, salt, black pepper, cayenne, sugar and parsley. Stir until combined; cook until tomatoes are broken down to a pulpy consistency, 20 minutes. Add okra and stock or broth; stir until combined. Cover and cook until okra is tender, 20 minutes, stirring often. Serve hot. Makes 4 to 6 servings.

For fluffy rice with separate grains, remember the following: Do not overfill pan; allow four or more inches between water level and top of pan. Do not use a pan larger than the heating element. After cooking, immediately place rice in a shallow container; fluff with a fork.

Minted Peas & Onions

Fresh mint, which grows beside just about every back porch in South Louisiana, is often cooked in vegetable dishes. Mint has a special affinity for green peas.

½ cup unsalted butter or margarine
2 (10-oz.) pkgs. frozen green peas, thawed
1 medium onion, halved lengthwise, thinly sliced

1 teaspoon salt
¼ teaspoon freshly ground pepper
1 teaspoon sugar
⅓ cup packed mint, minced

In a heavy 12-inch skillet over medium heat, melt butter or margarine; cook butter until nut-brown in color, about 7 minutes. Add peas and onion. Add salt, pepper, sugar and mint; cook until onion is wilted and transparent and peas are tender, about 10 minutes. Serve hot. Makes 4 to 6 servings.

Cajun Maquechou

Maquechou (pronounced mach shoe) is a Cajun dish that is based on corn. The remaining ingredients are a matter of individual choice, with every cook adding his or her own touches.

½ cup bacon drippings
Kernels from 6 ears fresh corn or 2 (17½-oz.) cans whole-kernel corn, drained
1 large onion, chopped
2 medium garlic cloves, minced
1 large green bell pepper, chopped
2 medium tomatoes, peeled, chopped

1 teaspoon salt
½ teaspoon freshly ground black pepper
1 tablespoon sugar
½ teaspoon red (cayenne) pepper
1 cup Louisiana Brown Poultry Stock, page 19, or canned chicken broth
1 cup milk
2 eggs

Heat bacon drippings in a heavy 12-inch skillet over medium heat. Add corn, onion, garlic and bell pepper; cook until onion is thoroughly wilted and transparent, about 10 minutes. Stir often to prevent sticking. Add tomatoes, salt, black pepper, sugar and cayenne; stir until combined. Add stock or broth. Reduce heat. Barely simmer, stirring often, until liquid has almost evaporated, about 30 minutes. The mixture will be thick and mushy. Stir in milk; cook until reduced by ½. Increase heat slightly. In a small bowl, beat eggs until frothy; stirring constantly, add to pan in a slow steady stream. Cook just to thicken, 3 to 4 minutes. Serve hot. Makes 4 to 6 servings.

Creole Sweet-Potato Pone

This classic Cajun dish is a must at holiday meals and the perfect accompaniment to any baked poultry dish.

4 large sweet potatoes (about 2 lbs.), peeled, quartered
½ cup unsalted butter or margarine
2 eggs, slightly beaten
½ pint whipping cream (1 cup)
1 teaspoon vanilla extract
2 tablespoons light-brown sugar
½ teaspoon ground cinnamon
½ teaspoon ground allspice

½ teaspoon ground cloves
Dash of freshly grated nutmeg
½ cup golden raisins
½ cup flaked coconut
1 teaspoon grated orange zest
1 teaspoon grated lemon zest
½ cup all-purpose flour
1 tablespoon baking powder
Topping, see below

Topping:
1 cup firmly packed light-brown sugar
½ cup unsalted butter or margarine, room temperature

½ cup finely chopped pecans
½ cup Grape Nuts cereal

Place quartered sweet potatoes in a heavy 5- to 6-quart saucepan; add enough water to cover. Bring to a boil over high heat. Reduce heat; simmer until potatoes are very tender, 20 minutes. Drain well; mash. Preheat oven to 350F (175C). Lightly butter a 13" × 9" baking dish. In a heavy 1-quart saucepan, melt butter or margarine over medium heat; cook until nut-brown in color, about 7 minutes. Stir browned butter or margarine and remaining ingredients except Topping into mashed sweet potatoes, blending well. Spread mixture into buttered baking dish; set aside. Prepare Topping. Sprinkle Topping evenly over sweet-potato mixture. Bake in preheated oven until golden brown and bubbly, 30 minutes. Serve hot. Makes 6 to 8 servings.

To prepare Topping, in a medium bowl, combine all topping ingredients.

Creole Corn Pudding

Corn Pudding is a delicious vegetable side dish that is very traditional in the Deep South. It is a perfect accompaniment to roast pork or poultry.

1 (20-oz.) can cream-style corn
1 tablespoon sugar
1 teaspoon salt
½ teaspoon freshly ground pepper
¼ cup unsalted butter or margarine, melted

5 eggs, well beatan
1 cup milk
½ pint whipping cream (1 cup)
1 tablespoon cornstarch mixed with 1 tablespoon cold water

Preheat oven to 350F (175C). Lightly butter a 13" × 9" baking dish. In a medium bowl, combine all ingredients. Spoon into buttered baking dish. Bake in preheated oven until custard is firm and knife inserted off center comes out clean, 1 hour. Serve hot. Makes 6 to 8 servings.

Sweet-Potato Puffs

For years this recipe has been served to dignitaries from around the globe. Its creation is attributed to Blanche Long, wife of former Louisiana governor, Earl K. Long. The puffs are made ahead and baked while still frozen.

4 large sweet potatoes
   (2 lbs.), peeled,
   quartered
¼ cup unsalted butter or
   margarine, melted
½ teaspoon salt
2 tablespoons light-brown
   sugar
1 teaspoon ground
   nutmeg

1 teaspoon ground
   cinnamon
2 egg yolks, slightly
   beaten
12 large marshmallows
2 cups cornflake crumbs
¼ cup unsalted butter or
   margarine, melted

Place sweet potatoes in a heavy 5- to 6-quart saucepan; add enough water to cover. Bring to a boil over high heat. Reduce heat; simmer until potatoes are very tender, 20 minutes. Immediately drain well; cool slightly. Mash cooled potatoes. In a medium bowl, combine mashed sweet potatoes, ¼ cup butter or margarine, salt, brown sugar, nutmeg, cinnamon and egg yolks. If mixture is too soft to shape, refrigerate until chilled. Flatten ⅓ cup sweet-potato mixture into a 3-inch circle; place a marshmallow in center. Gather sweet-potato mixture around marshmallow to enclose, leaving a small hole at top. Set aside. Repeat with remaining sweet-potato mixture and marshmallows. In a medium bowl, combine cornflake crumbs with remaining ¼ cup butter or margarine. Roll puffs in buttered crumbs, turning to coat well. Place on a baking sheet; freeze until solid. If not baking immediately, place frozen puffs in a plastic freezer container; store up to 2 months. To bake, preheat oven to 350F (175C). Bake frozen puffs 20 minutes; serve hot. Makes 12 puffs.

Creole Spinach Mousse

These tasty individual mousses will add an elegant touch to any meal. They are simple to prepare.

1½ (10-oz.) pkgs. frozen chopped spinach
2 tablespoons unsalted butter or margarine
1 large garlic clove, minced
2 green onions, minced
1 tablespoon all-purpose flour
½ cup milk

½ cup whipping cream
1 teaspoon Herbsaint
½ teaspoon salt
¼ teaspoon freshly ground black pepper
¼ teaspoon red (cayenne) pepper
2 eggs

Preheat oven to 350F (175C). Thoroughly butter 6 (½-cup) ramekins; set aside. Butter 1 side of a 13″ × 9″ parchment-paper sheet. Thaw spinach completely; press out all moisture from spinach. In a heavy 10-inch skillet over medium heat, melt butter or margarine; add pressed spinach, garlic and green onions. Cook 5 minutes; add flour, stirring to blend well. Cook 4 minutes, stirring constantly. Combine milk and cream; add to spinach mixture in a slow, steady stream. Add Herbsaint and seasonings; cook 5 minutes. Cool slightly. Lightly beat eggs; fold beaten eggs into spinach mixture. Pour into buttered ramekins. Place ramekins in a 13″ × 9″ baking dish. Add about 3 cups boiling water; put parchment paper, buttered-side-down, on ramekins. Bake in preheated oven until mousses are set, 25 to 30 minutes. Remove from water bath; unmold carefully onto serving plates. Serve hot. Makes 6 servings.

Variation

Sprinkle two sieved, hard-cooked egg yolks on a serving plate. Place mousses on egg yolks. Decorate with fresh thyme leaves and lemon-peel twists.

Chili-Cheese Grits Piquant

Grits are by no means just for breakfast in Cajun-Creole country. They're too good to be so limited! This spicy casserole makes an excellent vegetable dish for a buffet.

2¼ cups water
¾ cup slow-cooking grits
6 tablespoons unsalted
    butter or margarine,
    room temperature
6 oz. processed cheese,
    cut into ½-inch chunks

3 jalapeño peppers, seeds
    and veins removed,
    minced
1 medium, red bell
    pepper, chopped
4 green onions, chopped
1 teaspoon salt
2 eggs, slightly beaten

Preheat oven to 325F (165C). Butter a 13" × 9" baking dish. In a heavy 2-quart saucepan over medium-high heat, bring water to a boil; add grits. Reduce heat to medium; cook, stirring often, until mixture begins to thicken, about 20 minutes. Remove from heat; stir in butter or margarine, cheese, jalapeño peppers, bell pepper, green onions and salt. Blend well. Fold in eggs; spoon mixture into buttered baking dish. Bake in preheated oven until bubbly and lightly browned, 45 minutes. Makes 4 to 6 servings.

To easily remove moisture from thawed frozen spinach, place spinach in a pie pan. Set another pie pan over spinach. Over the sink, holding pie pans vertically in your hands, press pans together. Liquid will be pressed from spinach and drain into the sink!

Sweet-Sour Rutabagas

The rutabaga, like its cousin, the turnip, is not a front-runner among trendy foods—and what a shame. It's delicious and a nice change of pace.

4 medium rutabagas	½ teaspoon freshly
½ cup bacon drippings	ground pepper
1 large onion, chopped	1 tablespoon sugar
1 teaspoon salt	¼ cup cider vinegar
	6 green onions, chopped

Fill a 5-quart saucepan half full of water; bring to a boil over medium-high heat. Add rutabagas; cook until almost tender, about 10 minutes. Drain and cool to room temperature. Dice cooled rutabagas into ½-inch cubes; set aside. Heat bacon drippings in a heavy 12-inch skillet over medium heat. Add rutabaga cubes and onion; cook, stirring often, until onion is wilted and golden brown, about 15 minutes. Add salt, pepper and sugar; cook 5 minutes. Add vinegar; stir quickly, scraping up browned bits from bottom of pan. Cook until liquid has evaporated to a glaze, 6 to 7 minutes. Stir in green onions. Serve hot. Makes 4 to 6 servings.

Broccoli & Rice Casserole with Cress Sauce

Serve this robust-flavored vegetable dish with grilled steak, broiled fish or baked chicken for a most enjoyable meal.

3 cups tightly packed broccoli flowerets or 2 (10-oz.) pkgs. frozen chopped broccoli	1 large bay leaf, minced ½ cup dry bread crumbs 3 cups cooked white rice 3 hard-boiled eggs, sliced
½ cup unsalted butter or margarine	Cress Sauce, see below
3 large garlic cloves, minced	

Cress Sauce:

1 cup packed watercress leaves and tender stems

¼ cup chopped parsley, preferably flat-leaf

3 green onions, coarsely chopped

½ teaspoon dill weed or 1½ teaspoons minced fresh dill

½ teaspoon dried leaf basil or 1½ teaspoons chopped fresh basil

½ cup mayonnaise

1 teaspoon Creole mustard or other stone-ground mustard

⅛ teaspoon curry powder

¼ teaspoon red (cayenne) pepper

Salt to taste

Preheat oven to 350F (175C). Lightly grease a 3-quart casserole dish. Steam broccoli flowerets over rapidly boiling water until almost tender, 4 to 5 minutes. Cool slightly; coarsely chop. Or thaw and drain frozen broccoli. Set aside. In a medium saucepan, melt butter or margarine. Add garlic and bay leaf; cook over medium-low heat 5 minutes. Fold in bread crumbs, tossing to coat bread crumbs well. Stir in rice and chopped broccoli; turn into prepared casserole. Top with sliced eggs. Bake in preheated oven 20 minutes. While casserole is cooking, prepare sauce. Top casserole with sauce; bake 5 minutes. Serve hot. Makes 4 to 6 servings.

To prepare Cress Sauce, in a food processor fitted with the steel blade, combine all sauce ingredients. Process until pureed, stopping 2 or 3 times to scrape down side of bowl.

Scalloped Onion & Almond Casserole

Another great make-ahead dish for your next buffet dinner, this dish has a unique and delicate taste.

20 small pearl onions (about ½ lb.)
6 tablespoons unsalted butter or margarine
4 celery stalks, chopped
5 green onions, chopped
5 tablespoons all-purpose flour
1 teaspoon salt
½ teaspoon freshly ground pepper

1 teaspoon Tabasco sauce
2¼ cups half and half
⅔ cup sliced blanched almonds
½ cup grated Parmesan cheese (1½ oz.)
Toasted sliced almonds, if desired
Celery leaves, if desired

Preheat oven to 350F (175C). Lightly butter a 1½-quart casserole dish. Using a sharp knife, cut off and discard root end from each onion; set onions aside. Fill a 4- to 6-quart saucepan half full of water; bring to a boil over medium-high heat. Add onions; parboil 1 minute. Drain into a colander; place under running water to cool. When onions are cool enough to handle, peel by grasping between your thumb and forefinger at stem end and squeezing lightly. The peel should slip off easily. Set peeled onions aside. In a heavy 12-inch skillet over medium heat, melt butter or margarine. Add celery; cook 5 minutes. Add peeled onions and green onions; stir to blend. Sprinkle flour into skillet; stir until combined. Cook 3 to 4 minutes, stirring. Blend in salt, pepper and Tabasco sauce. Slowly stir in half and half. Cook about 5 minutes; fold in ⅔ cup almonds and cheese. Pour into buttered baking dish. Bake in preheated oven until bubbly and lightly browned, 25 minutes. Top with toasted almonds and celery leaves, if desired. Makes 6 to 8 servings.

Spinach & Artichoke Stuffed Tomatoes

This colorful vegetable dish is an excellent accompaniment to grilled fish, such as Grilled Shark Steak, page 136. The tomatoes can be completely prepared ahead of time and baked when ready to serve.

3 large, firm tomatoes
Salt to taste
Freshly ground black pepper
1 (6-oz.) jar marinated artichoke hearts
1 (10-oz.) pkg. frozen chopped spinach, thawed
4 green onions, chopped
⅔ (3-oz.) pkg. cream cheese, room temperature

1 tablespoon unsalted butter or margarine
2 tablespoons dairy sour cream
1 teaspoon dried leaf oregano or 1 tablespoon chopped fresh oregano
½ teaspoon salt
½ cup grated Parmesan cheese (1½ oz.)
2 tablespoons unsalted butter or margarine, melted
½ cup dry bread crumbs

Preheat oven to 350F (175C). Halve tomatoes crosswise. Carefully scoop out and discard pulp and seeds, taking care not to puncture shells. Sprinkle inside of each tomato with salt and pepper; set aside. Drain artichoke hearts; chop drained artichokes. Press out all moisture from spinach. In a medium bowl, combine pressed spinach, chopped artichoke hearts and green onions. In a food processor fitted with the steel blade, combine cream cheese, 1 tablespoon butter or margarine, sour cream, oregano, ½ teaspoon salt and Parmesan cheese. Process until pureed. Fold cream-cheese mixture into vegetables until blended. In a small bowl, combine 2 tablespoons butter or margarine and bread crumbs with a fork. Stuff tomato halves with spinach filling; top with buttered bread crumbs. Place in 13″ × 9″ baking dish; bake in preheated oven until heated through, 10 minutes. Do not overcook. Serve hot. Makes 6 servings.

Spinach Rice

Trust this easy-to-fix dish to add the perfect touch to any meal.

1 (10 oz.) pkg. frozen
  chopped spinach
½ cup unsalted butter or
  margarine
1 small onion, chopped
4 green onions, chopped
2 tablespoons minced
  parsley, preferably
  flat-leaf
1 teaspoon freshly ground
  black pepper

¼ teaspoon red (cayenne)
  pepper
½ teaspoon ground
  ginger
Salt to taste
3 cups cooked white rice
¼ cup dry sherry

Thaw frozen spinach thoroughly; press out all moisture. In a deep 12-inch skillet over medium heat, melt butter or margarine. Add onion; cook until slightly wilted and transparent, about 5 minutes. Add drained spinach, green onions, parsley, black pepper, cayenne, ginger and salt. Cook, stirring, 5 minutes. Add rice; stir until combined. Add sherry; cook until heated through and bubbly, about 5 minutes. Spoon into a serving dish. Makes 4 to 6 servings.

Cajun "Dirty" Rice

Cajuns and Dirty Rice are like pancakes and syrup—they just belong together. There is rarely an occasion involving food where Dirty Rice is not served. The dish meets the basic requirements for Cajun family fare: It is filling, it is cooked in one big pot, it will feed a lot of people for a little money and, most important, it is delicious. The authentic cooking method given here is time-consuming but well worth the effort. Even if you despise chicken livers and gizzards, you will love Dirty Rice. Neither livers nor gizzards are detectable as such. They become a part of the overall taste. Serve Dirty Rice as a side dish or as the main dish.

1 lb. chicken or turkey gizzards

½ lb. chicken, duck or turkey livers, or a combination

1 cup sausage or bacon drippings

2 medium onions, finely chopped

1 large green bell pepper, finely chopped

2 celery stalks, finely chopped

4 large garlic cloves, minced

3 cups Louisiana Brown Poultry Stock, page 19, or canned chicken broth

1 teaspoon freshly ground black pepper

¾ teaspoon red (cayenne) pepper or to taste

Salt to taste

¼ cup minced parsley, preferably flat-leaf

6 green onions, chopped

4 cups cooked white rice

Using a small, sharp knife, remove tough outer skin from gizzards by scraping meat from skin. Keep blade of knife at an angle against skin as you scrape. Place gizzards and livers in a food processor fitted with the steel blade; process until pureed. Heat drippings in a heavy 5- to 6-quart Dutch oven over medium heat; add gizzard-liver mixture. Cook, stirring, until mixture is browned, about 10 minutes. Add additional drippings, if necessary, to prevent sticking. Add onions, bell pepper, celery and garlic; cook until vegetables are slightly wilted and transparent, about 5 minutes. Add stock or broth, black pepper, cayenne and salt, scraping bottom of pan to release any browned bits of meat. Reduce heat to low; cook, stirring often, until thickened, about 45 minutes. Fold in parsley, green onions and rice, blending well. Cook just to heat through. Serve hot. Makes 6 to 8 servings.

Embellished Pecan Rice

There are several varieties of aromatic rice grown in Louisiana. Pecan rice is one of the tastiest. It is becoming widely available in specialty food stores throughout the country. Or see page 291 for mail-order information. Serve with game, poultry or curry dishes.

4⅔ cups water
3 tablespoons unsalted
    butter or margarine
1 teaspoon salt
2⅓ cups pecan rice
¼ cup unsalted butter or
    margarine
⅔ cup chopped pecans
1 small onion, finely
    chopped
1 large carrot, finely
    chopped

2 celery stalks, finely
    chopped
2 tablespoons minced
    parsley, preferably
    flat-leaf
1 teaspoon sugar
½ teaspoon salt
½ teaspoon
    Worcestershire sauce
½ teaspoon freshly
    ground pepper

In a heavy 3-quart saucepan with a tight-fitting lid, combine water, 3 tablespoons butter or margarine and 1 teaspoon salt. Bring to a boil over medium-high heat; stir in rice. Reduce heat to lowest setting. Cover and cook until rice is tender and all water is absorbed, 15 minutes. Meanwhile, melt ¼ cup butter or margarine in a 10-inch skillet over medium heat. Add remaining ingredients. Cook, stirring often, until onions are wilted and transparent and pecans are lightly browned, 7 to 8 minutes. Stir pecan-vegetable mixture into cooked rice until combined; serve hot. Makes 4 to 6 servings.

Range-Top White Rice

Rice is not only a mainstay of the diet in South Louisiana. Rice production accounts for a large chunk of the state's economy.

2 cups liquid, such as
    water or stock
1 cup long-grain white
    rice

1 tablespoon unsalted
    butter or margarine
1 teaspoon salt

In a 3-quart saucepan, bring liquid to a boil; add rice. Stir until combined. Stir in butter or margarine and salt. Reduce heat. Cover and simmer 15 minutes, stirring often. If rice is not quite tender or if liquid is not fully absorbed; cook 2 to 4 minutes longer. Makes about 3 cups.

Variation

Oven-Cooked Rice: Use boiling liquid. Place all ingredients in a baking dish. Stir; cover tightly. Bake in 350F (175C) preheated oven 25 to 30 minutes.

To refrigerate cooked rice, cover tightly to prevent drying out or absorbing other food odors. To reheat, add about 3 tablespoons water per cup of rice; heat in a 350F (175C) oven 10 to 15 minutes. To reheat rice in a microwave oven, add no water. Microwave on the highest setting 1½ minutes per cup of rice.

Desserts

Come Over for Dessert & Coffee

*Peach Pie topped with
Frozen Creole Cream Cheese
New Orleans Butter Pralines
Cafe Noir, page 284
Sugar-Fried Pecans*

The subject of desserts in South Louisiana needs no long-winded introduction. The Cajuns and Creoles like desserts. Fine restaurants throughout the area have extensive dessert menus offering a vast array of sinfully delicious, cream-and-butter-laden goodies. New Orleans' fine hotels and restaurants have been training grounds for some of the country's finest desserts and pastry chefs.

Fresh fruit is a favorite dessert ingredient, with the emphasis on Louisiana-grown varieties. Plaquemines Parish oranges, Ruston peaches and Ponchatoula strawberries are sliced, diced, mashed, pureed, sectioned and cooked into hundreds of irresistibly mouth-watering dessert dishes. Chocolate is another popular ingredient.

Many desserts which are considered passé in other areas of the country have never lost popularity in South Louisiana. This is a fact for which I give thanks each time I indulge in one of the dozens of rich and gooey crepe dishes popular in the area. Humble bread pudding is far and away the number-one dessert, and there are as

178

many recipes for it in South Louisiana as there are stoves. Each version has its own delightful personality.

One of the best desserts ever born of South Louisiana's cuisine is found only in Creole homes—which is unfortunate, because visitors rarely get to taste it. It is Frozen Creole Cream Cheese. It is one of the few dishes that will cut through the ravages of the unbearably hot and humid weather of South Louisiana to really cool your bones! It is like ice cream, but much richer. It is like frozen yogurt, but much better.

Of course, to make frozen Creole Cream Cheese, you must first have Creole cream cheese! The bad news is that it is usually not available outside of the New Orleans area. Produced by several of New Orleans' oldest creameries, Creole cream cheese is similar in taste and consistency to a combination of sour cream and cream cheese. It is often served for breakfast—right out of the container or topped with fresh fruit.

For years I have talked about Frozen Creole Cream Cheese all over the country—and I've fed it to anybody who came to visit, always with the underlying frustration of knowing they couldn't have it again. I finally took matters into my own hands and made a frontal assault on the creameries of New Orleans, "How is Creole Cream Cheese made?" I cried. Most, believe it or not, were very cooperative. After much testing—scaling things down from 500 gallons to 3 cups and substituting readily available ingredients—I determined that it is possible for anyone to make Creole Cream Cheese, and therefore, Frozen Creole Cream Cheese. The recipes repose quietly in the pages of this chapter—sleeping giants of taste.

Although the Cajun-Creole cuisine does indeed boast some very elegant and complicated dessert preparations, it is also loaded with rich-and-enticing down-home desserts, the likes of which can make a grown man cry. To ferret out the secrets of these desserts, I turned once again to the ultimate sources of great regional food—the covered-dish suppers, church socials, country fairs and treasured meals in private homes of every social strata. Researching this chapter I added 15 pounds, but I enjoyed every butter-dripping ounce of it!

Crepe Soufflé with Custard Sauce

Here is a delightfully light dessert that is the perfect ending to an elegant meal.

Custard Sauce, from Bittersweet-Chocolate Cake, page 196	**Filling, see below** **8 Sweet Crepes, page 199**

Filling:

6 egg whites, room temperature **3 cups powdered sugar, sifted**	**Grated zest of 1 large orange**

Prepare Custard Sauce as directed on page 197. Prepare Filling. Preheat oven to 400F (205C). Place crepes on a large ungreased baking sheet. Spread filling mixture over ½ of each crepe, then fold remaining half over to cover filling. Bake in preheated oven until filling has risen and browned lightly, about 10 minutes. Immediately place 2 crepes on each serving plate; cover with Custard Sauce. Serve immediately. Makes 4 servings.

To prepare Filling, in a medium bowl, beat egg whites with an electric mixer until very soft peaks form. Beat in sugar until smooth and glossy and stiff peaks form. Beat in orange zest.

Cajun-Country Bread Pudding with Rum Sauce & Soft Cream

No book written on the foods of South Louisiana would be complete (or authentic) if it did not contain a recipe for bread pudding. Many people believe Cajun and Creole children are made out of bread pudding! This version is light and airy rather than heavy and dense. It has an exciting combination of tastes and textures to please your mouth. It is sinfully rich and guaranteed to please the most ardent dessert fan.

7 tablespoons unsalted
    butter or margarine,
    melted
¼ cup unsalted butter or
    margarine, melted
16 cups lightly packed,
    very dry French-bread
    cubes (1 lb.)
3 eggs
1½ cups sugar
2 tablespoons vanilla
    extract

1 teaspoon freshly grated
    nutmeg
1½ teaspoons ground
    cinnamon
3 cups milk
¾ cup golden raisins
¾ cup flaked coconut
½ cup coarsely chopped
    toasted pecans
Rum Sauce, see below
Soft Cream, see below

Rum Sauce:
1 cup unsalted butter or
    margarine, room
    temperature
1½ cups sugar

2 large eggs, beaten until
    frothy
½ cup dark rum

Soft Cream:
1 pint whipping cream
    (2 cups)
⅓ cup powdered sugar,
    sifted
1 tablespoon vanilla
    extract

2 tablespoons cognac or
    other brandy
2 tablespoons Frangelico
    liqueur
¼ cup dairy sour cream

Pour 7 tablespoons butter or margarine into a 13″ × 9″
baking pan; swirl it around to coat bottom and sides.
Pour excess butter or margarine and additional ¼ butter
or margarine into a small bowl; set aside. Place bread
cubes in buttered baking dish; set aside. In a large bowl,
beat eggs and sugar with an electric mixer until thickened and light lemon-colored, 3 to 4 minutes. Add vanilla, nutmeg, cinnamon, milk, raisins, coconut, pecans
and reserved butter or margarine; beat on low speed to
combine. Pour liquid over bread in baking dish; stir to
distribute nuts, coconut and raisins evenly. Set pan aside
until bread has absorbed all of liquid, 30 to 45 minutes.
Press bread down into liquid often to cover all cubes
with liquid. Preheat oven to 350F (175C). Bake in preheated oven until crusty and golden brown on top, 45 to

60 minutes. While pudding is baking, prepare Rum Sauce and Soft Cream. Cool bread pudding to lukewarm. When bread pudding has cooled, slice into squares. Place a spoonful of rum sauce in bottom of each serving bowl; add a square of bread pudding. Top with a generous dollop of cream. Makes 15 to 18 servings.

To prepare Rum Sauce, using an electric mixer, cream butter and sugar mixture until light and fluffy. Put mixture in top of a double boiler over simmering water; cook 20 minutes, whisking often. The mixture should be silky smooth and light in color. Whisk 2 tablespoons hot butter mixture into beaten eggs, then 2 tablespoons more. Whisk warmed egg mixture slowly into remaining butter mixture. Cook mixture over barely simmering water until thickened, 4 to 5 minutes, whisking constantly. Cool slightly; whisk in rum. Sauce may be kept warm over hot water until served.

To prepare Soft Cream, chill beaters and a medium bowl until very cold. Place all ingredients in bowl; beat with an electric mixer on medium-high speed until soft, loose peaks form, 3 to 4 minutes. The cream should have a slightly runny, cloud-like consistency that softly drapes over the bread pudding. Do not overbeat. Cover tightly and refrigerate until served.

Fresh Peach Pie

You have to go far and wide to find a dessert better than peach pie made from ripe and juicy peaches just a few hours off the tree. If you do find such a dessert, I'll wager it's much more difficult to prepare than this one!

Double recipe Flaky Pie
    Pastry, below
½ pint whipping cream
    (1 cup)
¼ cup all-purpose flour
1 cup sugar
½ teaspoon ground
    cinnamon

½ teaspoon freshly grated
    nutmeg
6 large peaches, peeled,
    sliced, tossed with
    lemon juice
Vanilla ice cream or
    Frozen Creole Cream
    Cheese, page 190, if
    desired

Preheat oven to 350F (175C). Prepare pastry as directed
below; divide into 2 equal pieces. Wrap 1 pastry piece in
plastic wrap; refrigerate until ready to use. On a lightly
floured surface, roll out remaining pastry to a ¹⁄₁₆-inch-
thick circle. Roll pastry loosely around rolling pin; unroll
into a 9-inch pie pan. Gently lower pastry into bottom of
pan; lightly press against side. Do not stretch pastry. Cut
away excess pastry, leaving a ½-inch overhang at edge;
set aside. In a medium bowl, whisk cream, flour, sugar,
cinnamon and nutmeg until smooth. Pour ½ of cream
mixture into prepared pie shell. Add sliced peaches,
spreading evenly; pour remaining cream mixture over
top. On a lightly floured surface, roll out remaining
pastry as directed above. Place pastry over filling. Cut
off excess pastry, leaving about a 1-inch overhang at
edge. Tuck edge of top pastry securely under edge of
bottom pastry. Flute edges, if desired, or press pastry
against edge of pan using tines of a fork. Cut 2 rows of
steam vents in top of pastry. Bake in preheated oven
until golden brown, 35 to 40 minutes. Cool slightly. Serve
hot. For a sinfully rich addition, top each slice with a
scoop of vanilla ice cream or Frozen Creole Cream
Cheese. Makes 8 servings.

Flaky Pie Pastry

To make flaky pie pastry in a food processor, the butter
or margarine must be frozen.

| 1 cup all-purpose flour | Pinch of salt |
| ½ cup frozen unsalted butter or margarine, cut into 1-inch chunks | 3 to 4 tablespoons iced water |

Place flour, butter or margarine and salt in a food processor fitted with the steel blade. Turning on and off, process just until butter or margarine is in pea-sized chunks. With machine running, slowly add enough water through feed tube to form a soft, moist dough. Do not process until mixture forms a ball. Turn mixture out onto a lightly floured surface; using your hands and a pastry scraper, bring mixture together to form a ball. Do not overwork. Wrap in plastic wrap; refrigerate 30 minutes. Use as directed in recipe. Or roll out chilled dough and bake as directed below. On a lightly floured surface, roll out chilled dough in 1 direction only to ¹⁄₁₆-inch thick circle. Loosely roll pastry around rolling pin; unroll into an 8- or 9-inch pie pan, letting pastry fall into place. Gently ease pastry into bottom of pan; pat against side. Do not stretch. If stretched, pastry will shrink when baked. Preheat oven to 400F (205C). If baking pastry blind or without filling, prick pastry with a fork. Line with foil; fill with rice, dried beans or metal pie weights. Bake in preheated oven 15 minutes. Carefully remove foil and weights; bake until golden brown on bottom. Makes 1 (8- or 9-inch) pie crust.

Variation

For a sweet crust, add 2 teaspoons sugar along with flour, butter and salt.

Sweet Potato-Pecan Pie

The best of two South Louisiana favorites, sweet potatoes and pecans, are baked up into one delicious pie in this easy to prepare recipe.

1 recipe Flaky Pie Pastry,
   opposite

Filling:

2 tablespoons unsalted
   butter or margarine,
   melted
1 cup cooked, mashed
   sweet potatoes (1 large
   sweet potato)
2 eggs, slightly beaten
¾ cup firmly packed
   light-brown sugar
½ teaspoon ground
   ginger

Filling, see below
Topping, see below

½ teaspoon ground
   cinnamon
½ teaspoon freshly grated
   nutmeg
1 teaspoon vanilla extract
½ teaspoon salt
½ cup dark corn syrup
1 cup evaporated milk
1½ cups coarsely chopped
   pecans

Topping:

1 pint whipping cream
   (2 cups)
3 tablespoons powdered
   sugar

¼ cup Praline Liqueur or
   Frangelico
Pecan halves

To prepare Pastry, prepare pastry and chill as directed opposite. Preheat oven to 375F (190C). On a lightly floured surface, roll out chilled pastry into a ¹⁄₁₆-inch-thick circle. Gently roll pastry around rolling pin; unroll into a 9-inch pie pan. Gently ease pastry into bottom of pan; pat against side. Do not stretch pastry. Trim off and discard excess pastry. Flute edges, if desired. Refrigerate until ready to bake..

To prepare Filling, in a large bowl, stir butter or margarine into sweet potatoes. Add all remaining ingredients except pecans; blend well.

To assemble pie, pour sweet-potato filling into prepared pie crust; sprinkle chopped pecans evenly over top. Bake in preheated oven until filling is set and a knife inserted into center comes out clean, 40 to 45 minutes. Cool in pan on a rack to room temperature before slicing. Prepare topping. To serve, top with topping. Top with pecan halves. Makes 8 servings.

To prepare Topping, combine cream, powdered sugar and liqueur in a large bowl. Beat with an electric mixer until large, soft peaks form. Refrigerate, covered, until ready to serve.

New Orleans Butter Pralines

New Orleans pralines—and that's pronounced PRAH-leens, to set the record straight—are unique among pralines. They contain butter and milk to give them a softer, almost chewy texture. The taste is addictive.

2 cups granulated sugar
1 cup firmly packed light-
   brown sugar
½ cup unsalted butter or
   margarine

1 cup milk
2 tablespoons light corn
   syrup
3 cups pecan halves
2 teaspoons vanilla
   extract

Place 2 large parchment-paper sheets on baking sheets; butter parchment paper. Set aside. Combine all ingredients except vanilla in a heavy 2-quart saucepan over medium heat. Bring mixture to a boil, stirring often. Cook to soft-ball stage, 234F (114C). Remove from heat; stir in vanilla. Stir briskly until mixture loses its glossy sheen. **WORKING QUICKLY,** drop mixture by table-spoons onto buttered paper. Let pralines cool completely before removing from paper. Store at room temperature in an airtight container. Makes 24 pralines.

Louisiana Lemon-Cornmeal Pie

This classic country pie is a snap to prepare and is easy on the budget—two main considerations of its Cajun creators. It also tastes wonderful.

1 recipe Flaky Pie Pastry, pages 183–4	¼ cup unsalted butter or margarine, melted
2 cups sugar	1 cup milk
1 tablespoon all-purpose flour	¼ cup fresh lemon juice
¼ cup cornmeal	¼ cup grated lemon zest
4 eggs, slightly beaten	

Preheat oven to 350F (175C). Prepare pastry and chill according to directions on page 184. On a lightly floured surface, roll out pastry into a ½₃₂-inch-thick circle. Gently roll crust around rolling pin; unroll into a 9-inch pie pan. Gently ease pastry into bottom of pan; pat against side. Do not stretch pastry. Trim excess pastry off edges and discard. Flute edges, if desired. Refrigerate until ready to bake. In a medium bowl, combine sugar, flour and cornmeal with a fork. Add remaining ingredients; stir until blended. Pour filling into prepared pie crust. Bake in preheated oven until a knife inserted in center comes out clean, 45 minutes. Cool on a rack to luke-warm before slicing. Makes 8 servings.

Satsuma Cake

Satsumas are small, thin-skinned mandarin oranges grown in South Louisiana. They are wonderfully sweet and used in a wide variety of dishes. You may substitute other oranges in the recipe.

2½ cups cake flour, sifted
4½ teaspoons baking
  powder
1½ cups sugar
1 teaspoon salt
½ cup unsalted butter or
  margarine, room
  temperature
1 tablespoon grated
  Satsuma zest or other
  orange zest

1 teaspoon orange extract
1 tablespoon vanilla
  extract
¾ cup Satsuma or other
  orange juice
¼ cup milk
4 egg whites, room
  temperature
Satsuma Filling, see
  below
Satsuma Butter Cream,
  see below
Satsuma or other orange
  sections

Satsuma Filling:
¼ cup unsalted butter or
  margarine, room
  temperature
1¼ cups sugar
½ cup cornstarch
2 (12-oz.) cans frozen
  orange-juice
  concentrate, thawed

1 tablespoon grated
  lemon zest
2 tablespoons grated
  Satsuma or other
  orange zest
1 pint whipping cream
  (2 cups)
4 egg yolks, beaten until
  frothy

Satsuma Butter Cream:
⅓ cup all-purpose flour
1 cup milk
½ cup Satsuma or other
  orange juice

1½ cups sugar
2 teaspoons vanilla
  extract
1½ cups unsalted butter
  or margarine

Preheat oven to 350F (175C). Butter and flour 2 (9-inch)
springform pans, shake out all excess flour. Cut 2 (9-
inch) parchment-paper circles; place circles in pans.
Butter and flour circles in pans, again shake out excess
flour. Set pans aside. Sift all dry ingredients into a medium bowl. Add all ingredients through milk. Beat on
low speed 1 minute to blend. Increase speed to medium;
beat 2 minutes, scraping down side of bowl as necessary.
Add milk and egg whites. Beat 2 minutes on medium-
high. Pour equal amounts of batter into each prepared

pan. Bake in preheated oven until center of cake springs back when pressed lightly with fingertips, 20 minutes. Cool in pans on racks 10 minutes. Remove from pans; invert cakes on wire racks. Remove parchment. Cool layers completely. Prepare filling. Prepare butter cream. When layers have cooled completely, cut in half cross-wise using a serrated knife. Set 3 layers aside; place last layer on a serving plate; spread with a layer of filling. Carefully place a second cake layer on top. Spread with filling. On top of filling, spread a layer of Satsuma sections. Place a third cake layer over sections. Top with another layer of filling, and finally, place remaining cake layer on top. Frost cake with butter cream; decorate, if desired, with Satsuma sections. Makes 1 (9-inch) layer cake.

To prepare Satsuma Filling, using an electric mixer, in a medium bowl, cream butter or margarine and sugar until light and fluffy. Place mixture in top of a double boiler set over simmering water; melt mixture, whisking often. Meanwhile, in a medium bowl, stir cornstarch and orange-juice concentrate until cornstarch is completely dissolved. Add all remaining ingredients except egg yolks to orange-juice mixture. Add orange-juice mixture to melted butter mixture; whisk over simmering water until thickened. Cover and cook 5 minutes without stirring. Remove orange-filling mixture from heat. Add ½ cup hot filling mixture in a slow, steady stream to egg yolks, rapidly whisking yolks while pouring. Whisk warmed egg-yolk mixture slowly into remaining filling mixture; whisk 2 to 3 minutes. Cool slightly. Cover and refrigerate until chilled.

To prepare Satsuma Butter Cream, in a medium sauce-pan, combine flour and milk; whisk to dissolve flour lumps. Cook over medium heat until thick. Whisk in juice. Cool to room temperature. In a medium bowl, cream sugar, butter or margarine and vanilla with an electric mixer until light and fluffy. Add sugar mixture to

flour mixture; beat with electric mixer until light. Cover
and refrigerate until slightly chilled.

Homemade Creole Cream Cheese

Creole cream cheese is an old New Orleans treat which
is, unfortunately, not usually available outside of South
Louisiana. It is eaten for breakfast or dessert topped
with fresh fruit. Or it is enjoyed as Frozen Creole Cream
Cheese, below, a favorite New Orleans dessert. Making
cheese at home is a lengthy procedure, but it is worth the
effort. Rennet tablets are available in the baking-supply
section in supermarkets.

½ gallon skim milk	½ cup buttermilk
1 rennet tablet	1 cup nonfat dry milk

In a large saucepan, heat skim milk to 170F (75C); hold
at that temperature 20 minutes. This is most easily ac-
complished in a microwave oven with a temperature
probe and HOLD feature. Use a nonmetallic bowl for
the microwave. Immediately stir in rennet tablet, buttermilk and nonfat dry milk until blended. Cover with plastic wrap; let stand at room temperature 24 hours to
clabber. After 24 hours, carefully drain and discard liquid from cheese. Line a large, fine strainer with a double
thickness of cheesecloth; place over a deep bowl. Carefully turn clabber into strainer. Cover with plastic wrap
and refrigerate. Let drain 36 hours. Place finished cheese
in a bowl; use as desired. Creole cream cheese can be
covered and refrigerated up to 2 weeks. Makes 24
ounces.

Frozen Creole Cream Cheese

This dessert, enjoyed in Creole homes as a respite from
the beastly hot and humid weather, is one of New Orleans best kept secrets. Enjoy it right out of the ice-

cream freezer at backyard cookouts, or serve with sauces for a more elaborate presentation. Recipe can be halved.

3 recipes (72 oz.) Creole Cream Cheese, above	**3 cups sugar**
1 qt. milk	**3 teaspoons vanilla extract**
1 qt. whipping cream (4 cups)	

Using back of a wooden spoon, mash Creole Cream Cheese through a medium strainer into a large bowl. Add milk, cream and sugar; stir until blended. Stir in vanilla. Pour mixture into an ice-cream freezer; freeze according to manufacturer's directions. Keep frozen until ready to serve. Serve with Easy Strawberry Sauce, page 195, or Chocolate-Sherry Sauce, page 193, if desired. Makes 1 gallon or 12 to 15 servings.

Rennet is an enzyme used in cheese making.

Bananas Foster

Bananas Foster, next to bread pudding, is probably the most well-known of all South Louisiana dishes. Through the years, it has been flamed in some of the finest restaurants. It remains a strong favorite today.

⅓ cup firmly packed light-brown sugar	**½ cup dark rum**
1 teaspoon ground cinnamon	**4 bananas, halved lengthwise**
¼ cup unsalted butter or margarine	**4 scoops rich vanilla ice cream**
½ cup creme de banana or other banana liqueur	**Mint sprigs, if desired**

In a small bowl, combine brown sugar and cinnamon with a fork; set aside. In a heavy 12-inch skillet or flambé pan, melt butter or margarine over medium heat. Add cinnamon-sugar mixture; stir until sugar melts. Pour in banana liqueur and ¼ cup rum; cook, stirring, until syrupy and thickened, about 5 minutes. Add bananas; lightly coat with syrup. Add remaining ¼ cup rum. Swirl pan; ignite rum. Quickly swirl pan. Cook, basting bananas with sauce, until flame goes out. Remove from heat; place 2 banana slices on each of 4 plates, side by side. Place a scoop of ice cream on top of each serving; drizzle with sauce. Decorate with mint, if desired. Serve immediately. Makes 4 servings.

Creamy Chocolate & Bourbon Pie

Variations of this rich pie are served throughout the Deep South. It's right at home in South Louisiana, where folks do like their bourbon. The next time you bring dessert, bring this one. It'll be a hit!

Chocolate Crust, see below	**Topping, see below**
Filling, see below	**2 oz. semisweet chocolate, grated**

Chocolate Crust:

1¼ cups chocolate-wafer crumbs	3 tablespoons unsalted butter or margarine, melted
1 tablespoon sugar	

Filling:

21 large marshmallows	3 tablespoons bourbon
1 cup evaporated milk	½ cup chopped pecans
½ pint whipping cream (1 cup)	

Topping:

½ pint whipping cream (1 cup)	2 tablespoons powdered sugar
	1 teaspoon vanilla extract

To prepare Crust, preheat oven to 350F (175C). In a medium bowl, toss all ingredients with a fork until crumbs are moist. Spoon mixture into a 9-inch pie pan; pat into bottom and side. Bake crust in preheated oven 10 minutes. Cool slightly. Cover and refrigerate until chilled.

To prepare Filling, combine marshmallows and evaporated milk in a heavy 3-quart saucepan over medium heat. Cook until marshmallows melt, about 10 minutes, stirring often. Do not boil. Cool slightly; cover and refrigerate 1 hour. In a medium bowl, with an electric mixer, beat whipping cream and bourbon until medium-stiff peaks form. Fold pecans into chilled marshmallow mixture. Fold in whipped cream until blended.

To assemble pie, pour filling into chilled crust; smooth top. Cover and refrigerate until set, about 4 hours. To serve, prepare topping. Spread on chilled pie; top with chocolate. Makes 8 servings.

To prepare Topping, in a medium bowl, beat cream, sugar and vanilla until stiff peaks form.

Chocolate-Sherry Sauce

This sauce, in various versions, was the staple dessert sauce for cakes or pudding in the old South. Today it is equally good over pound cake and positively decadent on Frozen Creole Cream Cheese, page 190.

½ lb. unsweetened
    chocolate
½ pint whipping cream
    (1 cup)
6 tablespoons unsalted
    butter or margarine,
    room temperature

1 (1-lb.) box powdered
    sugar, sifted
½ cup cream sherry

In a heavy 2-quart saucepan over medium heat, combine chocolate and cream. Cook, stirring often, until chocolate melts and mixture is smooth and creamy. Set aside. In a medium bowl, with an electric mixer on medium speed, cream butter or margarine and sugar until light and fluffy, about 5 minutes. Spoon sugar mixture into the top of a double boiler set over simmering water; cook, whisking often, until silken and smooth, 20 minutes. Whisk in chocolate mixture; cook, whisking constantly, 5 minutes. Remove from heat; whisk in sherry. Serve warm. Makes 2 cups.

Ponchatoula Strawberry Shortcake

Ponchatoula strawberries are the best in the land. Grown in a small area around Ponchatoula, Louisiana, they are huge, sweet berries that need no adornment at all. I love to eat them right from the strawberry patch.

Shortcake Base, see
   below
3 pints strawberries
¾ cup granulated sugar
1 pint whipping cream
   (2 cups)

2½ tablespoons powdered
   sugar
2 teaspoons vanilla
   extract
2 tablespoons kirsch, if
   desired

Shortcake Base:
3 cups cake flour, sifted
1¼ cups all-purpose flour
1 tablespoon plus 1½
   teaspoons baking
   powder
2 tablespoons plus
   1 teaspoon sugar

1½ teaspoons salt
½ cup plus 1 tablespoon
   unsalted butter or
   margarine, cut into
   1-inch chunks
1¼ to 1½ cups whipping
   cream

Prepare Shortcake Base. Place ½ of berries in a medium bowl; add sugar. Using a potato masher, mash berries with sugar to form a chunky puree. Cut remaining ½ of berries into pieces, reserving 5 whole berries for decoration. Stir pieces into puree; set aside. Using an electric mixer, beat cream, powdered sugar, vanilla and kirsch, if desired, until medium-stiff peaks form. To serve, split shortcakes in half horizontally; place 1 bottom in each dessert dish. Spoon berries over bottoms; top with cream mixture. Set top of shortcake over cream. Slice reserved 5 berries in half; place a half berry, cut-side-down on each shortcake. Makes 10 servings.

To prepare Shortcake Base, preheat oven to 425F (220C). Lightly grease 2 heavy baking sheets. Sift flours, baking powder, sugar and salt into a 5-quart bowl; resift. With a pastry blender or 2 knives, cut butter or margarine into flour until mixture resembles coarse oatmeal in texture. Add 1¼ cups cream; blend with a fork just until all flour is moist. If mixture is too dry to roll out, add remaining cream until dough forms a ball and is slightly sticky. Turn out dough onto a lightly floured surface. Form dough into a ball; knead gently 2 or 3 times. Roll out into a ½-inch-thick circle. Using a 3-inch round cutter, cut dough into 10 circles. Place circles on greased baking sheets. Bake in preheated oven until golden brown and flaky, 12 to 15 minutes. Cool on racks.

Easy Strawberry Sauce

Nothing quite sums up the taste of summer like fresh strawberries. They really shine in this sweet and refreshing sauce.

3½ cups strawberries,   ¼ cup kirsch, if desired
   fresh or frozen
⅔ cup sugar

Place all ingredients in a food processor fitted with the steel blade. Process until pureed. Pour into a serving bowl. If sugar has not dissolved, let stand a few minutes; stir occasionally. Makes 2 cups.

Bittersweet Chocolate Cake

Chocoholics gather 'round—this is the cake you have been waiting for. Ultimately rich and fudge-like, it is guaranteed to satisfy even the strongest chocolate cravings. It is very attractive nestled in a pool of custard sauce and topped with a strawberry half.

1 lb. bittersweet chocolate, chopped	1½ tablespoons Grand Marnier or other orange-flavored liqueur
2 cups unsalted butter	
1¾ cups sugar	1 teaspoon vanilla extract
11 eggs, separated, room temperature	Custard Sauce, see below
	8 large strawberries, with tops, if desired

Custard Sauce:

1 cup milk	6 egg yolks, slightly beaten
½ pint whipping cream (1 cup)	
¾ cup sugar	2 tablespoons Grand Marnier or other orange-flavored liqueur

Butter and flour a 12-inch springform pan; shake out all traces of excess flour. Place rack in middle of oven. Preheat oven to 250F (120C). In a very heavy 3-quart saucepan over medium-low heat, combine chocolate and butter. Stir until melted. Cool to room temperature, stirring occasionally. In a large bowl, combine 1½ cups sugar and egg yolks. Beat with an electric mixer on medium speed until mixture is light, fluffy and lemon-colored, 8 to 10 minutes. Fold in cooled chocolate until blended. Set mixture aside. In a medium bowl, beat egg whites until soft peaks form. Beat in remaining ¼ cup sugar, liqueur and vanilla. Beat until medium-stiff peaks form, about 3 minutes on medium speed. Using a rubber spatula, fold in ¼ of beaten whites into chocolate mixture to lighten it. Fold in remaining beaten egg whites. Pour batter into prepared pan. Bake in middle of preheated oven until a wooden pick inserted into center comes out clean, 3 hours. Cool in pan on a wire rack 15 minutes. Remove side of pan; cool completely. When cool, remove bottom of springform pan; invert cake onto a serving plate. Refrigerate until chilled. Prepare sauce. To serve, slice strawberries in half. Cut cake into 16 equal pieces; place a strawberry half, cut-side down, on each slice. Pour some sauce onto each serving plate; arrange a slice of cake in middle of sauce. Serve at once. Makes 16 servings.

To prepare Custard Sauce, in a heavy 3-quart saucepan over medium-high heat, bring milk, cream and sugar to a full boil. Whisking constantly, add ¼ cup hot cream mixture in a slow, steady stream to egg yolks. Reduce heat to medium. Whisk warmed egg-yolk mixture slowly into remaining cream mixture. Whisking constantly, cook until mixture thickens and coats back of a metal spoon, about 3 minutes. This will happen rapidly; do not overcook and scramble eggs. Remove sauce from heat; whisk 3 minutes to cool slightly. Whisk in liqueur; strain sauce through a fine strainer into a 2-quart bowl. Place plastic wrap over custard; refrigerate until chilled. Custard Sauce will keep in the refrigerator 5 days or in the freezer 3 months. If frozen, thaw completely in refrigerator; whisk to smooth texture before serving.

Chocolate melts more easily if it is grated or chopped before melting. High temperature will cause chocolate to be dry and grainy.

Praline Crepes

If you keep a supply of crepes in the freezer, putting this dessert together is a breeze. It is so good that your guests will think you cooked all day.

Praline Sauce, see below
4 Sweet Crepes, opposite

4 scoops Frozen Creole
   Cream Cheese, page
   190, or rich vanilla ice
   cream

Praline Sauce:
¼ cup unsalted butter or
   margarine
½ cup powdered sugar

2 tablespoons dark corn
   syrup
¼ cup dark rum
½ cup chopped pecans

Prepare Praline Sauce. Working quickly, fill each crepe with a scoop of Frozen Creole Cream Cheese or ice cream. Place 1 filled crepe, seam-side down, on each serving plate. Drizzle sauce over crepes; serve at once. Makes 4 servings.

To prepare Praline Sauce, melt butter or margarine in a heavy 2-quart saucepan over medium heat. Add remaining ingredients; stir until blended. Cook, stirring often, until sauce is thick and syrupy, about 7 minutes. Set aside.

Sweet Crepes

Crepes freeze well. Place a layer of waxed paper between each cooled crepe, stack, and place in zip-sealing plastic freezer bags. The frozen crepes may be peeled off as needed! Thaw completely before using.

1 cup all-purpose flour
2 tablespoons sugar
¼ teaspoon salt
1 egg
1 egg yolk
1 cup milk

1 tablespoon unsalted
   butter or margarine,
   melted
½ cup water
1 teaspoon vanilla extract
Unsalted butter or
   margarine

In a medium bowl, combine flour, sugar and salt with a fork. Make a well in center of flour mixture; add egg and egg yolk. Using a fork, slowly begin to mix egg into flour. Continue until all flour has been moistened. Add milk slowly, stirring constantly to form a smooth batter. Stir in 1 tablespoon butter or margarine, water and vanilla until blended. The batter should be the consistency of light cream. If it is too thick, add 1 or 2 teaspoons more water; stir until blended. Cover and let batter stand at room temperature 30 minutes before using. To cook crepes, melt about 1 teaspoon butter or margarine in a 6-inch crepe pan over medium heat, swirling to coat bottom and side. Pour 3 tablespoons batter into pan all at once; swirl pan very quickly to cover bottom with batter. Cook until bottom of crepe is set and golden brown, about 2 minutes. Turn crepe; cook other side about 30 seconds. Cool crepes on paper towels. Repeat with remaining batter. Separate crepes with small sheets of wax paper, if desired. When serving crepes, fill so that first side cooked will be on outside. Makes 24 (6-inch) crepes.

Sugar-Fried Pecans

These irresistible little snacks will be the hit of your next party. They're guaranteed to be one of the most addictive party finger foods you will ever serve! Or serve them scattered over rich vanilla ice cream for a simple, yet delicious, dessert.

¼ cup sugar
2 tablespoons water
2 cups water

1 cup pecan halves
2 cups peanut oil

In a heavy 1-quart saucepan, combine sugar and 2 tablespoons water. Bring to a boil. Cover 1 minute to wash down any sugar crystals. Uncover; cook to jelly stage, 220F (105C), on a candy thermometer. While syrup is cooking, bring 2 cups water to a boil in a 2-quart saucepan. Add pecans; blanch 3 minutes. Drain in a colander; pat dry with paper towels. Immediately pour hot pecans into sugar syrup; stir until each piece is coated evenly. Remove nuts with a slotted spoon; place on a baking sheet in a single layer, not touching, to cool and dry, 30 minutes. When nuts are cool and dry, heat oil in deep skillet or wok to 240F (115C). Add pecans; fry until milk-chocolate-colored, 7 minutes, stirring gently and constantly. Remove with a slotted spoon; spread on a baking sheet in a single layer to cool. When cool, place on paper towels to remove excess oil. Store thoroughly cooled nuts in a container with a tight-sealing lid. Makes 1 cup.

Sicilian Ricotta Torte

This easy dessert is the perfect solution for those situations when you need a delicious dessert in a big hurry. No one needs to know you bought the pound cake!

1 pound cake, about
9″ × 3″
1 lb. ricotta cheese
(2 cups), drained
⅓ cup superfine sugar
2 tablespoons whipping
cream
1 teaspoon vanilla extract

1 tablespoon Grand
Marnier or other
orange-flavored
liqueur
⅔ cup finely chopped
toasted almonds
3 oz. miniature semisweet
chocolate pieces
Chocolate Glaze, see
below

Chocolate Glaze:
½ pint whipping cream
(1 cup)
8 oz. semisweet
chocolate, chopped

1 tablespoon Grand
Marnier or other
orange-flavored
liqueur

Using a serrated knife, trim end crusts from pound cake; level off top. Cut cake horizontally into ½-inch-thick slices; set slices aside, taking care not to break them. Cut a piece of cardboard the exact size of cake slices; set aside. Place cheese, sugar and whipping cream in a food processor fitted with the steel blade. Process until smooth, 1 minute. Add vanilla and liqueur; process just to blend. Place cheese mixture in a medium bowl; fold in almonds and chocolate pieces. Place a dab of cheese mixture on cardboard to fasten a cake slice to board. Spread slice with cheese mixture; add a second cake slice. Repeat until cake slices and filling have been used, ending with an unfrosted cake slice. Check that slices are perfectly aligned atop each other and that none of filling oozes out between layers. Refrigerate cake while preparing Chocolate Glaze. Prepare glaze. Place cake on a small rack over a sheet of foil. Drizzle chocolate mixture over cake, always working from top, to completely coat.

Place cake on a serving platter; refrigerate until ready to serve. Makes 10 to 12 servings.

To prepare Chocolate Glaze, in a heavy 2-quart saucepan over medium-low heat, combine cream and chocolate. Cook, stirring, until chocolate melts and mixture is smooth and uniform in color. Remove from heat; stir in liqueur.

Praline Cheesecake

This wonderfully rich and delicious cheesecake captures the very flavor of New Orleans.

Crust, see below   **Topping, see below**
Filling, see below

Crust:
1 cup graham-cracker   3 tablespoons unsalted
  crumbs   butter or margarine,
6 New Orleans Butter   melted
  Pralines, page 186, or
  New Orleans-type
  pralines

Filling:
2 (8-oz.) pkgs. cream   1 tablespoon fresh lemon
  cheese, room   juice
  temperature   1½ pints dairy sour cream
1 cup sugar   (3 cups), drained
1 tablespoon cornstarch   ½ cup Praline Liqueur or
3 eggs   Frangelico

Topping:
4 oz. semisweet   1½ cups Sugar-Fried
  chocolate, chopped   Pecans, page 200,
½ cup dairy sour cream   roughly chopped

To prepare Crust, in a food processor fitted with the steel blade, combine cracker crumbs and pralines. Process until pralines break into pieces the size of crumbs.

Empty mixture into a 2-quart bowl; stir in butter or margarine until crumbs are coated. Thoroughly grease bottom and side of an 8″ × 3″ round cake pan. Cut a 9-inch parchment paper-circle. Line bottom and part of side with circle; grease paper. Pat ¾ cup crumb mixture into bottom of pan, spreading evenly to cover. Refrigerate until ready to fill. Reserve remaining crumb mixture. Preheat oven to 350F (175C).

To prepare Filling, in a food processor fitted with the steel blade, process cream cheese and sugar until smooth, about 60 seconds. Add cornstarch; turn on and off 3 or 4 times to blend. Add eggs, 1 at a time, blending after each addition. Add remaining filling ingredients; process just until blended. Remove blade from processor.

To assemble and bake, pour batter into crust-lined pan. Set filled pan into a larger pan; pour in about 2 inches of boiling water. Bake in preheated oven until set, 1 hour. Turn oven off; leave cheesecake in closed oven 1 hour. Cool on a rack to room temperature. Cover and refrigerate 8 hours or until ready to serve.

To prepare Topping, in a heavy 1-quart saucepan over very low heat, melt chocolate, stirring. Remove from heat; fold in sour cream until blended. Fold in Sugar-Fried Pecans; set aside while unmolding cake.

To finish cake, run a thin knife around edges of pan to loosen cheesecake. Place a flat 10-inch plate over top of cake pan; invert cake onto plate. Carefully remove parchment paper and discard. The cake is now upside down. Carefully pat reserved crumb mixture into sides of cake. Place a serving plate over bottom of cake. Invert cake onto serving plate; spread topping over top using a metal spatula. Refrigerate until topping has set before serving. Makes 12 to 16 servings.

Cajun Country

Cajun food is good, hearty fare. It was created by people who work hard, play hard and love food. It has evolved over the years. The city motto of Lafayette, Louisiana, in the heart of Cajun country, is *"Laissez le bon temps rouller,"* or "Let the good times roll." Roll they do in the unique lifestyle of the Cajuns, and you can be certain that in the midst of every good time is FOOD.

What sort of food does a Cajun eat? The first time I asked that question many years ago, a larger-than-life Cajun mama told me: "Well, cher, me I tell you, we eat anything what can't get away from us." And they truly do eat every denizen of the wood and marshland, everything that swims in the water, and most creatures that fly.

To say that frogs proliferate in South Louisiana is like saying there are several people in Manhattan. There are frogs of every size and color—from the little bright green tree frogs that stick on your windows, to the granddaddy bullfrog, a huge, scary-looking creature whose nocturnal bellowings will keep you awake if you leave the windows open. It is not unheard of for South Louisiana frog legs to measure 12 inches in length. Now when you add a body, that is one fearsome frog!

Squirrel, rabbit, nutria and possum are no strangers to the Cajun family table, nor are alligators, terrapins or birds with names like coot, woodcock, jacksnipe or poule d'eau.

When cooking any type of wild game, take care to remove all traces of fat. A large measure of the "gamy" taste, which many people find objectionable, is found in the fat.

Cajun food is special, just like the people who created it. French in origin, the cuisine was broadened by Indian herbs and cooking methods, fiery Spanish spices and chilies and Black soul food. The result is spicy, down-home food with the subtle delicacy of haute cuisine lurking right under the surface.

Cajun cooking consists of many one-pot meals that, once started, can tend to themselves on the back burner for hours while mama tends to the chores of her usually large household. One-pot-meal cooking, as it evolved, fostered the practice of *cooking down*. Cooking down simply means cooking until the vegetables and perhaps pieces of seasoning meat have totally disintegrated and become part of the sauce. The sauce is served over the main meat and the rice that is always served with traditional Cajun dishes. Some of the most delicious examples of Cajun home cooking are dishes which consist solely of cooked-down vegetables served with a piece of meat. These dishes are referred to as *smothered*. Ask a Cajun for a recipe and he will no doubt tell you something like, "Well, first you make a roux, then add your seasonings, vegetables, meat and stock. Then you cook it all down and add shallots—green onions in Cajun country—and parsley at the end."

Part of the cooking-down process involves another taste-building technique called *layering of flavors* that goes something like this:

First, the roux is prepared and developed to its own depth of flavor. Then the vegetables, usually onions, garlic, celery and bell peppers, are added and sautéed in the roux. This adds a "fried" taste and a subtle sweetness if the onions are allowed to brown.

So far we have three layers of flavor—those of the roux, the fried vegetables and the onion sweetness. If tomatoes are used in the dish, they are added at this point to introduce an acid taste. Next come the herbs and spices for flavor and hotness, then the meat or seafood and a concentrated rich stock with its own dozens of tastes. Wine may be added and—I think we've lost the count! Then everything gets *cooked down* with each *layer* maintaining its own identity.

Oh, but good is never enough! After the dish has cooked down for a few hours or so, a second batch of vegetables is often added and gently poached 30 minutes or so, furnishing a second vegetable taste and a crunchy texture. Sometimes more meat or seafood is added here to further complicate the taste. The coup de grace is supplied about 10 minutes before serving with the addition of chopped green onions and minced flat-leaf parsley, both of which retain their crunch and most of their raw flavor.

To serve, the meat goes on the plate with steaming hot white rice cooked to perfection with moist, plump, nonsticky grains. The sauce goes on top. My friend, the taste is overwhelming.

There are several categories of traditional Cajun one-pot meals that are unique. Each deserves to have its story told.

Etouffée—(pronounced a-too-FAY), with the accent placed over the second "e," means a braised dish or a stew. When the Acadians first left France, their etouffée was probably quite different from the way it is prepared today. But underneath the mahogany roux and the cayenne, the dish is French. Cajun etouffées are dark-roux-based stews served over rice. The dish can be prepared from any meat, fish or shellfish. The liquid would, of course, be complementary to the meat. Tomatoes, tomato paste or tomato sauce may be included in etouffée depending upon personal opinion or what part of Cajun country you're from.

Jambalaya—(pronounced jahm-buh-LIE-ya) is generally believed to have been adapted from the classic Spanish dish, paella. However, the name was derived from the French *jambon*, or ham, an ingredient often used in the dish.

Jambalaya, like etouffée, may be prepared from any combination of meats, fish or shellfish that are on hand, using a complementary stock. The dish is not a roux-based dish. In the authentic version, the raw rice is cooked in hot fat, usually lard, along with the vegetables and meats, until golden brown. Then the stock is added and the dish is cooked until the rice is tender. Jambalaya is generally known to be a very spicy dish.

Sauce Piquant—(pronounced pee-KAWNT) is fairly unknown outside of Louisiana, but it is certainly as delicious as the more well-known Cajun dishes. Sauce piquants are often made from local game such as squirrel, alligator or turtle, but may be prepared using any meat, fish or shellfish.

Sauce piquant is roux-based and generally includes tomatoes. A great many sauce piquant aficionados include red wine in the recipe. As the name implies, the dish is definitely spicy. Sauce piquant is similar to the famous "Creole sauce" of New Orleans.

Courtbouillon—(pronounced COO-bee-yon) is presumed to have been inspired by the memory of the great French bouillabaisse. The Cajuns added their beloved roux and substituted local fish such as red snapper or redfish. Even catfish and perch make delicious courtbouillons. Like most Cajun dishes, it is highly seasoned.

If there is a fisherman in your family who can provide whole small fish such as perch, or *sac-a-lait* as they are known in Cajun country, use them whole, minus heads, in the courtbouillon for an impressive presentation. You may also use fish fillets to prepare the dish.

When dealing with the subject of Cajun country food, I always feel it prudent to discuss spiciness. Cajun food is spicy, the spiciness being an inherent part of its complex taste. Tolerance to spicy seasonings varies among individuals. I like mine plenty hot, but there are some Cajuns who make their food so hot that the only explanation for the fact that they can eat it must be that they have no feeling left!

My personal philosophy is that the food should never

be seasoned so highly that it detracts from the ability of the taste buds to distinguish the other elements of the dish. The sinus need not be draining for food to be considered authentically Cajun—unless that's the way you like it! I feel that after the first three or four bites, a warm glow should begin to radiate at the back of the throat. It should not intensify, but should remain gently teasing throughout the meal. You should know that something refreshingly exciting is going on in your mouth—something that makes you want more!

Cajun food is not fussy fare. Most of the traditional dishes are so colorful that they require no garnishing. Picture a plate of Crawfish Etouffée. On the bottom of the plate is a mound of snow-white rice, covered with the deep mahogany-roux gravy flecked with the red crawfish and bright green of the barely cooked parsley and green onions. The dish is a study in rich natural tones that reflect its honest taste.

Hungry? Well, that's what this book is all about.

Smoked-Duck Etouffée

This could be called the ultimate etouffée. The dish is worth all the effort. To make preparation easier, smoke duck the day before completing the dish.

1 recipe Cajun Roux, page 16
1 large onion, chopped
1 medium, green bell pepper, chopped
1 celery stalk, chopped
2 large garlic cloves, minced
½ recipe Mesquite-Smoked Duck, page 109
¼ teaspoon red (cayenne) pepper
½ teaspoon dried leaf thyme
¼ teaspoon dried leaf marjoram

⅛ teaspoon rubbed sage
½ teaspoon freshly ground black pepper
1¾ cups Louisiana Brown Poultry Stock, page 19, or canned chicken broth
Salt to taste
1 (14-oz.) can artichoke hearts, drained, quartered
6 green onions, chopped
¼ cup minced parsley, preferably flat-leaf
6 cups hot cooked brown rice

Make roux in a 12-inch skillet or Dutch oven as directed on page 16 using duck fat or lard, cooking until mahogany-colored. Add onion, bell pepper, celery and garlic; cook, stirring often, until vegetables are wilted and transparent, 10 minutes. Discard skin from duck; chop meat into bite-sized pieces. Add cayenne, thyme, marjoram, sage, black pepper and duck meat to pan; stir until blended. Slowly add stock or broth, stirring. Season with salt. Reduce heat; cover and simmer 45 minutes, stirring occasionally. Stir in artichoke hearts, green onions and parsley. Cook 10 minutes. To serve, place about 1 cup hot rice on each plate; spoon etouffée over top. Makes 4 to 6 servings.

Congri

This unusual dish was contributed to Cajun-Creole cuisine by the Spanish. It has a complex, somewhat mysterious taste. Serve with salad and French bread.

1 lb. dried black beans	¼ cup bacon drippings
3 tablespoons red-wine vinegar	8 bacon slices, finely chopped
4 qts. Brown Veal & Pork Stock, page 21, or canned beef broth	½ lb. tasso, page 24, finely chopped
2 medium, green bell peppers, chopped	1 large onion, chopped
2 teaspoons ground cumin	4 large garlic cloves, minced
2 teaspoons whole cumin seeds	2 cups long-grain white rice
1 teaspoon freshly ground black pepper	1 cup Brown Veal & Pork Stock, page 21, or canned beef broth
½ teaspoon red (cayenne) pepper	1½ lbs. chorizo sausage
Salt to taste	6 green onions, chopped

Sort through beans; discard any discolored ones. Soak beans overnight in water to cover. Drain beans. In a heavy 6-quart soup pot, combine drained beans, vinegar,

4 quarts stock or broth, bell peppers, cumin, cumin seeds, black pepper, cayenne and salt. Cook over medium heat until beans are very tender, about 1½ hours. Heat bacon drippings in a heavy 12-inch skillet over medium heat. Add bacon, tasso, onion and garlic; cook until onion is slightly browned, about 7 minutes. Add rice; cook 5 minutes, stirring to prevent sticking. Preheat oven to 350F (175C). Combine rice mixture, cooked beans and remaining 1 cup stock. Spoon mixture into a 13" × 9" baking dish; push sausage down into beans. Bake in preheated oven until rice is tender, 45 minutes. Sprinkle green onions over top. Serve hot. Makes 6 to 8 servings.

Ham & Sausage Jambalaya

Jambalaya is another of the wonderful Cajun dishes that can be prepared from whatever is on hand. Just follow the basic procedures and raid your refrigerator or freezer for ingredients to prepare a filling and economical supper. Serve with a tossed salad, French bread and wine. Or serve with cold beer as is traditional in Cajun Country.

⅔ cup bacon drippings or lard

2 medium onions, chopped

1 medium, green bell pepper, chopped

3 celery stalks, chopped

3 medium garlic cloves, finely minced

1 lb. ham, cut into bite-sized pieces

1½ lbs. smoked sausage, cut into bite-sized rounds

2 cups long-grain white rice

2 large tomatoes, peeled, chopped

3 cups Brown Veal & Pork Stock, page 21, or canned beef broth

½ teaspoon freshly ground black pepper

¼ teaspoon red (cayenne) pepper or to taste

Salt to taste

12 green onions, chopped

½ cup minced parsley, preferably flat-leaf

In a heavy 8-quart Dutch oven, melt drippings or lard over medium heat. Add onions, bell pepper, celery and garlic; cook until vegetables are wilted and transparent, about 5 minutes. Add ham and sausage; cook, stirring occasionally, until sausage is lightly browned, about 8 minutes. Add rice. Cook, stirring constantly, until rice is light golden-brown, about 5 minutes. Add tomatoes; stir until combined. Cook 2 minutes. Stir in stock or broth. Add seasonings. Reduce heat. Cover and simmer until rice is tender and no liquid remains, 45 minutes. Taste for seasoning; adjust if necessary. Add green onions and parsley. Cover and cook 5 minutes. Serve hot. Makes 6 to 8 servings.

Red Beans & Rice with Sausage

Everyone in South Louisiana knows that Monday is red beans and rice with sausage day, and what a treat! The custom originated because Monday was wash day, and the lady of the house had little time to prepare a supper which required a lot of her attention. Traditionally red beans and rice with sausage were put into one pot on the back of the stove and left to cook virtually unattended.

2 lbs. dried red kidney
   beans
¼ cup bacon drippings
2 large onions, chopped
1 large green bell pepper,
   chopped
4 large garlic cloves,
   minced
1 ham hock (about
   1½ lbs.)
Salt to taste
Freshly ground black
   pepper to taste
Red (cayenne) pepper to
   taste

½ teaspoon dried leaf
   marjoram or 1½
   teaspoons chopped
   fresh marjoram
2 bay leaves
1 tablespoon sugar
1 (12-oz.) can beer
2 lbs. chaurice or any hot
   sausage
3 tablespoons vegetable
   oil
Hot cooked white rice
12 green onions, thinly
   sliced
½ cup minced parsley,
   preferably flat-leaf

Sort through beans; discard any discolored ones. Rinse beans; set aside. Heat drippings in a large soup pot or Dutch oven. When drippings are hot, add onions, bell pepper and garlic. Sauté until vegetables are wilted. Add rinsed beans, ham hock, salt, black pepper, cayenne, marjoram, bay leaves, sugar, beer and enough water to cover. Bring to a boil. Reduce heat. Cover and simmer until beans are soft and juice has thickened, about 3 hours, stirring occasionally. Add more water, if necessary. Discard bay leaves. Prick sausage with a fork. Heat oil in a heavy 12-inch skillet over medium heat. When oil is hot, add sausage; cook, turning often, until browned, 10 to 15 minutes. To serve, spoon rice on each plate; ladle beans with liquid over top. Place a sausage on each plate. Sprinkle with green onions and parsley. Makes 6 to 8 servings.

Cajun Corn Bread

The traditional pan for baking corn bread in the South is made of cast iron. The pans usually yield 8 to 10 large portions of bread. They are sometimes round, with pie-shaped divisions. Or they may be rectangular with divisions in the shape of an ear of corn. A standard-size muffin pan may be substituted.

1 cup all-purpose flour
1 tablespoon baking powder
½ teaspoon salt
2 tablespoons sugar
1 cup yellow cornmeal, preferably stone ground
2 eggs, slightly beaten

¼ cup lard or vegetable shortening, melted
¼ cup whipping cream
¾ cup milk
½ cup finely chopped onion
3 canned or fresh jalapeño peppers, seeds and veins removed, minced

Preheat oven to 425F (220C). Generously grease 2 corn-bread pans or 18 muffin cups. If using cast-iron pans, place greased pans in hot oven 20 minutes while preparing batter. For a crispy outside crust, batter should sizzle and hiss when spooned into pans. Sift flour, baking powder, salt and sugar into a large bowl. With a fork, blend in cornmeal. Add remaining ingredients to bowl; stir just until all dry ingredients are moist. Do not overbeat. Pour batter into each division in pan, filling each about ⅔ full. Bake in preheated oven until top springs back when pressed with fingertips, 20 minutes. Serve hot. Makes 16 to 20 pieces.

Seafood-Stuffed Eggplant

Stuffed eggplant is truly one of the most delicious Cajun dishes. Use your imagination to dream up additional fillings using ground beef, ham, chicken or other fish or shellfish.

2 medium eggplants
1 cup bacon drippings or lard
3 medium onions, chopped
2 medium, green bell peppers, chopped
1 celery stalk, chopped
3 medium garlic cloves, minced
¼ cup all-purpose flour
1½ cups Seafood Stock, page 20, or 3 (8 oz.) bottles clam juice
¼ teaspoon dried leaf thyme or ¾ teaspoon minced fresh thyme
½ teaspoon dried leaf basil or 1½ teaspoons minced fresh basil
½ teaspoon dried leaf oregano or 1½ teaspoons minced fresh oregano

¼ teaspoon dried leaf marjoram or ¾ teaspoon minced fresh marjoram
¾ teaspoon red (cayenne) pepper
¾ teaspoon freshly ground black pepper
Salt to taste
Vegetable oil
1½ lbs. small, peeled uncooked shrimp
1 lb. lump crabmeat
4 green onions, chopped
¼ cup minced parsley, preferably flat-leaf
About 2 cups cornmeal
2 teaspoons salt
2 teaspoons freshly ground black pepper
2 teaspoons red (cayenne) pepper
About 2 cups all-purpose flour
2 eggs beaten with 1 cup milk

Slice eggplants in half; scoop out each half, leaving a shell about ¾-inch-thick. Set shells aside; chop pulp. Place chopped pulp in 2-quart saucepan; cover with water. Cook over medium heat until pulp is very tender, about 7 minutes. Drain thoroughly through a strainer. Melt bacon drippings or lard in a heavy 12-inch skillet over medium heat. Add onions, bell peppers, celery and garlic; cook until vegetables are very soft and start to break up, about 20 minutes, stirring often. Add ¼ cup flour all at once; stir until combined. Cook, stirring constantly, until flour is peanut-butter-colored, 15 minutes.

Stir in stock or clam juice, herbs, ¾ teaspoon cayenne, ¾ teaspoon black pepper and salt. Stir in drained eggplant pulp. Partially cover skillet; cook over medium heat 20 minutes, stirring often. Heat 3 inches oil in a heavy saucepan to 365F (185C) or until a 1-inch bread cube turns golden brown in 60 seconds. Add shrimp to eggplant mixture; cook 10 minutes. Meanwhile, using your fingertips, pick over crabmeat; remove and discard any small bits of shell or cartilage. Add crabmeat, green onions and parsley; stir gently to blend. Do not break up lumps of crabmeat. Cook 5 minutes to heat through. Cover to keep warm; set aside. In a shallow bowl, combine cornmeal, 2 teaspoons salt, 2 teaspoons black pepper and 2 teaspoons cayenne. Dredge reserved eggplant shells in flour; shake off excess. Dip floured eggplant into egg-and-milk mixture. Dredge in cornmeal mixture to coat well; shake off excess. Gently lower coated shell into hot oil; deep-fry, 2 at a time, until golden brown, turning once. Total cooking time is about 7 minutes per shell. Drain on paper towels. To serve, place 1 deep-fried shell on each plate; stuff with seafood mixture. Serve hot. Makes 4 servings.

Cajun Rabbit in Roux Gravy

Rabbit is a very popular meat in South Louisiana. It is cooked in every conceivable way from simply fried, to stews, to gumbos, to the rich and filling version below.

Rabbit has a delicate and pleasing taste. Domestic rabbit is available fresh or frozen in most parts of the U.S., at specialty meat markets or from home producers. Even though this dish is a earthy-type dish, I have served it to delighted guests on elegant occasions.

2 (3- to 3½-lb.) rabbits, cut into serving pieces
3 large garlic cloves, mashed
1 cup olive oil
2 teaspoons whole cloves
1 teaspoon peppercorns
1 teaspoon dried leaf thyme or 1 tablespoon chopped fresh thyme
1 bay leaf
About 2 cups California zinfandel wine
2 teaspoons each red (cayenne) pepper, salt, freshly ground black pepper
1 teaspoon rubbed sage or 1 tablespoon chopped fresh sage
1 teaspoon dried leaf basil or 1 tablespoon chopped fresh basil

1 teaspoon dried minced rosemary or 1 tablespoon minced fresh rosemary
1 teaspoon dried leaf thyme or 1 tablespoon chopped fresh thyme
About 5 cups all-purpose flour
1 lb. lard or vegetable shortening
2 large onions, chopped
3 large garlic cloves, minced
4 celery stalks, chopped
2 qts. Brown Veal & Pork Stock, page 21, or canned beef broth
1 tablespoon Creole mustard or other stone-ground mustard
6 green onions, sliced
Hot cooked white rice

Place rabbit pieces in a large baking dish. In a medium bowl, combine mashed garlic, olive oil, cloves, peppercorns and 1 teaspoon thyme. Pour over rabbit; add enough wine to cover. Cover and marinate in refrigerator 2 days, turning pieces often. Remove rabbit pieces from marinade; set aside. Strain marinade; reserve ½ cup. In a small bowl, combine cayenne, salt, black pepper, sage, basil, rosemary and 1 teaspoon thyme. Sprinkle marinated rabbit pieces lightly with some of seasoning mixture. In a large bowl, combine remaining seasoning mixture with flour. Melt lard or shortening in a large, heavy Dutch oven over medium heat. Dip rabbit pieces in seasoned flour; shake off excess, reserving seasoned flour. Place floured pieces in hot fat. Fry pieces slowly until crust is very crispy, 15 to 20 minutes on first side. Turn pieces; fry until crispy on other side, about 10 minutes. Using tongs, remove rabbit; set aside. Empty all fat from pan, leaving crispy browned bits at bottom. Reserve 1 cup fat; add it back to pan. Measure 1 cup seasoned flour; add to hot fat. Over medium heat, whisk to form a roux; cook until peanut-butter-colored, about 20 minutes. Add onions, garlic and celery; cook, stirring, until wilted and transparent. Meanwhile, in a large saucepan, heat stock or broth, mustard and reserved marinade. Slowly add hot liquid to roux mixture, stirring. Place browned rabbit pieces back in pan. Cover and cook over low heat 1 hour, stirring often to prevent sticking. Just before serving, gently stir in green onions. To serve, spoon rice on each plate; add rabbit and gravy. Makes 6 to 8 servings.

Variation

Substitute 2 broiler-fryer chickens for rabbit.

> To cut up a whole rabbit or squirrel, first cut and remove forelegs from body at shoulder. Cut and remove hind legs at hip. Finally separate rib section from loin.

Acadian Alligator Sauce Piquant

When alligators were taken off the endangered species list, enterprising Cajuns and restauranteurs developed ways to use the meat. There are now several plants in South Louisiana which process alligators under USDA inspection. There are three types of meat processed from the 'gator carcass, the choicest being tail meat. Tail meat is white and very much like veal in both taste and texture! The body meat is somewhat darker and has a stronger taste and slightly tougher texture. It is very similar to pork shoulder. The final grouping is leg meat, which is the strongest-flavored part of the carcass. The meat is very dark in color, resembling beef shank, and is very tough. Its use should be limited to braised dishes.

2½ lbs. mixed tail-and-body alligator meat or pork loin or shoulder, cut into cubes
Salt to taste
Finely ground black pepper
1 recipe Cajun Roux, page 16
2 medium onions, chopped
4 medium garlic cloves, minced
1 large green bell pepper, chopped
2 large celery stalks, chopped
3 medium tomatoes, peeled, chopped
2 tablespoons tomato paste
2 teaspoons Worcestershire sauce
1 teaspoon freshly ground black pepper
1½ teaspoons chili powder

1 teaspoon dried leaf oregano or 1 tablespoon chopped fresh oregano
1 teaspoon dried leaf basil or 1 tablespoon chopped fresh basil
1 teaspoon dried leaf thyme or 1 tablespoon chopped fresh thyme
½ teaspoon red (cayenne) pepper
Salt to taste
½ cup Burgundy wine
2 cups Brown Veal & Pork Stock, page 21, or canned beef broth
6 green onions, chopped
¼ cup minced parsley, preferably flat-leaf
Hot cooked white rice

Season alligator meat or pork with salt and black pepper. In a heavy Dutch oven over medium heat, make roux as directed on page 12, cooking until mahogany-colored. Add seasoned meat; cook quickly, stirring until lightly browned. Add onions, garlic, bell pepper, celery and tomatoes. Stir until vegetables are slightly wilted and transparent, about 5 minutes. Add tomato paste, Worcestershire sauce, black pepper, chili powder, oregano, basil, thyme, cayenne and salt; cook 5 minutes, stirring to prevent sticking. Stir in wine and stock or broth. Reduce heat. Cover and simmer until meat is tender and liquid is thick and rich, 1½ hours. Stir in green onions and parsley; remove from heat. Serve over rice. Makes 4 to 6 servings.

Smothered Cabbage with Sausage

This is one of the best of Cajun *cooked-down* dishes. If you wish to sample authentic Cajun home cooking, look no further.

2 qts. Louisiana Brown Poultry Stock, page 19, or canned chicken broth	8 links chaurice or other hot sausage
2 teaspoons salt	⅓ cup bacon drippings or lard
2 teaspoons freshly ground black pepper	1 large onion, halved lengthwise, sliced
1 medium head cabbage	½ teaspoon red (cayenne) pepper
1 (1-lb.) ham steak, trimmed	½ teaspoon freshly ground black pepper
	Salt to taste

Combine stock or broth, 2 teaspoons salt and 2 teaspoons pepper in a heavy 6-quart saucepan; bring to a boil. Meanwhile, cut cabbage into pieces about 1 inch wide and 2 to 3 inches long. Place cabbage in boiling stock. Reduce heat; simmer until cabbage is tender, 35 minutes. While cabbage is cooking, cut ham into bite-sized pieces; prick sausages several times with a fork. In a heavy 5- to 6-quart Dutch oven, heat drippings or lard. When fat is hot, add pricked sausages and ham pieces; cook until lightly browned, about 10 minutes. Add onion; cook until slightly wilted and transparent, about 5 minutes. Drain cabbage, reserving 1 cup cooking liquid. Add cabbage to ham mixture; add ¼ cup reserved cooking liquid. Season with cayenne, black pepper and salt. Reduce heat. Cover and simmer 1 hour, stirring occasionally. Add more reserved cooking liquid as necessary to prevent sticking. Cabbage should be fairly dry when served. Serve hot. Makes 4 to 6 servings.

Crawfish Pie

Crawfish pie is an institution in Cajun country, and the best to be had in a restaurant is found at the Crawfish Kitchen in Breaux Bridge, Louisiana, the Crawfish Capital of the World.

Double recipe Flaky Pie
    Pastry, page 183
¾ recipe Cajun Roux,
    page 16
1 large onion, chopped
2 large garlic cloves,
    chopped
1 small green bell pepper,
    chopped
2 celery stalks, chopped
½ cup minced parsley,
    preferably flat-leaf
½ teaspoon dried leaf
    basil or 1½ teaspoons
    chopped fresh basil
1 bay leaf, minced
½ teaspoon dried leaf
    oregano or 1½
    teaspoons chopped
    fresh oregano
½ teaspoon red (cayenne)
    pepper
¼ teaspoon freshly
    ground black pepper
1 tablespoon fresh lemon
    juice
1 medium tomato,
    peeled, pureed
1½ lbs. peeled crawfish
    tails
2 cups Seafood Stock,
    page 20, or 2 (8 oz.)
    bottles clam juice
Salt to taste
6 green onions, chopped

Prepare pastry as directed on pages 183–4. Divide into 2 equal pieces. Wrap with plastic wrap; refrigerate until chilled. Make roux in a heavy 12-inch skillet over medium heat, cooking until peanut-butter-colored. Add onion, garlic, bell pepper, celery, parsley, basil, bay leaf, oregano, cayenne and black pepper to hot roux. Cook, stirring, until vegetables are slightly wilted and transparent, about 5 minutes. Stir in lemon juice and tomato;

cook 5 minutes. Add crawfish tails. Slowly add stock or clam juice, stirring. Season with salt; cook 20 minutes, stirring often. Stir in green onions; remove from heat. Cool to lukewarm. Preheat oven to 375F (190C). On a lightly floured surface, roll out 1 chilled pastry piece to a 1/16-inch-thick circle. Roll pastry loosely around rolling pin; unroll into a 9-inch, deep-dish pie pan. Gently lower pastry into bottom of pan; lightly press against side, taking care not to stretch pastry. Cut away excess pastry, leaving a 1/2-inch overhang at edge. Pour cooled crawfish filling into pastry-lined pan; set aside. Roll out second pastry piece same as first; place over filling. Cut off excess pastry, leaving about a 1-inch overhang at edges. Tuck edge of top pastry securely under edge of bottom pastry; flute edges, if desired. Or press pastry against edge of pan using tines of a fork. Cut 2 rows of steam vents in top of pastry. Bake in preheated oven until pastry is golden brown and flaky, 20 minutes. Serve hot. Makes 4 to 6 servings.

Variation

For an alternative presentation, divide pastry into 12 equal pieces. Roll out 6 pieces as directed above into circles to fit 1-cup au gratin dishes; fit pastry into 6 dishes. Spoon crawfish filling into pastry-lined dishes. Roll out remaining 6 pastry pieces into circles for tops; place over filled dishes. Bake 20 minutes.

Crawfish Etouffée

Etouffée is one of the most delicious foods to grace a table in Cajun country, or perhaps in the universe. The dish derives its sultry richness from a deep mahogany-brown roux, so don't be timid about the depth of color when you prepare the roux for this dish.

1 recipe Cajun Roux,
    page 16
2 medium onions,
    chopped
3 medium garlic cloves,
    minced
1 large green bell pepper,
    chopped
2 celery stalks, chopped
1 tablespoon plus 1
    teaspoon tomato paste
½ teaspoon red (cayenne)
    pepper
½ teaspoon freshly
    ground black pepper

2 lbs. peeled crawfish tails
1 cup Seafood Stock,
    page 20, or 1 (8 oz.)
    bottle clam juice
Salt to taste
¼ cup minced parsley,
    preferably flat-leaf
8 green onions
6 cups hot cooked white
    rice

Make roux in a heavy 12-inch skillet as directed on page 16, cooking until mahogany-colored. Add onions, garlic, bell pepper and celery to hot roux. Cook, stirring often, until vegetables are slightly wilted and transparent, about 5 minutes. Stir in tomato paste, cayenne and black pepper. Stir in crawfish tails. Slowly stir in stock or clam juice. Season with salt. Reduce heat. Simmer, uncovered, 45 minutes. Stir in parsley and green onions; remove from heat. To serve, spoon about 1 cup rice on each plate; top with etouffée. Makes 4 to 6 servings.

Seafood Boudin with Green-Peppercorn Sauce

This is a delicious all-seafood version of the classic white Cajun sausage.

½ lb. sea scallops
1 lb. redfish fillets or other white-fleshed, non-oily fish
1 cup unsalted butter or margarine, cut into 1-inch cubes
3 eggs
½ lb. peeled uncooked shrimp, minced
1 lb. claw crabmeat
8 green onions, minced
1 medium, green bell pepper, minced

¼ cup minced parsley, preferably flat-leaf
12 garlic cloves, minced
2 teaspoons salt
1 teaspoon red (cayenne) pepper
2 tablespoons fresh lime juice
About 36 inches of sausage casings, medium diameter
Green-Peppercorn Sauce, see below
6 cooked crawfish or shrimp
Curly-parsley sprigs

Green-Peppercorn Sauce:
¼ cup white-wine vinegar
2 tablespoons green peppercorns
1½ teaspoons fresh lime juice
1½ cups whipping cream
½ teaspoon salt

¼ teaspoon freshly ground pepper
4 egg yolks, slightly beaten
1 cup unsalted butter or margarine, cut into 1-inch cubes

In a food processor fitted with the steel blade, combine scallops, redfish, butter or margarine and eggs; process until pureed. Scrape mixture into a medium bowl; fold in shrimp, crabmeat, green onions, bell pepper, minced parsley, garlic, salt, cayenne and lime juice until combined. Tie a firm knot in 1 end of sausage casing. Using a sausage stuffer or 14-inch pastry bag fitted with a 1-inch plain tip, stuff sausage casings. Do not pack too tightly, or they will burst during cooking. Sausages should actually appear to be a little understuffed; sausages expand during cooking. Twist sausages into desired lengths. Tie a firm knot in other end of casing. Set sausage aside. Add 3 inches water to a heavy 12-inch skillet; bring to a simmer over medium heat. Add sausages; poach 15 minutes. While sausages are cooking, prepare Peppercorn Sauce. Remove sausages from water; drain well. To serve, spoon some peppercorn sauce into each plate; top with desired number of sausages. Garnish with a cooked shrimp or crawfish and parsley sprigs. Makes 4 to 6 servings.

To prepare Green-Peppercorn Sauce, in a heavy 2-quart saucepan, combine vinegar, peppercorns and lime juice. Using a wooden spoon or a flat potato masher, crush peppercorns in liquid. Cook over medium-high heat until reduced to 1 tablespoon, about 5 minutes. Add cream, salt and pepper; cook until thickened and reduced slightly, 7 to 8 minutes. Whisk often. Reduce heat; whisk in egg yolks. Cook whisking constantly, until thickened, 3 to 4 minutes. Add butter or margarine cubes, a few at a time, whisking constantly, until all are added. Set aside. Makes about 1¼ cups.

Sac-a-Lait Courtbouillon

Courtbouillon (pronounced COO-be-yon) is one of the finest examples of country Cajun food. It holds a place of honor as a category of Cajun food. It is similar to other types of Cajun dishes, yet it has features that make it just a little bit different. It is one of the few Cajun dishes that is not served over rice. Courtbouillon may be prepared using any type of small, whole fish such as *sac-a-lait*, a tasty freshwater perch. You can substitute your favorite fish fillets or fish steaks. Serve with crisp French bread.

Broth, see below
6 (6- to 8-oz.) sac-a-lait or
   any small fish, fish
   fillets or fish steaks
About 2 cups all-purpose
   flour
⅔ cup lard or vegetable
   oil
¾ recipe Cajun Roux,
   page 16

Broth:
¼ cup lard or vegetable
   oil
2 large tomatoes, peeled,
   chopped
1 large onion, chopped
3 large celery stalks,
   chopped
1 medium, green bell
   pepper, chopped
2 large garlic cloves,
   chopped
2 bay leaves, minced
½ teaspoon dried leaf
   oregano or 1½
   teaspoons chopped
   fresh oregano
½ teaspoon dried leaf
   basil or 1½ teaspoons
   chopped fresh basil

1 small onion, chopped
1 small green bell pepper,
   chopped
1 celery stalk, chopped
1 teaspoon Tabasco sauce
Minced parsley,
   preferably flat-leaf
Lemon wedges

½ teaspoon dried leaf
   thyme or 1½ teaspoons
   chopped fresh thyme
1 tablespoon sugar
½ teaspoon red (cayenne)
   pepper
¼ teaspoon freshly
   ground black pepper
1 qt. Seafood Stock, page
   20, or 4 (8-oz.) bottles
   clam juice
½ cup Burgundy wine

Make broth. Meanwhile, in a heavy 12-inch skillet over medium-high heat, heat lard or oil. Dredge fish in flour, turning to coat well; shake off excess. When fat is hot, add fish; sear quickly on both sides just long enough to form a crispy crust. Drain on paper towels. Preheat oven to 375F (190C). Make roux in a heavy 10-inch skillet over medium heat as directed on page 16, cooking until mahogany-colored. Add onion, bell pepper and celery; cook 5 minutes, stirring. Remove from heat; stir in Tabasco sauce. Bring broth mixture to a rolling boil; stir in roux, a spoonful at a time. Reduce heat; cook 5 minutes. Remove pan from heat; add fried fish. Bake in preheated oven until fish turns from transparent to opaque, 15 minutes. To serve, place a whole fish or fillet in each soup plate; spoon some vegetables over top. Add a generous amount of broth to each serving. Garnish with parsley and lemon wedges. Serve hot. Makes 4 to 6 servings.

To prepare Broth, in an ovenproof Dutch oven, melt ¼ cup lard over medium heat; add all ingredients except stock and wine. Cook until vegetables are slightly wilted and transparent, about 5 minutes. Stir in stock or clam juice and wine. Reduce heat; cover and simmer 25 minutes, stirring occasionally.

Sauteéd Frog Legs with Cayenne

The Cajuns are masters at cooking with chili peppers, or capsicums, the botanical group to which cayenne peppers belong. These same hot peppers can be made to taste completely different by varying cooking times, cooking temperatures and companion ingredients. Cajun cooks use this principle to moderate the hotness level of fresh chilies. This delicious dish of sauteéd frog legs is topped with fresh cayenne peppers that have been treated by the "hotness-modifying principles" of cooking with sugar and slow sauteéeing. Without modification the diner would never live, much less enjoy the taste!

18 to 24 pairs large frog
   legs, skinned
1 qt. buttermilk
Seasoning Mixture, see
   below
18 fresh cayenne peppers,
   seeds, veins removed

¼ cup unsalted butter or
   margarine
½ cup olive oil
About 3 tablespoons
   sugar
3 cups all-purpose flour

Seasoning Mixture
1 teaspoon each salt,
   freshly ground black
   pepper, onion powder,
   garlic powder, paprika

Place frog legs in a large baking dish; add buttermilk. Cover and refrigerate at least 2 hours. Prepare Seasoning Mixture; set aside. Wearing rubber gloves, slice cayenne peppers into thin julienne strips; set aside. In a heavy 12-inch skillet over medium heat, heat butter and olive oil. Reduce heat; add cayenne-pepper strips; sprinkle with 3 tablespoons sugar. Cook slowly, stirring often, until strips are very wilted, about 15 minutes. Remove from heat. Remove 1 or 2 strips; taste degree of hotness. If a less intense taste is desired, sprinkle on 2 teaspoons more sugar; cook 5 minutes. Remove peppers with a slotted spoon, leaving oil in skillet. Cover to keep warm. Drain frog legs, discarding buttermilk. Rinse frog legs under running water. Pat dry on paper towels. Return skillet to medium heat. When oil is hot, dredge frog legs in flour, turning to coat well; shake off excess. Sauté frog legs in batches. Do not crowd pan. Sauté frog legs about 5 minutes on each side, turning once. As each batch is finished, drain on paper towels; sprinkle with Seasoning Mixture; keep warm. To serve, place frog legs on a platter; scatter sautéed peppers over top. Serve hot. Makes 4 to 6 servings.

To prepare Seasoning Mixture, in a small bowl, combine all ingredients.

Cajun Oyster Pie

Both Oyster Pie and Crawfish Pie, page 219, have their devoted followers. Each group will argue to the death that one or the other is best. Try them both and then decide. But if you love oysters as intensely as I do, this recipe will have a slight edge. This recipe is another example of the Cajun's love of oysters combined with pork.

1 recipe Flaky Pie Pastry,
page 190
½ recipe, Cajun Roux,
page 16, made with
bacon or sausage
drippings
⅔ cup finely chopped
smoked ham
½ lb. mushrooms,
chopped
1 small green bell pepper,
chopped
3 medium garlic cloves,
minced
6 green onions, chopped
½ teaspoon red (cayenne)
pepper
¼ teaspoon dried leaf
thyme or ¾ teaspoon
fresh chopped thyme
½ teaspoon dried leaf
basil or 1½ teaspoons
chopped fresh basil

½ teaspoon dried leaf
oregano or 1½
teaspoons
Worcestershire sauce
1 tablespoon fresh lemon
juice
36 shucked oysters with
their liquor, drained,
liquor reserved
½ cup Seafood Stock,
page 20, or bottled
clam juice
Salt to taste
½ cup grated Parmesan
cheese (1½ oz.)

Prepare and chill pastry as directed on page 190. Make roux in a heavy 12-inch skillet over medium heat as directed on page 16, cooking until peanut-butter-colored. Add ham, mushrooms, bell pepper, garlic and green onions; cook, stirring until vegetables are slightly wilted and transparent, 5 minutes. Add cayenne, thyme, basil and oregano; stir until blended. Stir in Worcestershire sauce, lemon juice and reserved oyster liquor. Slowly stir in stock or clam juice. Cook until thickened, about 15 minutes. Add oysters; stir into sauce. Season with salt. Cool to lukewarm. Preheat oven to 375F (190C). Spoon cooled filling into a 9-inch deep-dish pie pan; sprinkle with Parmesan cheese. Set aside. On a lightly floured surface, roll out chilled pastry to a ¹⁄₁₆-inch-thick circle. Roll pastry loosely around rolling pin; unroll over pie. Cut off and discard excess pastry; flute edges, if desired. Or press pastry onto edge of pan using tines of a fork. Cut 2 rows of steam vents in top of pastry. Bake in preheated oven until pastry is golden brown and flaky, 20 minutes. Serve hot. Makes 4 to 6 servings.

Variation

For an alternate presentation, spoon oyster filling into 6 (1-cup) au gratin dishes. Top each dish with 2 tablespoons Parmesan cheese; set aside. Divide pastry into 6 equal pieces; roll out as directed above into circles for tops. Top each dish with a pastry circle. Bake 20 minutes.

Creole-Italian

Creole-Italian Dinner Party

*Olive Salad
Pepper Breads
Italian Baked Oysters
Green Salad with
Creole Roquefort Dressing, page 83
Brucholoni with Wine Pasta
Spinach Bread
Sicilian Ricotta Torte, page 201*

In the late 1800s, large numbers of immigrants from Sicily began to settle in South Louisiana. Many stayed in New Orleans to establish businesses. With the arrival of the Italians, a new dimension was added to Creole food. Like the many other earlier influences, Italian cuisine contributed many subtle nuances of taste. From the Italians, the Creoles cultivated a love of garlic. Its sensuous, sultry presence is encountered just barely beneath the surface in many classic Creole dishes. My personal theory is that it was from these hearty, vivacious and fun-loving Sicilians that the Creoles inherited much of their intense love affair with fine food.

Conversely, the Spanish roots of the Creole cuisine had a profound impact on Sicilian-American foods. An entire sub-cuisine evolved within the Creole cooking of New Orleans. Today, some of New Orleans' finest restaurants are owned by descendants of these Creole-Italians. They serve excitingly different food which started out many years ago as robust Sicilian fare but which, through the years of Creole influence, developed its present piquant patina—this due largely to the Spanish love of ground chilies. After you've eaten two or three bites and a titillatingly warm glow has developed at the back of your throat, you realize that this is no ordinary spaghetti sauce!

The best examples of Creole-Italian cooking, of course, are found in the homes. But if you don't know a New Orleanian with a last name like Bonnitelli, try one of the city's great Creole-Italian restaurants. Tortorici's, La Louisiane, Broussard's, Impastato's, Pascal's Manale, Mosca's, La Riviera and Tony Angelo's are all classic examples of this sub-cuisine. There are two outstanding Creole-Italian restaurants on the North Shore of New Orleans across the Lake Ponchartrain Causeway—The Shadows in Mandeville and Sal and Judy's in Lacombe.

The most unique feature of the cuisine is its tomato sauce, commonly referred to as *red gravy* or *tomato gravy*. This rich sauce used over meats and pasta has dozens of variations from family to family. Some red gravies are based on a brown roux. Some contain eggplant. Others contain anchovies, whole boiled eggs or meat. Two consistent threads in red gravy are the addition of sugar and the frying of the tomato paste!

When I learned the secret of frying tomato paste, everything I cooked for a week contained fried tomato paste! The procedure produces a specific taste without which you simply do not have authentic Creole-Italian tomato gravy. After the vegetables are sautéed in olive oil, tomato paste is added and, literally, fried before the liquids are added.

Creole-Italians incorporate local fish and shellfish in their cooking with delicious results in dishes, such as Crawfish Fettuccine, Crabmeat in Garlic-Cream Sauce and many more. Some dishes were borrowed from Creole kitchens and topped with red gravy, as is the case with Creole Daube.

Other dishes, among them some of the best, came directly from the heart of the Creole-Italian homemaker's domain. Spinach Bread is such a dish. This entire chapter could be filled with nothing but the many versions of this delicious and versatile bread. You can bake loaves of the bread, slice them into inch-thick slices and serve them in bread baskets as party food. Or, for your best pasta-and-tomato-gravy meal, nothing gives a better complement than a hot loaf of Spinach Bread. When your guests lift the napkin covering of the basket, the aroma that rises says "Italian!"

The Creole-Italians are very serious about their pasta. My favorite New Orleans pasta is made from semolina flour, eggs and a little dry white or red wine, depending on the sauce. The taste of the wine is neither pronounced nor discernable in the overall taste of the dish. Rather, its addition combines Italian and Creole with a *lagniappe*, a little something extra—flavor.

Sweet & Sour Olives

This great relish is a must for the antipasta tray. Or use as a topping on your homemade pizza.

⅓ cup olive oil	1 qt. pitted ripe olives
2 medium onions, halved lengthwise, sliced	½ cup red-wine vinegar
	2 tablespoons sugar

Heat olive oil in heavy 12-inch skillet over medium heat. Add onions; sauté until thoroughly wilted and transparent, about 10 minutes. Add olives; stir until combined. Add vinegar and sugar; bring mixture to a boil. Reduce heat; simmer until liquid has thickened slightly to form a thin syrup, 10 minutes. Cool completely. Spoon into a jar with a tight-fitting lid. Refrigerate until served or up to 1 week. Serve at room temperature. Makes about 6 cups.

Spinach Bread

Spinach Bread is the very essence of Creole-Italian cooking. The bread freezes well, so make several loaves.

Serve with your favorite pasta dish for a satisfying meal.
Or slice the loaves into 1-inch rounds; serve as party
finger food.

¼ cup warm water (110F,
  45C)
1 cup milk, scalded,
  cooled to 110F, 45C
1 tablespoon sugar
1 (14-oz.) pkg. active dry
  yeast (about 1
  tablespoon)
About 4 cups bread flour

1½ teaspoons salt
2 tablespoons unsalted
  butter or margarine,
  room temperature
1 egg
Spinach filling, see below
About 6 tablespoons
  olive oil

Spinach Filling:
2 (10-oz.) pkgs. frozen
  chopped spinach
¾ cup grated Parmesan
  cheese (2¼ oz.)
4 large garlic cloves,
  minced
6 anchovy fillets, minced

2½ teasdpoons dried leaf
  oregano or 2
  tablespoons plus 1½
  teaspoons chopped
  fresh oregano
¼ cup olive oil

In a 2-cup glass measuring cup, combine water, milk and
sugar. Stir in yeast. Let stand until foamy, 5 to 10 minutes. In a food processor fitted with the steel blade,
combine 4 cups flour, salt, butter or margarine and egg.
Add yeast mixture. Process until dough forms a ball, 4 to
5 seconds. Stop machine; check consistency of dough. It
should be smooth and satiny. If dough is too dry, add
additional warm water, 1 tablespoon at a time; process
just until blended. If dough is too sticky, add additional
flour, 1 or 2 tablespoons at a time, process just until
blended. Process 20 seconds to knead. Pour 2 tablespoons olive oil into a large bowl; swirl to coat bottom
and sides. Place dough in oiled bowl; turn to coat all
sides with oil. Cover bowl with plastic wrap. Let rise in a
warm, draft-free place until doubled in bulk, 1½ hours.
Prepare filling. When doubled in bulk, punch down
dough; divide into 2 equal pieces. Lightly oil work surface with olive oil; roll out each piece of dough into a

15" × 12" rectangle. Place ½ of filling lengthwise in a line down center of each dough rectangle, leaving a border of 1½ inches at top and bottom. Fold top border down over filling and bottom border up over filling. Now fold sides of dough over filling to enclose, overlapping 1 side. Using your hands, rub all sides of loaves with olive oil. Place on an ungreased baking sheet, seam-side down, leaving 2 inches between loaves. Cover loosely with plastic wrap; let rise in a warm, draft-free place until almost doubled in bulk, 45 minutes. Place rack in center of oven. Preheat oven to 350F (175C). Remove plastic wrap. Bake in center of preheated oven until golden brown, 30 minutes. Carefully turn loaves; cook an additional 5 to 10 minutes to brown bottoms. Cool on wire racks until lukewarm before slicing. Refrigerate any leftovers. Makes 2 loaves.

To prepare Spinach Filling, thaw spinach completely; squeeze out all moisture. In a medium bowl combine all filling ingredients. Divide into 2 equal portions; set aside.

Pepper Breads

These garlicky little snack crackers laced with a sprinkling of pepper are very versatile munchies. Serve with salads or dips, top with Olive Salad, page 243, or eat them just as they are.

½ cup warm water (110F, 45C)
2 teaspoons sugar
1 (¼-oz.) pkg. active dry yeast (about 1 tablespoon)
About 4 cups all-purpose flour

2 tablespoons freshly ground pepper
2 teaspoons salt
About 1 cup olive oil
Salt
Garlic powder

In a 2-cup glass measuring cup, combine water and sugar. Stir in yeast. Let stand until foamy, 5 to 10 minutes. In a food processor fitted with steel blade, combine 4 cups flour, pepper and salt. Add yeast mixture; turn on and off 3 or 4 times to blend. With motor running, add ¾ cup olive oil through feed tube in a slow, steady stream. When all oil has been added, stop machine; check consistency of dough. It should be smooth and satiny. If dough is too dry, add more warm water, 1 tablespoon at a time; process just until blended. If dough is too sticky, add more flour, 1 or 2 tablespoons at a time; process just until blended. Process 20 seconds to knead. Place 3 tablespoons olive oil in a large bowl; swirl to coat bottom and side of bowl. Place dough in oiled bowl; turn to coat all sides with olive oil. Cover bowl with plastic wrap. Let rise in a warm, draft-free place until doubled in bulk, 1½ hours. Place rack in center of oven. Preheat oven to 400F (205C). Lightly oil work surface with olive oil. Punch down dough thoroughly; turn out onto oiled surface. Roll out dough to a 24-inch square. Using a sharp knife, cut dough into 16 (1½-inch-wide) strips. Cut strips into 1½-inch lengths. Place dough pieces on ungreased baking sheets. Using a pastry brush, lightly paint each square with olive oil; sprinkle with salt and garlic powder. Bake in center of preheated oven until light golden brown and crisp, 10 minutes. Cool on racks. Makes 256.

Sausage-Stuffed Zucchini

Creole-Italians produce some of the best Italian sausage this side of Italy. As with other "Creolized" Italian dishes, it has its own personality derived from the addition of chopped hot chilies and cayenne pepper. Italian sausage is usually sold in two varieties in New Orleans —hot and regular. It is used in all sorts of culinary concoctions, from the delicious Italian sausage po'boy, to stuffings, as in this recipe. The stuffed zucchini is a great do-ahead meal.

2 large zucchini (about 1
  lb. each)
¼ cup olive oil
¾ lb. hot Italian sausage,
  casings removed
1 small onion, chopped
1 small green bell pepper,
  chopped
3 medium garlic cloves,
  minced
1 large tomato, peeled,
  chopped
1 tablespoon minced
  parsley, preferably
  flat-leaf
1 teaspoon dried leaf
  oregano or 1
  tablespoon chopped
  fresh oregano

½ teaspoon salt
½ teaspoon freshly
  ground black pepper
¾ cup Italian-seasoned
  bread crumbs
4 green onions, chopped
1½ cups shredded
  mozzarella cheese
  (6 oz.)
1 lb. fettuccine, cooked
2 cups hot Creole-Italian
  Tomato Gravy, page
  242

Slice zucchini in half lengthwise; scoop out pulp, leaving a ¼-inch shell. Chop pulp; set aside. Preheat oven to 350F (175C). Heat olive oil in a heavy 10-inch skillet over medium heat. Crumble sausage into hot oil; add onion, bell pepper and garlic. Cook, stirring, until sausage has browned and onions are slightly wilted and transparent, about 7 minutes. Add reserved zucchini pulp, tomato, parsley, oregano, salt and black pepper. Cook, stirring often, until tomato liquid evaporates, about 10 minutes. Remove pan from heat; stir in bread crumbs, green onions and cheese. Pack sausage mixture into zucchini shells, mounding tops firmly. Place stuffed squash in an ungreased 13″ × 9″ baking dish. Bake in preheated oven until cheese has melted and stuffing is bubbly, 20 minutes. To serve, place a mound of fettuccine on each plate; place a stuffed zucchini on fettuccine. Drizzle hot tomato gravy over top. Serve hot. Makes 4 servings.

Spinach Pie

This Creole-Italian version of quiche bears no resemblance to its delicate French counterpart. Robust in flavor and hearty in substance, this pie captures the essence of New Orleans Italian food. Unbaked Spinach Pie freezes well, ready to be popped into the oven on a busy night. Serve with a salad of fresh fruits.

Double recipe of Flaky
  Pie Pastry, page 190
4 (10-oz.) pkgs. frozen
  chopped spinach
2 tablespoons unsalted
  butter or margarine
2 tablespoons olive oil
½ lb. prosciutto, finely
  chopped
6 anchovy fillets, minced
8 green onions, chopped
4 large garlic cloves,
  minced

1½ teaspoons dried leaf
  oregano or 4½
  teaspoons chopped
  fresh oregano
¼ teaspoon salt
¼ teaspoon freshly
  ground pepper
½ teaspoon Tabasco
  sauce
2 eggs beaten with ¼ cup
  whipping cream
1 cup grated Parmesan
  cheese (3 oz.)

Prepare pastry according to recipe, page 190. Separate into 2 pieces; wrap in plastic wrap. Refrigerate until ready to use. Thaw spinach; press out all moisture. In a deep 12-inch skillet over medium heat, heat butter or margarine and olive oil. Add prosciutto, anchovies, green onions, garlic, oregano, salt and pepper. Cook until onions are slightly wilted and transparent, about 5 minutes. Stir in pressed spinach and Tabasco sauce. Set aside. Preheat oven to 375F (190C). On a lightly floured surface, roll out 1 pastry piece to a ¹⁄₁₆-inch thick circle. Roll pastry loosely around rolling pin; unroll over a 9-inch pie pan. Gently lower pastry into bottom and side of pan; do not stretch. Trim excess pastry, leaving a ½-inch overhang. Pour spinach mixture into pastry; spread evenly. Pour egg-and-cream mixture over spinach mixture. Sprinkle cheese over top. Roll out remaining pastry as before. Roll loosely around rolling pin; unroll over filling. Trim off excess pastry, leaving a 1-inch overhang.

Pinch 2 pastries together at overhang; fold under, level with edge of pie pan. Flute edges, if desired. Or press tines of a fork into pastry all around edge to seal. Cut 2 rows of steam vents in top of pastry. Bake in preheated oven until pastry is golden brown and flaky, 25 to 30 minutes. To serve, slice in wedges; serve hot. Makes 6 to 8 servings.

Wine Pasta

Homemade pasta will spoil you. Once you have tasted those wonderful, egg-rich strands cooked to *al dente* perfection, it will be very hard to serve the store-bought variety again. It will seem somehow insulting to your homemade sauces. True to their reputation for uniqueness, Creole-Italians add a little *lagniappe* to the taste of their pasta. That something extra is wine. A little dry white or robust red wine added to the dough produces a rich pasta with a depth of taste that makes you want to simply add a bit of butter and eat the pasta otherwise unadorned.

1¾ cups semolina flour
2 eggs
1 teaspoon olive oil

About 1 tablespoon dry
    white or red wine
1 tablespoon salt
2 tablespoons olive oil

Combine flour, eggs, 1 teaspoon olive oil and 1 table-spoon wine in a food processor fitted with the steel blade. Process just long enough to form a smooth dough. Stop machine; check consistency of dough. If it is too dry, add more wine, 1 teaspoon at a time; process briefly after each addition. The dough should not be sticky, but must be moist enough to hold together in a smooth ball. If dough is too sticky, add more flour, 1 or 2 teaspoons at a time; process just until blended after each addition. Separate dough into 3 or 4 equal pieces. Cover with plastic wrap until ready to use. Using a pasta machine, knead pasta, 1 piece at a time. Start on number 1 setting; knead until smooth. Skip to middle setting; roll pasta through machine, cut pasta to desired size. Cook fresh, dry to store, or freeze, as desired. *To freeze pasta*, separate freshly made pasta, before it has begun to dry, into desired amounts. Freeze in plastic freezer bags up to 1 month. *To dry pasta*, spread strands on pasta drying racks, on wooden dowels or old broom handles. Separate strands as you spread them; dry several hours or overnight. Dry thoroughly to prevent spoiling. Each strand should be dry enough to snap when bent. Store in large, airtight containers. To cook fresh, frozen or fresh-dried pasta, fill a 6- to 8-quart pot ¾ full of water, add 1 tablespoon salt and 2 tablespoons olive oil. Bring to a boil; add cut pasta. Cook until al dente, about 1 minute for fresh or frozen pasta, longer for dry pasta. Drain; serve hot with your favorite sauce. Makes about 13 ounces.

Muffuletta Bread

In order to enjoy a New Orleans Muffuletta Sandwich at its best, you must have authentic Muffuletta Bread. In New Orleans you can buy the crusty loaves in any bakery, but don't forego this treat just because you can't find the bread—make it yourself!

1 cup warm water (110F, 45C)	About 3 cups bread flour
1 tablespoon sugar	1½ teaspoons salt
1 (¼-oz.) pkg. active dry yeast (about 1 tablespoon)	2 tablespoons vegetable shortening
	Sesame seeds

In a 2-cup glass measuring cup, combine water and sugar. Stir in yeast. Let stand until foamy, 5 to 10 minutes. In a food processor fitted with the steel blade, combine 3 cups flour, salt and shortening. Add yeast mixture. Process until dough forms a ball, about 5 seconds. Stop machine; check consistency of dough. It should be smooth and satiny. If dough is too dry, add more warm water, 1 tablespoon at a time, processing just until blended. If dough is too sticky, add more flour, 1 or 2 tablespoons at a time, processing just until blended. Process 20 seconds to knead. Lightly oil a large bowl, swirling to coat bottom and sides. Place dough in oiled bowl; turn to coat all sides. Cover bowl with plastic wrap. Let rise in a warm, draft-free place until doubled in bulk, about 1½ hours. Lightly grease a baking sheet. When dough has doubled in bulk, punch down dough; turn out onto a lightly floured surface. Form dough into a round loaf about 10 inches in diameter; place on greased baking sheet. Sprinkle top of loaf with sesame seeds; press seeds gently into surface of loaf. Cover very loosely with plastic wrap; let rise until almost doubled in bulk, 1 hour. Place rack in center of oven. Preheat oven to 425F (220C). Remove plastic wrap. Bake loaf in center of preheated oven 10 minutes. Reduce heat to 375F (190C); bake 25 minutes. The loaf is done when it sounds hollow when tapped on bottom. Cool completely on a rack before slicing. Makes 1 loaf.

Muffuletta Sandwich

A visit to New Orleans without eating a Muffuletta would be like a trip to Ireland without kissing the Blarney Stone! A Muffuletta, one of life's great pleasures, is a 10-inch round sandwich stuffed with meats and cheese and topped with a concoction known as Olive Salad, page 243. In New Orleans the two best Muffulettas, bar none, can be had at Central Grocery or at Napoleon House on Chartres Street. At Central Grocery, you stand in line at the counter to shout your order. You can eat your sandwich while wandering through the tiny, crowded grocery. You'll find open barrels of flours and beans, wooden crates of dried salt cod, huge jars of olive salad and oil-cured olives, every brand of olive oil imaginable along with boxes of every size and shape of pasta made. The Napoleon House is a real cafe and bar located in one of the French Quarter's oldest buildings. Here you may dine unmolested by elbows and tromping feet.

1 (10-inch) Muffuletta
    Bread loaf, above, or
    French bread
2 oz. Genoa salami, thinly
    sliced

2 oz. Italian ham, thinly
    sliced
2 oz. Provolone cheese,
    thinly sliced
1 cup Olive Salad, page
    243

Cut bread in half crosswise. Pile several layers of salami
and ham over bottom layer. Add layers of cheese. Top
with Olive Salad and top of loaf. Press down slightly. Cut
sandwich in quarters. Use wooden picks to secure
layers, if desired; remove before eating. Makes 1 to 4
servings, depending on the appetite!

Veal & Pork Meatballs

It is truly hard to beat a plate of pasta cooked *al dente*,
or "to the tooth," and topped with tomato gravy. Throw
in these combination meatballs and you have a feast—
Creole-Italian style.

¾ lb. ground veal
¾ lb. lean ground pork
1 medium onion,
    chopped
5 medium garlic cloves,
    minced
½ cup grated Parmesan
    cheese (1½-oz.)
6 anchovy fillets,
minced
1 teaspoon dried leaf
    oregano or 1
    tablespoon chopped
    fresh oregano
1½ teaspoons salt
1 teaspoon freshly ground
    pepper

4 (1-inch-thick) French-
    bread slices, torn into
    tiny pieces
2 eggs, slightly beaten
2 tablespoons ketchup
1 tablespoon minced
    parsley, preferably
    flat-leaf
Olive oil
1 qt. Creole-Italian
    Tomato Gravy,
    opposite or favorite
    tomato sauce
1 lb. pasta, cooked

Combine all ingredients except olive oil, tomato gravy or
tomato sauce and pasta in a large bowl. Divide mixture

into 10 to 12 portions. Form round balls by rolling each portion between your hands. In a heavy 12-inch skillet, heat about ¼-inch olive oil over medium heat. Add as many meatballs as will fit comfortably without touching. Sauté quickly until browned on all sides; remove with a slotted spoon. Brown remaining meatballs. Heat tomato gravy or tomato sauce in a Dutch oven over medium heat. Add meatballs; cook 30 minutes, stirring often to prevent sticking. Serve meatballs and sauce over your favorite pasta. Makes 5 to 6 servings.

Roux-Based Red Gravy

Roux-Based Red Gravy forms the very soul of Creole-Italian cuisine. The taste is rich and mysterious, and it says "More." One thing for sure, it was born in New Orleans. Serve gravy over meat dishes or pasta.

½ recipe Cajun Roux,
    page 16
1 large onion, finely
    chopped
4 medium garlic cloves,
    minced
1 (6-oz.) can tomato paste
1½ teaspoons sugar
2 cups Brown Veal &
    Pork Stock, page 21,
    or canned beef broth

1 teaspoon salt
¼ teaspoon red (cayenne)
    pepper
1 teaspoon freshly ground
    black pepper
1 teaspoon
    Worcestershire sauce
⅓ cup grated Parmesan
    cheese (1 oz.)

Make roux in a deep 12-inch skillet over medium heat, cooking until mahogany-colored. Add onion and garlic to hot roux; cook, stirring, until onion is completely wilted, about 10 minutes. Blend in tomato paste and sugar; cook, stirring, 5 minutes. Slowly stir in stock or broth. Stir in salt, cayenne, black pepper, Worcestershire sauce and cheese. Reduce heat. Cover and simmer 35 minutes, stirring often. Puree gravy, in batches, in a blender or food processor fitted with the steel blade; serve hot. Makes 4 cups.

Creole-Italian Tomato Gravy

This vegetable-and-tomato-laden sauce will delight even the most ardent connoisseur of Sicilian food. Tomato gravy freezes well. Make this large batch and have plenty on hand to serve over meat dishes or pasta.

½ cup olive oil
½ medium eggplant, peeled, finely chopped
6 anchovy fillets, minced
3 celery stalks, chopped
2 medium onions, chopped
6 large garlic cloves, minced
4 green onions, chopped
2 bay leaves, minced
2 teaspoons dried leaf oregano or 2 tablespoons chopped fresh oregano
2 teaspoons dried leaf basil or 2 tablespoons chopped fresh basil
2 teaspoons dried leaf savory or 2 tablespoons chopped fresh savory
½ teaspoon dried leaf marjoram or 2 tablespoons chopped fresh marjoram

½ teaspoon minced dried rosemary or 1½ teaspoons minced fresh rosemary
1½ tablespoons sugar
1¼ cups tomato paste
3 (28-oz.) cans Italian plum tomatoes, drained, chopped
1¾ cups tomato sauce
1½ teaspoons salt
1 teaspoon freshly ground black pepper
1 teaspoon red (cayenne) pepper
2 tablespoons minced parsley, preferably flat-leaf
½ cup grated Parmesan cheese (1½ oz.)
3 qts Brown Veal & Pork Stock, page 21, or canned beef broth

Heat olive oil in a heavy 8-quart Dutch oven. Add eggplant, anchovies, celery, onions, garlic, green onions, bay leaves, oregano, basil, savory, marjoram and rosemary. Cook, stirring often, until vegetables are thoroughly wilted, about 10 minutes. Add sugar and tomato paste; cook 5 minutes, stirring. Add remaining ingredients; stir until combined. Reduce heat. Barely simmer, uncovered, 1 hour. Puree in batches in blender or food processor; serve hot. Makes 5 quarts.

Olive Salad

No respectable Creole-Italian home would be without a container of Olive Salad in the refrigerator. The number one use for Olive Salad in New Orleans is as a dressing for the famous Muffuletta Sandwich. It also makes a delicious addition to tossed green salads and a great relish to spread on party crackers.

1 (32-oz.) jar broken
   green (unstuffed)
   olives
6 garlic cloves, minced
2 (3¼-oz.) jars marinated
   cocktail onions,
   drained (1 cup)
4 celery stalks, halved
   lengthwise, thinly
   sliced

1 (4-oz.) jar chopped
   pimentos, drained
2 tablespoons chopped
   capers, drained
1 tablespoon dried leaf
   oregano or 3
   tablespoons chopped
   fresh oregano
1 teaspoon finely ground
   pepper
3 tablespoons red-wine
   vinegar
⅓ cup olive oil

Drain olives; reserve 3 tablespoons brine. In a medium bowl, combine olives, garlic, onions, celery, pimentos and capers. In a small bowl, whisk reserved olive brine, oregano, pepper and vinegar until combined. Add olive oil in a slow, steady stream, whisking constantly. Pour dressing over salad; toss. Spoon into a jar with a tight-fitting lid. Refrigerate until served or up to 3 weeks. Serve at room temperature. Makes about 5 cups.

Crawfish Fettuccine

Even crawfish have managed to get themselves blended into Creole-Italian cuisine. This dish provides an elegant, but simple, dinner. Serve with Spinach Bread, page 231, and a lettuce salad.

3 cups Seafood Stock,
    page 20, or 3 (8-oz.)
    bottles clam juice
2 pints whipping cream (4
    cups)
½ cup unsalted butter or
    margarine
1 medium onion,
    chopped
1 medium, green bell
    pepper, chopped
3 medium garlic cloves,
    minced
1 teaspoon dried leaf
    basil or 1 tablespoon
    minced fresh basil
1 lb. peeled crawfish tails

Salt to taste
¼ teaspoon freshly
    ground black pepper
½ teaspoon red (cayenne)
    pepper
3 tablespoons unsalted
    butter or margarine
    blended with 3
    tablespoons all-
    purpose flour
6 green onions, chopped
1 lb. fettuccine, cooked
Grated Parmesan cheese

In a heavy 4-quart saucepan over medium-high heat, reduce Seafood Stock by ½. Add cream; reduce again by
½. Meanwhile, in a deep 12-inch skillet over medium
heat, melt ½ cup butter or margarine; add onion, bell
pepper, garlic and basil. Cook until onion is slightly
wilted and transparent, about 5 minutes. Add crawfish
tails, salt, black pepper and cayenne. Cook 2 to 3 minutes, stirring. Set aside. Bring reduced cream-and-stock
mixture to a boil; whisk in butter-and-flour mixture, a
small piece at a time. Whisk until all has been added and
sauce has thickened slightly. Stir cream sauce into crawfish mixture; cook until heated through. Stir in green
onions; remove from heat. Serve over fettuccine; top
with cheese. Makes 4 servings.

Italian Sausage Oysters

A dynamic combination of every Creole-Italian's favorite
foods—oysters, Italian sausage and fresh basil—this
dish will win raves at your table.

24 shucked oysters, drained, liquor reserved

6 green onions, finely chopped

1 cup dry white wine

½ pint whipping cream (1 cup)

1 teaspoon dried leaf basil or 1 tablespoon chopped fresh basil

1 tablespoon parsley, preferably flat-leaf, finely chopped

2 tablespoons unsalted butter or margarine blended with 2 tablespoons all-purpose flour

Salt to taste

Freshly ground pepper

Dash of Tabasco sauce

4 Italian-sausage links

¼ cup olive oil

4 green onions, chopped

½ cup fresh bread crumbs

½ cup grated Parmesan cheese (1½ oz.)

Preheat oven to 325F (165C). Pat oysters dry with paper towels; set aside. In a heavy 2-quart saucepan over medium-high heat, combine oyster liquor, 6 green onions and wine. Cook until reduced by ½. Add cream, basil and parsley; reduce again by ½. Reduce heat to medium. Whisk in butter-and-flour mixture, a small piece at a time. Whisk until all has been added and mixture is slightly thickened. Season with salt, pepper and Tabasco sauce. Set aside. Meanwhile, remove casings from sausage; crumble meat. Heat olive oil in a heavy 10-inch skillet over medium heat; add crumbled sausage. Sauté, breaking up any lumps with a wooden spoon or fork, until all traces of red are gone and sausage is lightly browned. Drain off and discard fat from sausage. Stir in 4 green onions. In a large au gratin dish or casserole, arrange oysters in a single layer on bottom. Pour reduced cream mixture over oysters. Scatter cooked sausage and green onions over top. In a small bowl, combine bread crumbs and cheese with a fork. Sprinkle bread-crumb mixture over sausage. Bake in preheated oven until bubbly and light golden brown, 15 minutes. Serve at once. Makes 4 first-course servings of 6 oysters with topping per person.

Italian Baked Oysters

Every oyster lover in the world should be able to have this dish. It is proof that often the simplest combination of fresh ingredients yields the finest taste. The finished product has a complex taste usually associated with dishes that have been "fussed with" for hours.

Seasoned Bread Crumbs,
     see below
½ cup unsalted butter or
     margarine
1 large onion, chopped
4 garlic cloves, minced
½ teaspoon dried leaf
     thyme or 1½ teaspoons
     chopped fresh thyme
¾ teaspoon dried leaf
     oregano or 2¼
     teaspoons chopped
     fresh oregano

2 tablespoons minced
     parsley, preferably
     flat-leaf
¼ teaspoon red (cayenne
     pepper
¼ teaspoon freshly
     ground black pepper
1 teaspoon salt
48 shucked oysters with
     their liquor
1 cup grated Parmesan
     cheese (3 oz.)

Seasoned Bread Crumbs:
1½ cups dry bread
     crumbs
2 teaspoons dried leaf
     basil or 2 tablespoons
     chopped fresh basil
1 teaspoon dried leaf
     oregano or 1
     tablespoon chopped
     fresh oregano

1 teaspoon minced dried
     rosemary or 1
     tablespoon minced
     fresh rosemary

Prepare Seasoned Bread Crumbs; set aside. Grease a 3-quart casserole dish. Preheat oven to 375F (190C). In a heavy 10-inch skillet over medium heat, melt butter or margarine. Add onion, garlic, herbs, cayenne, black pepper and salt. Sauté until onion is wilted and transparent, about 5 minutes. Add oysters and their liquor, stirring gently to blend. Simmer mixture over medium heat just until oysters begin to curl at edges. Stir in Seasoned Bread Crumbs; spoon mixture into greased dish. Sprinkle top of casserole evenly with Parmesan cheese. Bake in preheated oven until bubbly and lightly browned on top, 15 minutes. Serve hot. Makes 6 to 8 servings.

To prepare Seasoned Bread Crumbs, in a medium bowl, combine all ingredients.

Brucholoni

There are as many ways to spell this New Orleans delight as there are recipes for making it! Brucholoni is a favorite family meal in Creole-Italian homes. However, you may share it with very good friends on less formal occasions. Serve with pasta of your choice.

2 beef for veal top round steaks, ¼ inch thick
1 cup Italian-seasoned bread crumbs
2 eggs, slightly beaten
4 large garlic cloves, minced
½ cup grated Parmesan cheese (1½ oz.)
1 medium onion, halved lengthwise, thinly sliced

1 medium, green bell pepper, thinly sliced
2 hard-cooked eggs, thinly sliced
Salt to taste
Freshly ground black pepper
½ cup olive oil
1 recipe Roux-Based Red Gravy, page 241

Place steaks on a cutting board; trim all fat from edges. Using a meat pounder, pound steaks to about ⅛-inch-thick, taking care not to tear. Preheat oven to 375F (190C). In a medium bowl, combine bread crumbs, eggs, garlic and cheese. Pat mixture evenly over pounded steaks, leaving a 1-inch border at long edges. Scatter onion and bell pepper over bread-crumb mixture; top with hard-cooked eggs. Beginning at long edges, roll tightly, jelly-roll fashion. Tie securely with kitchen string. Salt and pepper rolled steaks. Heat olive oil in a heavy 12-inch skillet over medium heat. Add steak rolls,

1 at a time; brown on all sides. Place browned rolls in a 13″ × 9″ baking dish; pour gravy over top. Bake in preheated oven until meat is fork tender, 45 minutes. To serve, remove string; slice Brucholoni into ½-inch-thick slices. Spoon gravy over each serving. Makes 4 to 6 servings.

Veal Thomassina

This is a simple dish to prepare, but the taste is scrumptious. Serve with buttered pasta and a green vegetable for a very elegant meal.

Salt to taste
Freshly ground pepper
4 (4- to 5-oz.) veal cutlets
1½ cups dairy sour cream
1 egg
2 tablespoons red-wine vinegar

2 tablespoons unsalted butter or margarine
3 tablespoons vegetable oil
3 cups Italian-seasoned bread crumbs
Mushroom Garnish, see below

Mushroom Garnish:
¼ cup unsalted butter or margarine
½ lb. small button mushrooms
3 large garlic cloves, minced

Salt to taste
Freshly ground pepper
1 tablespoon minced parsley, preferably flat-leaf

Salt and pepper both sides of veal cutlets; place in a 13″ × 9″ baking dish. In a medium bowl, whisk together sour cream, egg and vinegar. Pour over cutlets; marinate 1 hour. In a heavy 12-inch skillet over medium heat, heat butter or margarine and oil. Remove cutlets from marinade; gently scrape off excess marinade. Dredge meat in bread crumbs; shake off all excess. Sauté meat in hot butter mixture about 3 minutes per side, turning once. Prepare garnish. To serve, place a sautéed cutlet on each plate; top with garnish. Serve hot. Makes 4 servings.

To prepare Mushroom Garnish, in a medium skillet, melt butter or margarine; add mushrooms and garlic. Cook, stirring, 5 minutes. Season with salt and pepper; stir in parsley.

Crabmeat in Garlic-Cream Sauce

A rich and sumptuous example of the Creole-Italian use of shellfish, this dish is a great do-ahead meal for company. Serve with a green salad.

1 lb. backfin lump
    crabmeat
2 tablespoons minced
    parsley, preferably
    flat-leaf
6 green onions, chopped
4 large garlic cloves,
    minced
⅔ cup dairy sour cream

3 tablespoons dry white
    wine
½ teaspoon salt
1 teaspoon freshly ground
    pepper
1 cup Italian-seasoned
    bread crumbs
½ cup grated Parmesan
    cheese (1½ oz.)

Preheat oven to 350 F (175C). Using your fingertips, carefully pick through crabmeat; remove and discard any bits of shell or cartilage. In a medium bowl, combine crabmeat, parsley, green onions and garlic; set aside. In a small bowl, combine sour cream, wine, salt and pepper. Gently fold cream mixture into crabmeat mixture; do not break up lumps of crabmeat. Divide crabmeat mixture among 4 (1-cup) au gratin dishes. In a small bowl, combine bread crumbs and cheese with a fork. Sprinkle bread-crumb mixture over top of each dish. Bake in preheated oven until golden and bubbly, 20 minutes. Makes 4 servings.

Creole Daube with Red Gravy

Creole Daube is one of the most classic beef dishes existing within this cuisine. Daube uses the beef rump roast, a cut which benefits from the Creole long-cooking

methods. The vinegar marinade and the spices used in
this dish suggest that its roots may have been in the soil
of Cote des Allemands or "German Coast." This area,
upriver from New Orleans, was settled by German immigrants in the early 1700s. The dish in itself provides a
delicious and filling meal, but it becomes an exquisite
buffet item when chilled in its own rich broth and served
as Daube Glace. The Creole-Italians took it one step further by preparing the dish in its classic form, then serving it topped with Red Gravy and accompanied by pasta.

4 large garlic cloves,
  minced
¼ lb. salt pork, diced into
  ½-inch cubes
1 teaspoon ground cloves
1 teaspoon ground
  allspice
1 teaspoon dried leaf
  thyme or 1 tablespoon
  fresh chopped thyme
1 teaspoon red (cayenne)
  pepper
1 (5-lb.) beef round rump
  roast boneless
1 cup red-wine vinegar
Salt to taste
Freshly ground black
  pepper
⅓ cup vegetable oil
4 large carrots, thinly
  sliced
3 medium onions, halved
  lengthwise, sliced

1 large turnip, diced
½ cup Burgundy wine
6 green onions, chopped
3 bay leaves, minced
2 tablespoons minced
  parsley, preferably
  flat-leaf
1½ teaspoons freshly
  ground black pepper
½ teaspoon salt
½ teaspoon red (cayenne)
  pepper
2 qts. Brown Veal & Pork
  Stock, page 21, or
  canned beef broth
1 lb. pasta, cooked
1 recipe hot Roux-Based
  Red Gravy, page 241

In a medium bowl, combine garlic, salt pork, cloves, allspice, thyme and 1 teaspoon cayenne with a fork. Toss
until salt pork is coated with seasoning mixture. Using a
small sharp knife, make slits in meat; insert seasoned
salt-pork cubes into slits, leaving remaining seasoning
mixture in bowl. Add vinegar to remaining seasoning
mixture. Salt and pepper meat; place in a large bowl.

Pour vinegar mixture over top. Cover with plastic wrap; refrigerate 3 days, turning occasionally. Remove meat from marinade; pat very dry with paper towels. Discard marinade. In a heavy 8-quart Dutch oven, heat oil over medium-high heat. When oil is very hot, add meat; sear quickly on all sides to form a crisp brown crust. Remove meat; set aside. Add carrots, onions and turnip to hot oil; cook quickly, tossing constantly, to lightly brown vegetables, about 7 minutes. Carefully pour off oil from pan. Return pan to heat; add wine, scraping up browned bits from bottom. Return meat to pan; add green onions, bay leaves, parsley, black pepper, salt, ½ teaspoon cayenne and stock or broth. Reduce heat. Cover and simmer until meat is fork tender, 3 hours. Place meat on a cutting board; cut, across grain, into serving slices. To serve, place meat slices and pasta on each plate. Spoon some sauce and cooked-down vegetables over meat; top with red gravy. Makes 6 to 8 servings.

Brunch

Even today, amidst the hustle and bustle of everyday life, the Deep South has managed to hold onto a few precious relics of quiet times gone by. South Louisianians live life at a slower "internal" pace, with great emphasis placed on enjoying each moment to its fullest.

The Cajuns and Creoles work hard, often six days a week, but you can bet your red beans that they have arranged their lives to make the absolute best of the one day of the week on which they may do exactly as they please. Since the early days of settlement in Louisiana, Sunday brunch has remained a pleasant tradition. Sunday is known as a day for morning worship at church, after which a full day looms ahead for relaxing, visiting with family and friends and, best of all, enjoying good food.

The tradition of the full-meal breakfast in New Orleans began in the late 1800s in fine restaurants such as

Madame Begue's. The French Quarter merchants started their workday long before dawn and by "breakfast time" were hungry for a full meal.

With the 1884 Cotton Exposition, the fame of such dishes as Eggs Benedict and fancy stuffed and sauced omelettes spread. French Market coffeehouses opened, serving New Orleans famed Cafe au Lait with beignets or *rice calas*—tasty deep-fried rice fritters made from a yeast starter.

Brunch or breakfast in South Louisiana includes some of the most unique dishes in the cuisine. Virtually the same dishes would be served on a French Quarter balcony rich with "iron lace" railings and on the houseboat where a Cajun trapper and his family live, moored to a rickety dock. The difference is that one meal would be served from antique china and crystal on cut-work linens adorning a 17th-century French table. The other would be eaten from graniteware and mismatched canning jars and mugs placed securely in one's lap to avoid accidental spilling from the gentle rocking of the boat.

A hearty Cajun-Creole brunch may be served on any occasion and on any day. It is a great celebration of the bounties of life—and a wonderful excuse for overeating.

A simple weekend brunch would consist of one or two breads, a seasonal fruit in heavy cream laced with a complimentary liqueur, a meat dish and an egg dish. Cafe au Lait is a must. Brandy Milk Punch, though certainly optional, is ethereal and reminiscent of lazy afternoons on the deck of a slow-moving paddle-wheeler headed upriver to Natchez.

If you serve a Cajun-Creole brunch on New Year's Day, tradition dictates that you add a pot of purple hull or black-eyed peas for good luck and smothered cabbage for wealth during the coming year.

Many of the classic New Orleans brunch dishes are structured around egg-based sauces—hollandaise and béarnaise and their variations. Once you master these sauces, you can serve Eggs Benedict to rival "breakfast at Brennan's."

Crawfish Folklore

Within their fascinating "lore" the Cajuns have a delightful story about the origin of the crawfish. The story, of course, centers around the Cajuns, and it goes like this. It seems that when the Acadians were exiled from Nova Scotia in the mid-1700s, they packed up and started walking all the way to Louisiana. Now, they had grown especially fond of the delicious lobsters indigenous to the region. Therefore, they decided to bring lots of lobsters to Louisiana so that they could continue to enjoy them. They tied strings on all the lobsters and off they went, Cajuns and lobsters, heading for Louisiana and a new life.

Well, you know, my friend, it was a long trip from Nova Scotia to Louisiana. By the time they got here, those poor lobsters had lost so much weight that they were just pitiful little things only a fraction of their original size. Why, they looked just like bugs! But, like the Cajuns, they had found a new home, and they were happy. They just made themselves at home in the muddy bayous and marshlands. That's where they've been ever since, but they never grew big again.

Pain Perdu

Pain Perdu, or *lost bread*, is a sinfully rich and delicious dish concocted by frugal Cajuns to make use of the household's leftover French bread. If only all leftovers tasted this good!

⅓ cup vegetable oil
6 eggs
3 tablespoons Grand
   Marnier or other
   orange-flavored
   liqueur
2 tablespoons milk
⅓ cup sugar

Grated zest of 1 large
   lemon
8 to 12 slices leftover
   French bread, cut
   ¾-inch-thick
Powdered sugar
Butter
Syrup

In a heavy 12-inch skillet over medium heat, heat oil. In a medium bowl, combine eggs, liqueur, milk, sugar and lemon zest. Whisk until eggs are frothy and sugar is dissolved. When oil is hot, dip bread slices into batter, turning to coat well. Place coated bread in hot oil in batches. Fry until golden brown on both sides, turning once, 5 to 6 minutes. Drain on paper towels; sprinkle with powdered sugar. Keep warm while frying remaining slices. Serve hot with butter and your favorite syrup. Or, use real cane syrup. Makes 4 to 6 servings.

Cajun Coush-Coush

Coush-Coush is a thick breakfast cereal made from cornmeal. The name, derived from the Moroccan grain dish, couscous, was given by African slaves. It is hearty and delicious Cajun fare when served with butter, milk and sugar or—to be authentic—real cane syrup.

2 cups yellow cornmeal
1½ teaspoons salt
1 teaspoon freshly ground
  pepper
2 teaspoons baking
  powder
½ cup bacon drippings or
  lard

1½ cups boiling water
Butter
Sugar or cane syrup
Milk or half and half

In a medium bowl, combine cornmeal, salt, pepper and baking powder with a fork. In a heavy 10-inch skillet over medium heat, heat bacon drippings or lard. Pour boiling water into cornmeal mixture; stir to form a smooth paste. Spoon mixture into hot fat; fry until a light crust forms on bottom, about 10 minutes. Stir mixture, breaking up crust and distributing browned bits throughout. Cook 10 minutes, without stirring. To serve, scoop Coush-Coush into individual bowls. Add your choice of butter, sugar or cane syrup and milk or half and half. Serve hot. Makes 4 servings.

Quail in Sherry Sauce over Fluffy Eggs

Quail was a favorite among the plantation owners, who presented lavish and sumptuous Sunday brunches for neighbors and friends. Neighbors often lived several miles away and were ready for hearty food after the long trip. Dishes such as these are still found on the brunch menus of some of New Orleans finer restaurants and hotels. Serve with biscuits or French Bread.

6 quail
About 2 cups all-purpose
   flour
2 teaspoons salt
2 teaspoons freshly
   ground black pepper
2 teaspoons red (cayenne)
   pepper
2 tablespoons unsalted
   butter or margarine
½ cup bacon drippings
½ lb. mushrooms, sliced

2½ cups Louisiana Brown
   Poultry Stock, page
   19, or canned chicken
   broth
½ cup dry sherry
½ teaspoon freshly
   ground pepper
Salt to taste
Fluffy Eggs, see below
6 green onions, chopped
Minced parsley,
   preferably flat-leaf

Fluffy Eggs:
8 eggs
½ cup warm water
1 teaspoon salt

½ teaspoon freshly
   ground pepper
1 teaspoon Tabasco sauce
2 tablespoons unsalted
   butter or margarine

Pat quail dry with paper towels; set aside. In a medium bowl, combine flour, 2 teaspoons salt, 2 teaspoons black pepper and cayenne with a fork. In a heavy 12-inch skillet over medium heat, heat butter or margarine and bacon drippings. When fat is hot, dredge quail in seasoned flour, turning to coat well; shake to remove excess flour. Reserve 3 tablespoons seasoned flour. Add floured quail to hot fat in batches. Cook quail until browned on all sides, 6 to 7 minutes. Remove from skillet; set aside. Add mushrooms to skillet; sauté until wilted, about 5 minutes. Add reserved 3 tablespoons flour all at once; stir until combined. Cook, stirring constantly, 3 to 4 minutes. Slowly stir in stock or broth. Add sherry, ½ teaspoon black pepper and salt. Bring to a boil. Return quail to skillet. Reduce heat. Cover and barely simmer quail until tender, 20 minutes, stirring often. Meanwhile prepare eggs. Remove quail from heat; stir in green onions. Cover; let stand 2 to 3 minutes. To serve, place a mound of eggs in center of each plate; nest 1 quail in middle of eggs. Drizzle sauce over top; sprinkle with minced parsley. Serve hot. Makes 6 servings.

To prepare Fluffy Eggs, in a medium bowl, combine eggs, water, salt, pepper and Tabasco sauce. Whisk until eggs are very frothy. In a heavy 12-inch skillet over medium heat, melt butter or margarine. Add egg mixture; cook, stirring constantly, until eggs are cooked, dry and fluffy.

Marchand de Vin Sauce

Marchand de Vin is but one of the rich and flavorful sauces born of High-Creole cuisine. The sauce originated at Antoine's Restaurant, a New Orleans institution with a reputation for fine cuisine. This is a time-consuming sauce, but, alas, excellence cannot be rushed. Canned stock simply will not do in this recipe. Before tackling the sauce, have a supply of Brown Veal & Pork Stock, page 21, for the Espagnole Sauce from which you then prepare Marchand de Vin Sauce!

For those students of the classic French way of doing things, let me state up front, that through the years, Creole chefs have taken a few liberties with classic dishes. These subtle changes were made to adapt to local ingredients and taste. Forgive us, Monsieur Escoffier, but then, if you could have dined on fine Creole cuisine, you would know why we took these liberties. Marchand de Vin is one of two sauces used in the classic brunch dish, Eggs Hussarde, page 263. But this wonderful sauce is not limited in use to one egg dish. The sauce, served over beef tournedos at Antoine's, is one of the restaurant's most popular dishes. This sauce freezes well, a fact that helps compensate for the time involved in its preparation.

Espagnole Sauce, see below
6 tablespoons unsalted butter
2 medium onions, finely chopped
1 lb. mushrooms, finely chopped

6 large garlic cloves, finely minced
¼ lb. ham, finely chopped
6 tablespoons all-purpose flour
2½ cups red wine
Salt to taste
Freshly ground pepper

Espagnole Sauce:

1¼ recipes Cajun Roux, page 16
4 qts. Brown Veal & Pork Stock, page 21
2 medium onions, finely chopped
2 carrots, finely chopped

2 celery stalks, finely chopped
1 teaspoon dried leaf thyme or 1 tablespoon chopped fresh thyme
1 bay leaf, minced
4 large tomatoes, peeled, seeded and chopped

Prepare Espagnole Sauce; set aside. In a 4-quart Dutch oven over medium heat, melt butter. Add onions, mushrooms, garlic and ham. Cook, stirring often, until onions are thoroughly wilted and lightly browned, about 12 minutes. Add flour all at once; stir until blended. Cook 3 to 4 minutes, stirring constantly. Stirring, add wine in a slow, steady stream. Bring to a boil. Puree sauce mixture in blender or food processor fitted with the steel blade. Return pureed sauce to pan over medium heat. Add Espagnole Sauce; season with salt and pepper. Simmer 30 minutes. Serve hot. Makes about 2 quarts.

To prepare Espagnole Sauce, make roux in a heavy 4-quart Dutch oven as directed on page 16, cooking until mahogany-colored. Meanwhile, heat 3 quarts stock in a heavy 6- to 8-quart saucepan over medium-high heat. Add onions, carrots, celery, thyme and bay leaf to roux. Cook, stirring, until onions are wilted and transparent, about 10 minutes. When stock comes to a simmer, rapidly whisk about 2 cups hot stock into roux mixture. When blended, pour mixture into remaining hot stock; whisk until combined. Bring to a boil. Reduce heat. Barely simmer, uncovered, 1 hour, skimming surface often to remove grey foam. Strain sauce through a fine strainer, pressing down hard on vegetables to remove all moisture. Discard vegetables. Return strained stock to a clean pot over medium-high heat. Add remaining 1 quart stock; bring to a boil. Reduce heat. Barely simmer, uncovered, 1 hour. Skim grey foam from surface often. Add tomatoes. Simmer, uncovered, 1 hour, skimming surface frequently. Line a strainer with cheesecloth or clean kitchen towel; strain sauce into a clean 5-quart saucepan. Cook over medium-high heat until sauce is reduced to 6 cups. Makes 6 cups.

Hollandaise Sauce

This regal and delicious sauce has an important role in Cajun-Creole brunches. It is easy to make a perfect hollandaise that is as smooth as silk if you are mindful of two things: First, relax! If you fret yourself into a state of disarray over making the sauce, you can't concentrate and are doomed to failure. Second, and most important, do not think of hollandaise as a HOT sauce. Keep in mind that egg yolks coagulate—or curdle—at about 180F (80C)—considerably below the boiling point 212F (100C). The temperature of the finished ready-to-serve sauce should be tepid. If you try to serve it hot, it will curdle, plain and simple.

3 egg yolks, room
   temperature
2 teaspoons fresh lemon
   juice
¾ teaspoon salt

¼ teaspoon red (cayenne)
   pepper
⅔ cup unsalted butter,
   melted

Place bottom of a double boiler containing water over medium-low heat; bring water to a simmer. Reduce heat to low. Water should be hot while cooking, never simmering. Add all ingredients except butter to top of double boiler. Whisk rapidly. Continue whisking as egg mixture thickens and lightens in color, 7 to 8 minutes. Egg mixture should be light lemon-yellow. Drizzle butter into egg mixture, 1 drop at a time, whisking rapidly. Continue adding butter in a slow, steady stream, whisking constantly. Remove from heat; keep warm until served. Makes 1 cup.

Béarnaise Sauce

Béarnaise sauce, like hollandaise sauce, must be cooked in a double boiler. A whisk is important for making these egg-based sauces. Select a whisk made of stainless wire, making sure that wires are flexible. Now all you need are eggs, butter and some energy for whisking.

Herb Mixture, see below
3 egg yolks, room temperature
2 teaspoons tepid water
½ teaspoon Creole mustard or other stone-ground mustard

¾ teaspoon salt
¼ teaspoon red (cayenne) pepper
¾ cup unsalted butter, melted

Herb Mixture:
4 green onions, finely minced
2 medium garlic cloves, finely minced
1 tablespoon dried leaf tarragon or 3 tablespoons chopped fresh tarragon
1 tablespoon dried leaf chervil or 3 tablespoons chopped fresh chervil

¼ cup fresh lemon juice
¼ cup dry white wine
1 teaspoon Tabasco sauce
¾ teaspoon freshly ground pepper

Prepare Herb Mixture; set aside. Place bottom of a double boiler containing water over medium-low heat; bring water to a simmer. Reduce heat to low. Water should be hot while cooking, never simmering. Add egg yolks, water, mustard, salt and cayenne to top of double boiler. Whisk rapidly. Continue whisking as egg mixture thickens and lightens in color, 7 to 8 minutes. Egg mixture should be light lemon-yellow. Drizzle butter into egg mixture, 1 drop at a time, whisking rapidly. Continue adding butter in a slow, steady stream, whisking constantly. Remove pan from heat; whisk in Herb Mixture. Keep warm until served. Makes 1 cup.

To prepare Herb Mixture, combine all ingredients in a heavy 2-quart saucepan over medium-high heat. Cook until reduced almost to a glaze, about 10 minutes. There should be about 2 teaspoons of liquid remaining.

Poached Eggs

To be a successful New Orleans brunch cook, you must master the art of poaching eggs. Most of the classic brunch dishes are built around poached eggs. Fortunately, egg poaching is a task that is simple to master.

**¼ cup white vinegar or   3 to 6 eggs
  lemon juice**

In a heavy, deep 12-inch skillet, combine 1½ quarts water and vinegar or lemon juice. Bring liquid to a simmer. Break 1 egg into a saucer, taking care not to break yolk; slide egg into simmering water. Repeat with remaining eggs. *To serve at once*, cook eggs 3 minutes; remove with a slotted spoon. Use as directed in recipe. *To make ahead*, before you begin cooking eggs, prepare a large bowl of water and ice cubes. Cook eggs as directed above 2 minutes only. Remove at once with a slotted spoon; place in iced water. Set aside up to 2 hours, adding ice cubes as necessary. To serve, heat fresh water to a simmer in deep skillet. Remove eggs from iced water with a slotted spoon; place in simmering water. Cook 1 minute; remove with slotted spoon. Serve at once. Makes 3 to 6 servings.

Eggs Sardou

This now-famous dish was created by Antoine Alciatore, proprietor of Antoine's Restaurant, for a dinner he hosted for French playwright Victorien Sardou in 1908. It has remained a popular dish throughout the years.

Creamed Spinach, see
  below
¼ cup unsalted butter or
  margarine
4 large artichoke bottoms
8 anchovy fillets

¼ cup minced baked ham
  (about 2 oz.)
4 Poached Eggs, above
2 recipes warm
  Hollandaise Sauce,
  page 259
Orange slices

Creamed Spinach:
1 (10-oz.) pkg. frozen
  chopped spinach
3 tablespoons unsalted
  butter or margarine
4 green onions, chopped
2 tablespoons all-purpose
  flour
⅔ cup whipping cream

2 teaspoons Herbsaint
½ teaspoon sugar
½ teaspoon salt
¼ teaspoon freshly
  ground pepper
¼ teaspoon freshly grated
  nutmeg

Prepare spinach; keep warm. In a 10-inch skillet, melt butter or margarine over medium heat. Add artichoke bottoms; sauté just until heated through. Remove from skillet. Set aside. Add anchovy fillets to skillet; cook 3 minutes; set aside with artichoke bottoms. Add ham to skillet; toss to coat with butter or margarine. To assemble, place a mound of spinach in center on each of 4 serving plates. Nest an artichoke bottom into each mound; crisscross 2 anchovies across each artichoke bottom. Place a poached egg in each artichoke bottom over anchovies; top each egg with ½ cup Hollandaise Sauce. Sprinkle with ham. Garnish plates with orange slices; serve at once. Makes 4 servings.

To prepare Creamed Spinach, cook frozen spinach according to package directions; drain and press out as much moisture as possible. Set aside. Melt butter or margarine in a 10-inch skillet over medium heat. Add green onions; sauté 4 minutes, stirring. Add flour all at once; stir until blended. Cook 3 minutes, stirring. Add cream, stirring; cook until thickened. Stir in Herbsaint, sugar, salt, pepper and nutmeg. Stir in cooked spinach; remove from heat.

Eggs Hussarde

A New Orleans original, this variation of Eggs Benedict adds a second sauce to the traditional hollandaise, rich and flavorful Marchand de Vin.

2 tablespoons unsalted
   butter or margarine
4 baked-ham slices,
   trimmed to fit rusks or
   bread crumbs
4 (⅜-inch-thick) tomato
   slices
Salt to taste
Freshly ground black
   pepper

4 Holland Rusks or 4
   (3-inch) rounds cut
   from white bread
   slices, toasted
1 cup Marchand de Vin
   Sauce, page 257
4 Poached Eggs, opposite
2 recipes warm
   Hollandaise Sauce,
   page 259
Minced parsley,
   preferably flat-leaf
Orange slices

In a 10-inch skillet over medium heat, melt butter or margarine. Add ham slices; sauté on both sides until lightly browned, about 5 minutes. Remove from skillet; keep warm. In same skillet, sauté tomato slices just until heated through, about 30 seconds per side, turning once. Salt and pepper tomato slices. To assemble dish, place a toasted rusk or bread round on each plate; top with a browned ham slice. Spoon ¼ cup Marchand de Vin Sauce over each; add a hot tomato slice and a poached egg. Top each egg with ½ cup Hollandaise Sauce; sprinkle with minced parsley. Garnish plates with orange slices. Serve at once. Makes 4 servings.

Eggs Benedict

Eggs Benedict is the number one dish across the country. Although this dish probably originated at New York's famed Delmonico's, it is most often associated with breakfast at Brennan's.

2 English muffins	4 Poached Eggs, page 261
2 tablespoons unsalted butter or margarine	2 recipes warm Hollandaise Sauce, page 259
4 baked-ham slices, trimmed to fit English muffins	Paprika Orange slices
2 tablespoons Madeira	Curly-parsley sprigs

Halve English muffins. Toast and butter halves; keep warm. In a 10-inch skillet over medium heat, melt butter or margarine. Add ham slices; sauté on both sides until lightly browned, about 5 minutes. Pour Madeira over ham; cook until liquid evaporates. To assemble dish, place a toasted English-muffin half on each plate; top with a browned ham slice. Place a poached egg on top of ham; pour ½ cup Hollandaise Sauce on each egg. Sprinkle with paprika; garnish plates with orange slices and parsley. Serve at once. Makes 4 servings.

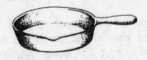

Cajun Skillet-Baked Eggs

Here's a delicious, no-fuss breakfast dish for those times when you need a hearty family breakfast in a hurry. Slice into pie-shaped wedges; serve with biscuits or toast.

6 eggs
½ cup water
½ pint whipping cream
    (1 cup)
1 teaspoon salt
2 teaspoons Creole
    mustard or other
    stone-ground mustard
½ teaspoon freshly
    ground black pepper
1 teaspoon Tabasco sauce

¼ cup unsalted butter or
    margarine
7 green onions, chopped
1½ cups sliced
    mushrooms
1 medium, green bell
    pepper, chopped
3 medium garlic cloves,
    minced
6 crisp-cooked bacon
    slices, crumbled
1 cup shredded Cheddar
    cheese (4 oz.)
2 teaspoons paprika

Preheat oven to 300F (150C). In a medium bowl, combine eggs, water, cream, salt, mustard, black pepper and Tabasco sauce. Whisk until eggs are very frothy; set aside. In a 12-inch ovenproof skillet, melt butter or margarine. Add green onions, mushrooms, bell pepper and garlic. Cook, stirring often, until onions are slightly wilted and transparent, about 5 minutes. Stir in beaten egg mixture and bacon; blend well. Remove pan from heat; sprinkle cheese over eggs. Garnish with paprika. Bake in preheated oven until eggs are set and a knife inserted off center comes out clean, 35 minutes. Serve hot. Makes 4 to 6 servings.

Eggs Nouvelle Orleans

Shirred eggs have declined in popularity in recent years, but they are still found on the menu at a few of New Orleans' finer hotels. This dish is one of my favorites for a casual brunch. The sauce may be completed ahead of time, and the eggs assembled, ready to bake.

Creole Sauce, see below
2 tablespoons unsalted
   butter or margarine
⅓ cup finely chopped
   tasso, page 24, or
   smoked ham (about
   3 oz.)
⅔ cup whipping cream
1 teaspoon dry mustard

2 teaspoons
   Worcestershire sauce
4 eggs
Salt to taste
Freshly ground pepper
Minced parsley,
   preferably flat-leaf

Creole Sauce:
¼ cup vegetable oil
4 green onions, chopped
1 medium onion,
   chopped
1 medium, green bell
   pepper, chopped
1 large celery stalk,
   chopped
2 medium garlic cloves,
   chopped
2 large tomatoes, peeled,
   chopped
½ teaspoon dried leaf
   thyme or 1½ teaspoons
   chopped fresh thyme

1 bay leaf, minced
½ teaspoon salt
¼ teaspoon freshly
   ground black pepper
¼ teaspoon red (cayenne)
   pepper
1 cup Louisiana Brown
   Poultry Stock, page
   19, or canned chicken
   broth
⅔ cup Burgundy wine
2 teaspoons fresh lemon
   juice

Prepare Creole Sauce; keep warm. Preheat oven to 375F
(190C). In a small skillet, melt butter or margarine. Add
tasso or ham; sauté until heated through, 3 to 4 minutes.
Set aside. In a small bowl, combine cream, mustard and
Worcestershire sauce. Pour equal amounts of mixture
into 4 individual au gratin dishes. Break 1 egg into each
dish, taking care not to break yolks. Top each dish with a
sprinkling of tasso or ham. Salt and pepper. Bake in preheated oven just until eggs are set, about 7 minutes. To
serve, spoon a generous amount of hot Creole Sauce
over each egg, sprinkle with minced parsley. Serve hot.
Makes 4 servings.

To prepare Creole Sauce, in a heavy 12-inch skillet over
medium heat, heat oil until hot. Add green onion, onion,

bell pepper, celery and garlic. Cook, stirring often, until vegetables are slightly wilted and transparent, about 5 minutes. Add tomatoes, thyme, bay leaf, salt, black pepper and cayenne. Stir to blend well. Add stock or broth; cook until reduced by ½, about 15 minutes, stirring often. Add Burgundy and lemon juice; cook until reduced by ½ again, about 20 minutes.

Grillades & Grits

Grillades (pronounced GREE-odds) & Grits is just about the best breakfast South Louisiana has to offer. Grillades are pounded pieces of round steak which are seasoned, seared quickly in hot fat, then cooked slowly in a rich, roux-based gravy with vegetables and tomatoes. The grillades and thick, rich gravy are served with old-fashioned slow-cooking grits.

2 teaspoons salt
1½ teaspoons freshly ground black pepper
1½ teaspoons red (cayenne) pepper
About 2 cups all-purpose flour
1½ lbs. beef round steak, trimmed, cut into 2-inch squares
⅓ cup lard or bacon drippings
1 recipe Cajun Roux, page 16
2 medium onions, chopped

1 large green bell pepper, chopped
4 large garlic cloves, minced
1 large celery stalk, chopped
3 tomatoes, peeled, chopped
2 cups Brown Veal & Pork Stock, page 21, or canned beef broth
1 tablespoon cider vinegar
Old-Fashioned Grits, see below
6 green onions, chopped

Old-Fashioned Grits:
5 cups water
1 teaspoon salt
1 cup slow-cooking grits

¼ cup unsalted butter or margarine, room temperature
1 egg, slightly beaten

In a medium bowl, combine salt, black pepper, cayenne and flour with a fork. Sprinkle seasoning mixture over both sides of meat squares. Using a meat pounder, pound meat until doubled in size, taking care not to tear meat; set aside. In a heavy 12-inch skillet over medium-high heat, heat lard or bacon drippings. When fat is hot, add pounded meat in batches; brown quickly on both sides. Remove from heat; set aside. Make roux in a heavy 12-inch skillet as directed on page 16, cooking until mahogany-colored. Add onions, bell pepper, garlic and celery to hot roux; cook, stirring, until vegetables are slightly wilted and transparent, about 5 minutes. Stir in tomatoes. Slowly stir in stock or broth and vinegar. Add browned meat. Reduce heat. Cover and simmer until meat is tender, 1 hour, stirring occasionally. Meanwhile, prepare grits. To serve, remove grillades from gravy with a slotted spoon; place on individual plates. Stir green onions into gravy; remove from heat. Spoon grits on each plate; top grillades and grits with gravy. Serve hot. Makes 4 to 6 servings.

To prepare Old-Fashioned Grits, combine water and salt in a heavy 3-quart saucepan over medium-high heat; bring to a boil. Stir in grits; reduce heat to low. Cover; cook until thickened, 30 to 35 minutes, stirring occasionally. Remove from heat; quickly stir in butter or margarine and egg until blended.

Pecan Crescents

These easy-to-make little rolls are one of my favorite
things to eat for breakfast—or for any occasion.

2 cups sifted all-purpose
   flour
¼ teaspoon salt
1 cup frozen unsalted
   butter or margarine,
   cut into 1-inch pieces

1 egg yolk, slightly beaten
¾ cup dairy sour cream
Pecan Filling, see below

Pecan Filling:
¾ cup sugar
1½ teaspoons ground
   cinnamon

¾ cup coarsely chopped
   pecans

In a food processor fitted with the steel blade, combine
flour and salt. Add butter or margarine. Turn on and off
to break butter or margarine into chunks the size of peas.
In a small bowl, combine egg yolk and sour cream; add
to flour mixture. Process just until combined. Place
dough on a lightly floured surface; gather into a ball.
Divide dough into 4 pieces; pat into small circles. Wrap
each circle in plastic wrap; refrigerate overnight. Prepare
filling; set aside. Preheat oven to 375F (190C). Remove 1
circle of dough, at a time, from refrigerator. On a lightly
floured surface, roll out dough into a 12-inch circle. Cut
circle into 8 wedges. Sprinkle filling evenly over surface
of dough. Roll up each wedge, starting at outside edge.
Place on ungreased baking sheet; bend into crescent
shapes, curving ends in toward each other. Repeat with
remaining circles. Bake in preheated oven until golden
brown and crispy, 20 to 25 minutes. Cool on a rack.
Makes 32 crescents.

To prepare Pecan Filling, in a medium bowl, combine
sugar, cinnamon and pecans.

Peaches in Soft Brandy Cream

Starting in late June, sweet and scrumptious Ruston, Louisiana peaches are available at roadside stands. We all do our best to get our fill of them fresh. We put a bushel or so in the freezer, and we put up dozens of jars of peach preserves to remind us of summer throughout the year. They are especially pleasing on a wet and cold winter's day. Of all the ways to eat peaches, however, this is my favorite. It is a great eye-opener for a weekend brunch.

6 large peaches, peeled, sliced	½ cup peach brandy
1 cup powdered sugar, sifted	1 teaspoon vanilla extract
1 pint whipping cream (2 cups)	Mint sprigs

Place peaches in a medium bowl; sprinkle with ½ cup powdered sugar. Stir gently to coat all slices. Set aside. In a medium bowl, beat cream with an electric mixer on medium-high speed until peaks just begin to form, about 3 minutes. Beat in remaining ½ cup powdered sugar, peach brandy and vanilla. Beat just until soft peaks form, about 2 minutes. Fold whipped-cream mixture into peaches; serve in glass bowls. Garnish with mint sprigs. Makes 4 to 6 servings.

Creole Rice Calas

At the turn of the century, Rice Calas sellers made their way through the marketplace in the French Quarter with their baskets of delightful rice fritters calling "Belles calas! Belles calas tout chauds." The name *calas* came from an African word for rice. Sadly, calas vendors are gone. The secret for preparing rice calas was kept alive in Creole homes where the dish originated as a means of using leftover rice. If you are serving a New Orleans-style brunch, add calas for a delicious note of authenticity.

½ cup warm water (110F, 45C)

2 tablespoons granulated sugar

1 (¼-oz.) pkg. active dry yeast (about 1 tablespoon)

1½ cups leftover cooked white rice

3 eggs, slightly beaten

1½ cups sifted all-purpose flour

½ teaspoon salt

½ teaspoon vanilla extract

¼ teaspoon freshly grated nutmeg

Vegetable oil

Powdered sugar

The night before you wish to serve calas, combine water and granulated sugar in a 2-cup glass measuring cup. Stir in yeast. Let stand until foamy, 5 to 10 minutes. In a medium bowl, combine yeast mixture and rice. Cover bowl with plastic wrap; set aside in a warm, draft-free place overnight. This step forms a **soured-rice starter** for calas. Do not be alarmed by its less than enticing aroma the next morning! Next morning, stir rice mixture thoroughly. Add eggs, flour, salt, vanilla and nutmeg. Beat mixture with a wooden spoon until combined. Cover with plastic wrap. Let rise in a warm, draft-free place 1 hour. Heat 3 inches oil in a large saucepan over medium heat to 365F (180C) or until a 1-inch bread cube turns golden brown in 60 seconds. Drop rice mixture by rounded tablespoons into hot oil. Do not crowd pan. Fry until golden brown, 5 to 6 minutes, turning once. Drain calas on paper towels; sift powdered sugar over hot calas. Serve hot. Makes about 24.

South-Louisiana Buttermilk Biscuits

The very mention of southern biscuits makes my mouth water and sends visions of biscuits with heavenly soft, fluffy layers floating through my mind. Biscuits are so much a part of the southern way of living that we even have several different kinds! Biscuits freeze beautifully, uncooked, so make lots.

4 cups soft, southern
   wheat flour, page 290,
   or all-purpose flour
2 tablespoons plus
   2 teaspoons baking
   powder

2 teaspoons salt
¼ cup lard or vegetable
   shortening
1 cup buttermilk

Lightly grease 2 baking sheets. Preheat oven to 400F
(205C). Sift flour, baking powder and salt into a large
bowl. Work in lard or shortening with your fingertips
until mixture resembles coarse cornmeal. Add buttermilk
slowly, stirring with a fork until blended. When dough is
smooth, turn out onto a floured surface. The dough will
be sticky, so flour work surface and surface of dough
fairly heavily; do not work more flour into dough itself.
Roll out to ½ inch thickness. Using a 2-inch biscuit cutter, cut dough into rounds. Place on greased baking
sheets. Gather scraps of dough together. Repeat rolling
and cutting until all dough has been used. Bake in preheated oven until light golden brown, 15 to 18 minutes.
To freeze, freeze unbaked biscuits, unwrapped, on baking sheets just until firmly frozen; place in freezer bags
to store up to 1 month. To bake, preheat oven as directed
in recipe; place frozen biscuits on a baking sheet. Bake
in preheated oven, allowing 3 to 5 minutes longer. Serve
hot. Makes 24 biscuits.

Bayou-Country Beignets

One of the most enjoyable aspects of living in New Orleans is being able to sit under the softly whirring ceiling
fans at Cafe du Monde in the French Market eating beignets and sipping Cafe au Lait. The whole experience has
a way of removing your mind from the realities of the
day. It allows you to peacefully contemplate the passing
world as powdered sugar filters silently into your lap. I
have never met anyone who didn't like beignets. Children are positively transformed into models of good behavior with the mere promise of beignets for breakfast.
No Cajun-Creole brunch is complete without them.

¾ cup water
2 teaspoons sugar
½ cup evaporated milk
1 (¼-oz.) pkg. active dry yeast (about 1 tablespoon)
3 to 3½ cups soft, southern wheat flour, below, or all-purpose flour

⅓ cup sugar
1 egg
2 tablespoons lard or vegetable shortening
1 teaspoon salt
½ teaspoon freshly grated nutmeg
Vegetable oil
Powdered sugar

In a medium saucepan over low heat, combine water, 2 teaspoons sugar and evaporated milk; heat to 110F (45C). Pour into a 2-cup glass measuring cup. Stir in yeast. Let stand until foamy, 5 to 10 minutes. In a food processor fitted with the steel blade, combine 3 cups of flour and all remaining ingredients except oil and powdered sugar. Turn on and off 3 or 4 times to blend ingredients. Add yeast mixture. Turn on and off 4 or 5 times to bring dough together. Check consistency of dough. It should be fairly smooth and nonsticky. If additional flour is needed, add 1 to 2 tablespoons at a time; process just until blended. Process 15 seconds to knead dough. Turn out dough on a lightly floured surface; form into a smooth ball. Lightly oil a large bowl. Place dough in oiled bowl, turning to coat all sides. Cover with plastic wrap. Let rise in a warm, draft-free place until doubled in bulk, about 1½ hours. Punch down dough. Turn out onto a lightly floured surface. Roll out dough into a rectangle about ½ inch thick. Working at a diagonal to rectangle, with a sharp knife, cut dough into 2-inch-wide strips, moving from left to right. Starting at top left and moving toward bottom of rectangle, cut dough diagonally into 2-inch-wide strips to form diamond shapes. See photos for Crawfish Beignets, page 42. Carefully place all completed diamonds ½ inch apart on ungreased baking sheets. Cover loosely with plastic wrap. Gather up remaining dough scraps; knead together. Cover loosely with plastic wrap; let rest 15 minutes to relax dough. Roll out and cut as before. Repeat until all dough has been used. Cover beignets loosely with plastic wrap; let rise in warm, draft-free place until almost doubled in bulk, 45 minutes. In a large saucepan, heat 3 inches oil to 365F (185C) or until a 1-inch bread cube turns golden brown in 60 seconds. Carefully slide beignets into hot oil, 3 or 4 at a time; do not crowd. Fry until puffy and golden brown on both sides, turning once with tongs. Cooking time is about 2 to 3 minutes per side. Remove with a slotted spoon; drain on paper towels. Sift powdered sugar over hot beignets; serve hot. Makes about 36.

In the South, flour from soft wheat is often used for biscuits and other baked goods. This soft, southern wheat flour has a gluten content of about 8 percent. All-purpose flour is an acceptable substitute, or mail order, page 290.

Beverages

Sandwich Buffet Football Party

Cajun Party Punch
Home-Smoked Sausage with
Horseradish Sauce, page 38–9
Cajun Party Spareriblets, page 31
New Orleans Oyster Loaves, page 137
Muffuletta Sandwiches, page 239
Marinated Cole Slaw, page 76
Cajun Deviled Eggs, page 78
Satsuma Cake, page 187

South Louisianians have long been noted for their love of strong drink even if the "drink" happens to be coffee! Chicory adds a rich color to coffee and an indescribably sweet and pungent flavor. Coffee with chicory is available by mail order, page 289.

The chicory that is added to coffee is the roasted and ground chicory root. The root resembles parsnips and is an off-white color. It was the Dutch who first added chicory to coffee when the beverage was introduced to Europe in the 1600s. The combination soon became popular all over Europe and was brought to the New World, and eventually, to South Louisiana by the Acadians.

Cafe au Lait, the famous coffee-and-milk drink sipped with French Quarter beignets, is a New Orleans favorite among residents and tourists alike. The elegant Cafe

Brulot is an after-dinner flambéed coffee drink that is still served in grand style at some of New Orleans finest restaurants. It is quite a rewarding experience.

As early as the first part of the 18th century, when New Orleans was no more than a walled city of mud streets in a cypress swamp, its residents enjoyed their fine French wines and brandies. Indeed, the early order of Ursuline nuns had already classified the area as being possessed by the demon spirits of alcohol.

As New Orleans grew and prospered, the social custom of imbibing also grew. The *cocktail* was born in the city. In 1793, a French refugee from Santo Domingo arrived in New Orleans with a secret formula for a tonic which he called *bitters*. Antoine Amdee Peychaud opened an apothecary shop in the Vieux Carre where he served his concoction with cognac. The potion was served in an egg cup, or "coquetier." The Americans gradually mispronounced the word into its present form, cocktail.

In the heyday of the plantation era, fine cognacs, brandies and heady Jamaica rum were popular drinks, while the French Quarter boasted world-famous bars serving the most popular European liqueurs. No social affair was complete without a huge sterling silver punch bowl filled with gigantic portions of alcohol, fruit and spices. After the Civil War, New Orleans became more Americanized and bourbon whiskey became increasingly popular.

Pairing South Louisiana foods with beverages can be a complex matter. For the refined foods of New Orleans restaurants follow traditional guidelines for wine service. With fish, veal and poultry, serve a dry white wine, such as chardonnay. With beef, pork and game dishes, serve a red wine, such as Bourdeaux or cabernet sauvignon. For a delightful luncheon or light supper, serve rosé wine with chilled dishes and salads. Champagne (extra-dry rather than brut) may be served with any food, including desserts, but for a specific dessert-course wine, select a Sauterne, cream sherry or malmsey Madeira. You may also serve a Spatlese or Auslese Rhine wine with desserts. Port should not be served with the dessert, but rather with nuts after dessert.

Now we seem to have beverage service taken care

of—or do we? When the country Cajun dishes enter the picture, the standard rules of beverage etiquette do not apply. These robust and spicy dishes totally overwhelm delicate wines.

Beer is often the beverage chosen by locals to accompany gumbo, barbecue and other roux-based dishes. If you wish to serve wine, select a full-bodied red wine, such as cabernet sauvignon or zinfandel. The French wines of the Rhone Valley, such as Chateauneuf du Pape, are also good choices.

If you are serving fish, shellfish, poultry or veal dishes that are moderately spicy, try serving a dry California gewurztraminer, chardonnay, a French vouvray or one of the Sancerre wines.

For those who do not partake of alcoholic beverages, the fog vanishes. Iced tea is wonderful with everything, and nothing sets off dessert better than coffee—of whatever strength you prefer.

Planter's Rum Punch

Rum Punch was the gentleman's drink during the plantation era. Untold numbers of dollars, acres, crops and what-have-you changed hands over this potent drink in the owner's private study. It is still popular in many parts of the Deep South, but it is delicious anywhere.

1 teaspoon light-brown sugar	2 tablespoons rosé wine (1 oz.)
2 teaspoons water	Mint sprig
¼ cup dark Jamaican rum (2 oz.)	Maraschino cherry
Juice of 1 lemon	Orange-slice half
⅔ cup cracked ice	

In a small bowl, dissolve brown sugar in water; pour into a cocktail shaker or jar with a tight-fitting lid. Add rum, lemon juice and ice; shake until well chilled. Pour in a glass. Float wine on top by pouring over the back of a spoon. Decorate with mint sprig, cherry and orange slice. Serve cold. Makes 1 drink.

Cajun Party Punch

This old Louisiana recipe will be a hit the next time you serve punch.

1 qt. strong tea
1½ cups sugar
10 mint sprigs
4 (3-inch) cinnamon
   sticks
1 teaspoon whole cloves
1 qt. dark rum
2 cups unsweetened
   pineapple juice

1 cup fresh lime juice
2 (1-qt.) bottles club soda
Ice ring or large block of
   ice
1 lemon, sliced
1 lime, sliced
1 orange, sliced

Place tea in a heavy 3-quart saucepan over medium heat. Add sugar, mint, cinnamon and cloves. Cook, stirring, until sugar dissolves. Cool slightly; refrigerate until chilled. To serve, strain tea into a punch bowl; discard spices. Add rum, pineapple juice, lime juice and club soda. Stir until blended. Add ice and fruit slices. Ladle into punch cups. Makes about 5 quarts.

The Ultimate Egg-Nog Punch

Egg Nog is a traditional American punch served during the Christmas holiday season. Not to be outdone, New Orleanians also serve this rich and highly spirited version at their gala holiday parties.

12 eggs, separated
2 cups sugar
2 cups bourbon whiskey
½ pint whipping cream
   (1 cup)

1 qt. milk (4 cups)
1 teaspoon vanilla extract
Cracked ice
Freshly grated nutmeg

In a large bowl, beat egg yolks with an electric mixer on medium-high speed until thick and lemon-colored, about 5 minutes. Slowly beat in sugar; beat 5 minutes. Slowly beat in bourbon in a slow, steady stream. Beat in cream and milk; add vanilla. In a medium bowl, beat egg whites until medium-stiff peaks form. Fold beaten egg whites into yolk mixture. To serve, add ¼ cup ice to punch cups. Add punch; top with nutmeg. Makes about 5 quarts.

Brandy Milk Punch

No matter how many times I make the trip, I never tire of the tourist-oriented Mississippi River excursions on the steamboat Natchez. The river is fascinating, and each time I am reminded of how exciting it is to live in such a unique area. But just perhaps my favorite part of the trip is sitting at the fine old bar sipping Brandy Milk Punch, the southern "nectar of the gods."

2 cups brandy	½ gallon milk
¾ cup white creme de cocoa	1 qt. whipping cream (4 cups)
1 teaspoon vanilla extract	Freshly grated nutmeg
1¾ cups Simple Bar Syrup, page 282	3 cups cracked ice

In a large bowl, combine all ingredients except cream, nutmeg and ice. Cover and refrigerate until ready to serve. Just before serving, in a medium bowl, beat cream with an electric mixer on medium speed until medium-stiff peaks form. Fold whipped cream into brandy mixture; pour into a punch bowl. To serve, add ice to punch cups. Add punch; top with nutmeg. Makes 12 (8-oz.) servings.

Cajun Mimosas

If you want to immortalize your next social affair, serve this delightfully spicy and different drink. The citrus juice moderates some of the fire from the chilies so that you can actually taste their flavor! It's a must for a Cajun-style cookout.

1 qt. orange juice
6 pickled jalapeño
   peppers, brine packed,
   drained

1 magnum Champagne,
   well chilled
Cracked ice

Place orange juice in a 1-quart, non-metallic container with tight-fitting lid. Slice well-drained peppers into rounds; add to juice. Do not remove seeds. Place lid on container; shake well. Refrigerate 3 days. When ready to serve, strain juice; discard peppers. Fill glasses half full of ice. Fill halfway with orange juice; add enough Champagne to fill glass. Stir and serve. Makes 8 servings.

Minted Brandy Ice

Fresh mint and mint-flavored liqueurs play a big role in the beverage selection of South Louisiana. Mint is very refreshing, and combined with ice cream in this recipe, it makes a drink so delicious it makes you feel wonderful all over.

1 qt. rich vanilla ice
   cream
¾ cup brandy
½ cup white creme de
   cocoa

¼ cup white creme de
   menthe
10 ice cubes
6 to 8 mint sprigs

Combine all ingredients except mint in a blender; process until smooth. Serve in brandy snifters or Old Fashioned glasses; garnish with mint. Makes 6 to 8 servings.

Sazerac

This potent cocktail was invented in New Orleans and named for the bar in which it made its debut. The drink was originally prepared using brandy. But American tastes eventually won out, and the drink is now prepared with either bourbon or rye whiskey. At the Sazerac Bar in the Fairmont Hotel, Sazeracs are still prepared in the grand style of the past. The Herbsaint is added to the glass, which is then twirled into the air to coat with the liqueur. Try it only if you happen to be a very good catcher!

1 teaspoon sugar	1 cup cracked ice
2 drops Peychaud Bitters	¼ cup bourbon or rye
1 teaspoon water	whiskey (2 oz.)
2 drops Angostura Bitters	1 teaspoon Herbsaint
	Lemon twist

In a cocktail shaker or jar with a tight-fitting lid, muddle sugar with Peychaud Bitters and water. Add Angostura Bitters, ice and whiskey; shake until well chilled. Pour Herbsaint into an Old Fashioned glass; swirl to coat bottom and sides. Strain drink mixture into glass; add lemon twist. Makes 1 drink.

Ramos Gin Fizz

This light-as-a-cloud and deceivingly non-alcoholic-tasting drink was born in New Orleans in the late 1800s. The drink, now world-famous, has often been a frustration to those who try to duplicate it at home. The secret to its taste is the addition of a few drops of an obscure ingredient, orange-flower water. It is available at large liquor stores throughout the country. The egg white must be beaten until very frothy. Then the entire drink must be shaken madly until thickened and creamy. Use a container with a screw-top lid to prevent the drink from spilling over.

1 egg white, beaten until very frothy	2 tablespoons whipping cream
1 teaspoon powdered sugar	¼ cup gin (2 oz.)
3 drops orange-flavor water	2 tablespoons club soda
Juice of ½ lime	1 cup cracked ice
1 drop vanilla extract	1 orange slice

Combine all ingredients except orange slice in a cocktail shaker or jar with a tight-fitting lid. Shake until thickened and creamy, about 3 minutes. Pour into a tall glass. Decorate with orange slice. Serve immediately. Makes 1 drink.

Simple Bar Syrup

Keep this simple syrup on hand to sweeten all your drinks.

2 cups sugar   **1 cup water**

Combine sugar and water in a 3-quart saucepan. Bring to a boil, stirring. Boil 5 minutes. Cool before using. To store, pour into a jar with a tight-fitting lid. Refrigerate until needed. Makes 3 cups.

Absinthe Drip

Absinthe is a liqueur which originated in Switzerland but became very popular in the bars of New Orleans in the mid-1800s. The original Brennan's restaurant was called The Old Absinthe House in the 1860s. The city became known as the absinthe capital of the world.

The original absinthe was made of wormwood, anise seed, fenel, star anise, coriander seeds, hyssop and 190-proof alcohol! After large numbers of absinthe devotees succumbed to madness or death, it was determined that wormwood was a narcotic with devastatingly addictive properties. The substance was subsequently banned in most areas of Europe, and in the United States, in 1912.

Several anise-flavored liqueurs, made without wormwood, are produced today, including Pernod, anisette, Ojen and Herbsaint. The latter was created by a New Orleans pharmacist, J. Marion Legendre. It is marketed today by his heirs. The Absinthe Drip was the fashionable drink of the day when absinthe was in its heyday.

Cracked ice   2 tablespoons Herbsaint
1 sugar cube   (1 oz.)
                                     2 tablespoons club soda

Fill a brandy snifter with cracked ice; set a small strainer over mouth of snifter. Place sugar cube in strainer; drip Herbsaint over it onto ice. Then drip club soda through. Remove strainer; stir drink. Discard any remaining sugar. Serve immediately. Makes 1 drink.

Absinthe Suissesse

This is another of the famous absinthe cocktails created in the 1800s. Though not as fashionable as it once was, it is still a delightful drink.

2 egg whites, beaten until   2 tablespoons whipping
   very frothy   cream
2 tablespoons Herbsaint   2 drops orange-flower
   (1 oz.)   water
½ teaspoon orgeat syrup   2 tablespoons club soda
                                  Cracked ice

Combine all ingredients except ice in a cocktail shaker or jar with a tight-fitting lid. Shake until frothy. Fill glass with cracked ice. Serve immediately. Makes 1 drink.

New Orleans Rye Old Fashioned

Leave it to the mixologists of New Orleans, the city that invented the cocktail and spread the fame of bitters, to add its unique touch to this old standby drink.

1 sugar cube   3 tablespoons rye whiskey
3 dashes Angostura   (1½ oz.)
   Bitters   Cracked ice
1 whole clove   1 tablespoon club soda
1 (3-inch) orange-peel   Maraschino cherry
   strip   Orange-slice half

In an Old Fashioned glass, combine sugar, bitters, clove and orange peel. Muddle together with a wooden spoon, crushing sugar cube and bruising clove and orange peel. Add whiskey; stir until blended. Fill glass with ice; add club soda and enough water to fill glass. Stir until blended; add cherry and orange-slice half. Serve immediately. Makes 1 drink.

Cafe Noir

At any time of the day or night, dark roasted coffee with chicory is the universal drink in South Louisiana. Both Cajuns and Creoles like it strong. Tourists can't abide it, and natives can't live without it. But one thing can be said for sure—it WILL wake you up in the morning. To make the best quality coffee, use either a traditional French drip pot, called a *biggin*, or one of the modern electric coffee makers which drip hot water slowly over the grounds.

Pinch of salt
¾ cup drip-grind dark-
   roast coffee with
   chicory

2½ quarts boiling water

Place salt and coffee in top of drip pot. Pour ½ cup water over coffee; let drip through completely. Add remaining water, ½ cup at a time, letting each addition drip through completely before adding more. Serve hot. Makes 12 cups.

Cafe au Lait

Cafe au Lait is an integral part of New Orleans society. Beignets are just not the same without it. No visit to the French Quarter is complete without a stop at the Cafe du Monde, New Orleans' famous bastion of coffeedom, for a cup or two. The secret to real New Orleans Cafe au Lait is the caramel milk! The extra large pot for preparation of the caramel is very important. When the boiling milk is added to the caramel, it boils, froths, spits and sputters ferociously. It would overflow a smaller pan and could result in serious burns.

3 tablespoons sugar	2 cups hot dark-roast
2 cups boiling milk	coffee with chicory

Place sugar in a heavy 8-quart pan over medium heat. Cook until sugar caramelizes, stirring once or twice after sugar begins to dissolve. When caramel is a deep hazelnut color, about 7 minutes, remove pan from heat; slowly add boiling milk. When all milk has been added, wait for foam to subside; stir until blended. Add coffee; stir. Serve hot. Or for a truly authentic presentation, place caramel-milk in 1 coffeepot and hot coffee in a second coffeepot. Pour equal amounts of each into cups at the same time. Special cafe au lait pots are available. Makes 4 cups.

Cafe Brulot

For a very special occasion, this spectacular after-dinner coffee drink may be prepared at the table with great fanfare. The Creoles have special *brulot bowls* in which to prepare the drink, but you may use a round chafing dish. Serve in demitasse cups.

Finely grated zest of 2 oranges	½ cup pecan halves
Finely grated zest of 1 lemon	12 sugar cubes
2 (3-inch) cinnamon sticks, broken into small pieces	¾ cup cognac or other brandy
2 teaspoons whole coriander seeds	¼ cup Grand Marnier or other orange-flavored liqueur
1 large bay leaf	8 cups hot dark-roast coffee with chicory
6 whole cloves	

Using a mortar and pestle or grinder, mash together orange and lemon zest, cinnamon, coriander, bay leaf, cloves, pecans and sugar. Transfer mashed spices, zest and sugar to brulot bowl or chafing dish. Place bowl or dish over a heat source; add cognac and liqueur. Just as liquid starts to simmer; ignite. Using a long handled spoon, stir mixture. As flame begins to subside, stir in coffee. Ladle into demitasse cups; serve hot. Makes 8 servings.

Metric Chart

Comparison to Metric Measure

When You Know	Symbol	Multiply By	To Find	Symbol
teaspoons	tsp	5.0	milliliters	ml
tablespoons	tbsp	15.0	milliliters	ml
fluid ounces	fl. oz.	30.0	milliliters	ml
cups	c	0.24	liters	l
pints	pt.	0.47	liters	l

When You Know	Symbol	Multiply By	To Find	Symbol
quarts	qt.	0.95	liters	l
ounces	oz.	28.0	grams	g
pounds	lb.	0.45	kilograms	kg
Fahrenheit	F	5/9 (after subtracting 32)	Celsius	c

Liquid Measure to Milliliters

¼ teaspoon	=	1.25 milliliters
½ teaspoon	=	2.5 milliliters
¾ teaspoon	=	3.75 milliliters
1 teaspoon	=	5.0 milliliters
1¼ teaspoons	=	6.25 milliliters
1½ teaspoons	=	7.5 milliliters
1¾ teaspoons	=	8.75 milliliters
2 teaspoons	=	10.0 milliliters
1 tablespoon	=	15.0 milliliters
2 tablespoons	=	30.0 milliliters

Liquid Measure to Liters

¼ cup	=	0.06 liters
½ cup	=	0.12 liters
¾ cup	=	0.18 liters
1 cup	=	0.24 liters

1¼ cups	=	0.3 liters
1½ cups	=	0.36 liters
2 cups	=	0.48 liters
2½ cups	=	0.6 liters
3 cups	=	0.72 liters
3½ cups	=	0.84 liters
4 cups	=	0.96 liters
4½ cups	=	1.08 liters
5 cups	=	1.2 liters
5½ cups	=	1.32 liters

Fahrenheit to Celsius

F	C
200–205	95
220–225	105
245–250	120
275	135
300–305	150
325–330	165
345–350	175
370–375	190
400–405	205
425–430	220
445–450	230
470–475	245
500	260

Mail-Order Sources

Cajun Sausages & Seasoning Meats

K-Paul's Louisiana Kitchen
406 Chartres, Apartment 2
New Orleans, LA 70130
1-800-654-6017

Tasso and andouille sausage. 48-hour delivery.

Poché's Meat Market
Rt. 2, Box 415
Breaux Bridge, LA 90517
(318) 332-2108

Tasso, pickled marinated pork, andouille, smoked Cajun sausage, pure pork sausage, boudin. Chaurice in winter only. Will ship fastest and best way for area.

Coffee

Neighbors Coffee Company
P.O. Box 46
Covington, LA 70434
(504) 892-2741

Dark Roast Coffee with Chicory, Special Blend Dark Roast, Dark Roast Decaffeinated. Uniquely packaged in amounts to make 8 and 12 cups. Eliminates the guess-work!

Corn Flour (Unseasoned fish fry)

Louisiana Fish Fry Product
5267 Plank Rd.
Baton Rouge, LA 70805
(504) 356-2905

Corn flour. Write or call for prices.

Community Kitchen
Box 3778
Baton Rouge, LA 70821-3778
(504) 381-3900

Community Dark Roast Coffee, New Orleans Blend with Chicory. Write or call for catalog.

Luzianne-Blue Plate Foods
P.O. Box 60296
New Orleans, LA 70160
1-800-692-7895

Luzianne Dark Roast Coffee with Chicory, CDM Dark Roast Coffee with Chicory. Call or write for brochure.

Merchant Coffee Company
P.O. Box 50654
New Orleans, LA 70150
(504) 581-7515

Union Coffee and Chicory, French Market Dark Roast Coffee and Chicory. Call or write for brochure.

Flour

White Lily Flour Company
Box 871
Knoxville, TN 37901

Soft, southern wheat flour. Write for prices

War Eagle Mill
Route 6, Box 127
Rogers, AR 72756

Stone-ground flours and cornmeals. Write for catalog and price list.

Pecan Rice

Konriko Company Store
301 Ann St.
New Iberia, LA 70560
1-800-551-3245

Pecan rice available in 7-oz. boxes, 2-lb. and 10-lb. bags. Write for catalog and prices.

Seafood

Harlon's Old New Orleans Seafood
126 Airline Highway
Metairie, LA 70001
(504) 831-4592

All types of Gulf Coast fish and shellfish, including turtle meat, frog legs, alligator meat and shark meat. Will air freight and arrange for delivery to your door. Accepts all major credit cards.

Index

293

About the Author

Terry Thompson's background in Cajun-Creole cuisine comes from years of seeking out the techniques, recipes, and traditions of the Cajun families of the bayou country and the Creoles of New Orleans. Her resulting style, which she refers to as Haute Cajun-Creole, combines the best of classic French with the best of Cajun-Creole. Mrs. Thompson's fresh and innovative recipes have been shared with over 10,000 students in cooking classes and seminars all over the United States.

The author lives and works in Mandeville, Louisiana, on the north shore of Lake Pontchartrain with her husband and daughter, who are as enthusiastic about food as she is.